Praise for *I Didn't Know I Needed This*

"Eli Rallo's debut is not to be missed. Her writing is fresh, funny, and honest. *I Didn't Know I Needed This* will be a bible to those navigating the sticky, confusing, and often accidentally hilarious world of modern dating."

—TARA SCHUSTER, author of *Glow in the F*cking Dark* and *Buy Yourself the F*cking Lilies*

"Funny, charming, and real, *I Didn't Know I Needed This* is the book every young woman definitely needs. Like a wise, compassionate, and highly entertaining big sister, Eli takes lessons she learned the hard (and often hilarious) way about navigating modern relationships and gaining self-worth, cutting through the confusion and saying: You are more than enough, and it will all be okay."

—LORI GOTTLIEB, *New York Times* bestselling author of *Maybe You Should Talk to Someone* and cohost of the *Dear Therapists* podcast

"*I Didn't Know I Needed This* is exactly what you're hoping it will be—compulsively readable, hugely helpful, and deeply relatable. Written in Eli Rallo's signature unabashed, authentic, and unapologetic voice, *IDKINT* will hold your hand through your twenties and pull you toward the person you've always known you could be."

—HALEY JAKOBSON, author of *Old Enough*, a *New York Times Book Review* Editors' Choice

Does Anyone Else Feel This Way?

Does Anyone Else Feel This Way?

Essays on Conquering the Quarter-Life Crisis

Eli Rallo

HARVEST
An Imprint of WILLIAM MORROW

Without limiting the exclusive rights of any author, contributor or the publisher of this publication, any unauthorized use of this publication to train generative artificial intelligence (AI) technologies is expressly prohibited. HarperCollins also exercise their rights under Article 4(3) of the Digital Single Market Directive 2019/790 and expressly reserve this publication from the text and data mining exception.

The names and identifying characteristics of the individuals discussed in this book have been changed to protect their privacy.

DOES ANYONE ELSE FEEL THIS WAY? Copyright © 2025 by Eli Rallo. All rights reserved. Printed in the United States of America. No part of this book may be used or reproduced in any manner whatsoever without written permission except in the case of brief quotations embodied in critical articles and reviews. For information, address HarperCollins Publishers, 195 Broadway, New York, NY 10007. In Europe, HarperCollins Publishers, Macken House, 39/40 Mayor Street Upper, Dublin 1, D01 C9W8, Ireland.

HarperCollins books may be purchased for educational, business, or sales promotional use. For information, please email the Special Markets Department at SPsales@harpercollins.com.

hc.com

FIRST EDITION

Library of Congress Cataloging-in-Publication Data has been applied for.

ISBN 978-0-06-341753-3

25 26 27 28 29 LBC 5 4 3 2 1

To the eldest daughters,
may you turn this light onto yourselves.

Contents

Introduction   xi

Does Anyone Else Have No Plan?   1

Does Anyone Else Know WTF to Do About Imposter Syndrome?   23

Does Anyone Else Feel Like a Faux Adult?   45

Does Anyone Else Feel Like Relationships Take Work?   63

Does Anyone Else Feel Like They're Having a Quarter-Life Crisis?   87

Does Anyone Else Feel Like They Need to Stop Scrolling?   115

Does Anyone Else Avoid the OB-GYN?   149

Does Anyone Else Feel Like All Their Friends Hate Them?   173

Does Anyone Else Hate Socializing?   197

**Does Anyone Else Fear Moving Away and
Growing Apart?** 219

Does Anyone Else Feel Like They're in a Funk? 243

**Does Anyone Else Feel Like It's Okay
Not to Know Everything?** 263

Acknowledgments 285

Introduction

Today I am twenty-six years old, and a lot of times I feel as though I know less than I did at sixteen.

Today I am twenty-six years old, and I pay for my own phone bill, which feels like an adult thing for me to do.

Today I am twenty-six years old, and I am a cavern of joy and ambition, and I am awash in gratitude. Today I am twenty-six years old, and I feel awkward at the party I am invited to. I wish I had never come. I overthink so much about everything that it interferes with my ability to live. I am scared that I am losing my mind.

I am planning for my future. What is a future? How do you plan for one? I am afraid that no matter how hard we resist, women are forced to assume a series of titles throughout our lives—we are girls and then we are wives and then we are mothers—and I feel guilty for wanting more.

Today I am twenty-six years old, and I don't have my shit together, but sometimes I pretend to. I feel like I am behind.

Today I am twenty-six years old, and I feel too old. I also feel too young. I am cold all the time. I like to listen to jazz music when I cook dinner, which is something I like to do now, cook dinner. That wasn't something I liked to do the last time I saw you here, on the page.

This is my way of telling you that I have changed. In many

ways I have also remained the girl you always knew. The girl my childhood best friend knew. The baby my mom raised. I am all of them, all of me. You have changed too. Think about it for a second. Wow.

Today I am twenty-six years old and writing you a short note that I hope you'll read before you begin this book, a book I would call mine, but is now just as much yours. Stories I have lived that you will hopefully see your own reflection in.

I'm not sure how many of you read my debut, *I Didn't Know I Needed This*, but I was freshly twenty-three when I started to write it, and was eighteen, nineteen, and twenty when I lived the many experiences I shared within those pages. I had so much distance from those experiences to process them, time to realize they maybe weren't that deep, space to grow up a lot, and as a result, writing that book was purely fun for me. Like riding on a flirty pink cloud (drinking a margarita, wearing a glittery dress). The challenge with my first book was not the content but learning the form. I did my best, and I am so proud of that. I am here today, a different woman than I was at twenty-three. But in so many ways I am the same woman I have been on every birthday, every time I've blown out the candles. I have written you a book that is wildly different than my first—a book that was a challenge to write because I was processing the emotions, fresh and hot, as I wrote. I cried a lot while writing this book. It felt like a release. It felt like pushing a boulder up a mountain. I am protective of this book because it feels like handing over my soul, whereas *I Didn't Know I Needed This* felt like handing over my heart. Now you have so much of me, and yet I still have so much left. Nonfiction writing will do that to you. Force you to dissect yourself. Force you to write about the hard things. Force you to break yourself down and hand over your messy parts. I once heard someone say, "You know you're writing something good when your family hates it." I'm not sure this fits the bill, but maybe it does.

This book is my ode to the unspoken loneliness of our twenties, even when we are surrounded by our friends at a party we do actually want to be at. This book is a love letter to feeling stuck, lost, unmoored, and untethered as people in adulthood who felt forgotten in childhood, confused when it all changed around us. This book is for the overextended, the afraid, the unsure, the ready, the fearless twentysomething or thirtysomething or beyond. This book seeks to answer the question: Will we ever have it all figured out?

Spoiler alert: this book does not answer this question.

My experience of being in my twenties will be different than yours. Your experience will be different than that of the girl you inevitably see reading this on the subway (manifesting). I do not believe any of us can be fully "in touch" with the reality of others, as we can only be present in our realities—shaped by our unique lived experiences. I do not claim to speak for all of us, or on behalf of all of us. I wanted to use this space to work through the difficult emotions I've processed, many of which felt unprecedented, many of which came out of nowhere—many of which I've realized, through speaking up, are incredibly universal, even when our daily lives are not the same.

I Didn't Know I Needed This is not required reading before *Does Anyone Else Feel This Way?* but I do think that if you read both, you will see the way a girl can mature, grow, and change in three years. You will also see the same realization slowly be had, in many ways—that you need to put yourself first. That you are yours first—to have and to hold. To care for. To prioritize.

In these pages I lament on so many of the things I've carried with me through the years. I crack open questions and hunt for answers I both do and do not find. I went on my own journey writing this book, laying down the bricks for the road you will travel in the pages ahead. I was reminded, throughout this process, that I am the girl who was once five years old, and then sixteen. One day I will be lucky enough to still be the girl I was today. My baggage is in the form of interests and hobbies, great loves and tastes that have never changed, unpacked meticulously, across state lines. My sweet tooth, love for Ariana Grande, nervous disposition, big heart, and stubborn demeanor travel with me from one chapter to the next, even as everything else flips upside down.

Sometimes, when I feel like my feet aren't planted firmly in today, or I feel like I can't find my way, I ask the universe for a sign. Just give me a sign that everything is going to be okay.

And then a few hours later, when I run into the grocery store to buy Claritin, "My Favorite Things" from *The Sound of Music* will be playing, which has always been my song (much like how couples have a song, and whatnot). And I will take a moment and realize that this is my sign. That the signs are everywhere. In the familiar creaks of your home's floorboards, the eyes you've gazed into for years, the first sip of a drink across the table from an old friend, the so rare and so real privilege of having an old friend.

Maybe if you've been looking for one—a sign, that is—this could be yours.

I have no requests for you before you read. Just that you be good to yourself, good to other people, good to our world. I love you. I trust you. I believe in us. And thank you. The show is about to begin.

Does Anyone Else Have No Plan?

I'm on the subway going to my friend Lizzie's twenty-seventh birthday party. Twenty-seven always sounded like a good age to be. She doesn't agree, and because I'm twenty-five, I don't get to have a say. I'm wearing vintage kitten heels and reading a book while balancing a tote bag full of wine bottles between my legs. I think my outfit is cool until the doors push open and a gaggle of preteen girls bounds toward the seats directly across from me—three conversations going at once, voices ecstatic and half shriek, half shrill. They move together as one, tossing hair and taking selfies, affirming one another's quips like a five-headed picture of girlhood. They wear the same outfits in different colors: Converse sneakers or heeled black boots, short skirts and long-sleeve shirts. I watch them watch me, their eyes running over my face and the outfit I now feel is incredibly dumb.

I was you once, I want to say, but don't. I let them go over me with their eyes before they grow bored and launch into various discussions—whose house they will sleep over at after the party, who will be there and who is drinking, what designer bags they wish they had and which lip glosses they do. One of them proudly exclaims that she is the group's "mom friend." I pause my music and listen to their musings, the PG version of conversations I'll have at the twenty-seventh birthday party. They are thirteen, in the early throes of awkward stages and first kisses. Halfway to twenty-five. Halfway to me. They live inside me and they race toward me; they wish they were twenty-one, and I wish I was twelve. I half focus on the book in my lap, keeping a soft glance on them and their airy innocence. They look around like they know everything, and I'd like to tell them to hold on to that feeling as long as they can; it'll slip through their fingers one day without the faintest warning. Pantomiming heartbreak with their math class crushes, challenges chaperoned by their parents; their world is just this party, and for now, they are friends. I envy them briefly, envy thirteen. When my mind was a glass castle. My virgin heart and braided hair and the memorized home phone number of a girl I don't talk to anymore. On the 1 train, their fearless laughs are a soundtrack to my inner monologue, and I am twice their age. My mind is a shattered snow globe, and my heart is taped together with Band-Aids. I am trying to grow out the bangs I cut on a whim, and my friend is turning twenty-seven, and I felt like I knew everything when I was thirteen, and somehow I know more now but feel like I know less. The sparkly confidence of being a girl in a group has faded, and I have been left with no answers. One of them says she hates Kyle, another one says she wishes she had a Prada bag, one is engrossed in her pink-cased iPhone, and two have their arms around each other like soulmates. I know these girls because I am these girls, was these girls, yet they are strangers.

Stay thirteen forever, I want to say, but I don't. Instead, I see bits of myself in them, and I wish the best for them, and I get to my stop and get up. I feel them watch me go, and then the subway throttles on, into the future and into the night.

•

The best part of being thirteen was imagining what life would be like when I was seventeen and had a set of car keys with multicolored, jingly key chains like the older girl who lived next door. The best part of being seventeen was imagining what life would be like when I was twenty-one and about to graduate from college. I looked forward to the day the fog of adolescence would lift and everything would click naturally into place, when the perpetual unknown I'd been living in would finally cease. The worst part about being twenty-one was that my attic bedroom had carpet beetles and the guy I wanted to be with forever only wanted to be with me when it was time to leave the bar. I looked forward to becoming a *real adult* on my twenty-second birthday. I assumed that by twenty-two, you graduated from training wheels to a two-wheel bike—metaphorically of course—and you finally felt like the adult you had technically become at the age of eighteen.

My senior year of college, I lived with five girls who had their postgrad plans lined up by the end of first semester. One going to grad school, one working in finance, one doing Teach for America, one going to work in sales in California, and the final going to work in consulting in Chicago. And then there was me, a planless loser, the queen of racking up rejection emails and changing her mind. One Friday, on the first day of spring, I sat in my playwriting workshop brimming with pride for my thesis—a play about Rosie the Riveter. It was the perfect March day. The air smelled like grass and potential, and it was my turn to get feedback from a circle of my peers—fellow writers, actors, and directors—who'd be working on the senior thesis plays that semester. Everyone held frayed copies of my work and proceeded to share (what felt like) a million things that were wrong with my one hundred pages of writing. I smiled politely, distractedly scrolling to the pages they referenced, halfheartedly jotting down notes about unfinished characters and confusing plot points and gender politics. It's always the writing you think is good that your workshop will make sure to tell you they hate. About halfway through, it became clear that I might be better off just starting over. On my laptop screen, Gmail flashed a new notification. I was waiting for an email with a decision from the *Wall Street Journal*'s prestigious Bartley Fellowship in the arts. I had gone through a five-round interview process for the second year in a row. The committee had narrowed the thousands of applications down to a handful—and for the second time, I was one of them. I was hesitant but confident about getting the role. I knew the team, had demonstrated interest, visited the offices that summer for an informational interview, and felt like I'd improved from the prior year—I'd asked the editor of the section what I could work on before applying again and focused all my energy on each bullet point he gave. While my classmates shared polite, generic compliments and specific, granular critiques about my thesis, I hovered my mouse over the new email and clicked, revealing a curt rejection email. They said that while they felt like "the Eli Rallo who applied this year was a completely different applicant than the one who applied last year," they'd decided to go in a "different direction." I swallowed hard and tried to snap back into the present moment, where everyone was agreeing that I should rewrite the entire first scene because there was "room for improvement." Class came to a close on that note, and I didn't feel saved by the bell. It was a Friday in March, and everyone was entranced by tulips and iced coffees and glee, languidly packing their bags and exchanging weekend plans. I shoved everything into my backpack, put my head down, and avoided eyes as I made my way to the bus. Rejection never bothered me much, nor did workshop. I actually felt that both made me a better creative and a stronger writer. But this rejection and this workshop, coming on the heels of months of rejection and reminders of ways I could be better, pounded in my skull, making me wish I could crawl out of my skin or turn my brain off.

I entered the University of Michigan pursuing a bachelor's degree in theater art, with a concentration in performing arts management and entrepreneurship, which felt practical and adultlike. I took minors in playwriting, creative writing, and political science, married to the idea that I'd probably never make it as a creative and needed a backup plan. I chose to pursue entertainment producing to be practical, when the truth was that I wanted to be an author and a creative, not a girlboss in a pantsuit. I feared the unconventional path of the artist for years—and had no idea how anyone got a play produced or a book published anyway. Being an artist lacked a one-size-fits-all equation or a set of steps to follow to achieve success—it was like making a DIY project into a career. But senior year, the eleventh hour, I realized I was abandoning my passions to be *practical*, and now I was desperately trying to hunt down a creative job. A job in culture, entertainment, arts, journalism, or writing that could pay my bills but be a sensible step toward the artistic dreams I had for myself—the far-off dream of seeing my very own book in a bookstore or my play on a real stage. But even when I was trying to be brave and take the leap, I was still forcing myself to be practical and pragmatic. I couldn't rip the Band-Aid off. Instead, I peeled it in slow motion, watching in agony as it tore up tiny pieces of arm hair.

On the bus I tried to just go blank, to avoid the run-on sentence in my mind, reminding me I had no job—despite the over fifty applications I'd sent out. The guy I liked had opened my Snapchat without responding hours ago. My thesis was nobody's favorite and apparently needed to be completely redone. My best friend was moving to San Francisco in May. I was afraid to admit I wanted to be an artist or a creative, and at this point, I didn't feel like I was capable anyway. It felt more like I was delusional. I didn't believe in myself, and I wasn't sure I could find anyone else who believed in me either. I trudged home from the bus stop, firing off a brief email to Lisa—the hiring manager at the fellowship, desperately letting her know I'd love to be considered if anything changed, or for any other position. I joked with my mom that I was always "more of a *New York Times* girl" as I wondered who, if anyone, was going to hire a theater student and aspiring playwright, poet, and author for a legitimate adult job in journalism.

At home, my best friend, Sadie, sat on our deflated couch with a few of our roommates. They plotted the Friday night ahead, scrolled Instagram, and gossiped about the guys who lived across the street. I came in like a thunderstorm, a torrent of anxious emotion, suddenly disrupting their joy like a lightning crack. They looked at me and I looked at them and then they asked me how the workshop went. I was angry at first—it was not good, I had a lot of work to do, I was expecting them to like it, but even the actors assigned to the final performance seemed unmotivated by the material. They cooed empathetically, they were sure I'd figure it out, they bet it wasn't as bad as I thought. And then, out of nowhere, my voice cracked and tears streamed down my cheeks—I didn't get the job, the *dream job*, the job I was sure was mine. Not only that, I feared I wouldn't get any job at this point, and wasn't that my own fault? I came to college and told myself the creative stuff was a hobby and a side hustle and I had to focus on something practical. I had reached this point of despair through a lack of belief in myself. What would be different if I'd spent the last few years working toward my dreams instead of pretending like they were a silly hobby? What would be different if I grew a set of metaphoric balls? I blubbered and whimpered, lamenting MFA program rejections and job after job saying "no thanks," collapsing into the couch opposite them, sending up a waft of the upholstery's permanent fruit-flavored-vodka smell. I wanted to become the couch. I wanted to stop all this feeling, especially in front of anyone besides Sadie. Sadie is cool like lake water, sharp and shiny like a sword, all honest truths and simple pleasures rolled into one firecracker redhead I call my best friend. I didn't cry in front of these other girls. We were housemates, and we went out together and made seductive Instagram stories in the bar's bathroom. We didn't bare our souls to one another on our disgusting couch in our dilapidated living room on the first Friday afternoon of spring. Here I was, saying I felt like both a freak and a failure—a mess who had always been too afraid to take the leap, to be honest about what she wanted—but when I finally found the courage, the world turned red like a stop sign and held me in place. For a second that felt like an eternity, nobody said anything. And then it was Sadie—coming over to me so our knees were touching, putting her hand on top of mine—who broke the ugly silence.

"You don't know how lucky you are. I'm so jealous of you," she said, and I turned my puffy eyes up to look at her. I wasn't expecting that, but then again, a Sagittarius is hardly one to say something expected.

"Do you know how much I wish I was passionate about something the way you're passionate about writing?" she asked, and I wanted to break her cool gaze.

"Most of us are going to go work at desks or in offices, and it's fine, I'll like my job and be happy and motivated, but it isn't like I'm all that passionate about it. At the end of the day, I'll work to live, to make money." She paused.

"But you write because you feel like you have to. Because you couldn't live with yourself if you didn't try. Don't you realize how lucky you are to be that passionate about something?"

Nobody else said anything for a while. I don't know when the clock started turning again or when we got up from the couches and went to our rooms and did our hair and picked out outfits from one another's closets. But I know my world kept turning, because my best friend looked at me with ice in her eyes and said, "Do you realize how lucky you are?"

•

I didn't realize how lucky I was. Now, exactly four years later, I want to clamp my hands on my twenty-one-year-old self's shoulders and shake and shake and shake. I swam in a sea of fear of rejection and failure back then. I danced an elaborate dance with the anxiety that I wasn't good enough to be an artist. And then, when that dance partner got tired, I danced with the anxiety that I'd never forgive myself if I didn't try. I was waiting for the permission to jump when the permission slip simply needed my own signature. I truly did not understand or recognize the privilege it is to be artistically passionate—and the privilege it is to pursue an artistic career path.

Most creatives—most artists—create out of necessity, and for me, writing and creating has always been second nature. Even if not for an audience or not for a job, I was always just doing it. Toiling with a story or a half-finished poem after class, jotting down ideas for a play or a feature film in my notebook on a Saturday afternoon. Even when I told myself, *This is just your side hustle, this is just your hobby*, I had a constant, intrinsic instinct to create. I'd be on the bus to a business producing class in my *Hamilton* crewneck listening to a playlist full of show tunes, writing a poem in my notes app, selling myself a lie that show tunes and poems were unserious and silly, so it was imperative to be practical. But creating was necessary for my survival—it wasn't something I could just turn away from. Yet the idea of being a professional creative, and that way of life—seemingly so fluid and free and unconventional—was at direct odds with, the antithesis of, the practical path higher education and teachers and parents pushed on me when I neared eighteen. Throughout my childhood and young adulthood, the world was not affirming artists and writers the way they did doctors and lawyers. Nobody would've called being an artist practical or sensible, and there was certainly no one clear path to a career in the arts. Funny boys were class clowns, and funny girls were like puppets or show ponies. Everyone wanted to be in on the joke, but nobody wanted to take us seriously, nobody wanted to take us home, nobody wanted to sign a contract and have us sign too. I'd make everyone laugh or marvel at the way the wheels in my mind turned, but I wasn't their parents' idea of a good influence, just a good time and a free spirit. For most of my life, everyone around me sucked up all my creativity and theatricality and left me bare—sure, Eli was funny and creative, but surely a man would end up taking care of her. *Nobody makes it in the arts. And who does she think she is, Tina Fey?* I basked in my fair share of pity smiles from Uber drivers and neighbors and my parents' friends alike when I said I wanted to be an author, or a playwright. Nobody applauded you for going to college to major in theater the way they did with business and biochemistry majors. Instead they'd get this twisted smile on their face, like they just ate something sour. They'd look at you with a gaze of slight embarrassment and say something like,

"Well, good for you. Can't hurt to try." I could see it behind their condescending glance; they looked at my acting class like I was burning money, and my creative writing seminar like I was playing the slots in Vegas.

I decided to major in performing arts management and entrepreneurship with minors in playwriting and creative writing—that way I was marrying my passions with the advice of the practical voices swirling around me, telling me that to make it as a writer was one in a million, so I needed a backup plan. The world tells you over and over and over—in movies and TV shows, through books and people you know—not to pursue a career in the arts. And even when they're not telling you to your face, there's a clear message being pushed at you from all sides: this is not practical, this is not legitimate, this is not serious. You are not serious. I watched my high school take funding from the band and the choir and the drama club and reallocate it to the football team. The irony—most of the kids in the band and the choir and the drama club would go on to pursue something creative, while most of the football players wouldn't touch a football again past the age of eighteen.

But I listened anyway. I was always an obedient kid. Always craved the approval of the well-intentioned adults around me. And I chose to listen to the world. I'd be practical. Be serious. Potentially be miserable. I'd take the business classes and the legal classes and the performing arts management classes. I could be a producer or an administrator or a casting director. Writing could be a side hustle. It could just be for fun. But there was a deep pit growing in my stomach, gnawing away at me through my early years of college, causing me to question whether this was the right decision. I forced myself to fall in love with practicality and accept that my deep desire to tell stories could be a passion project.

They were right: I'd never make it. It wasn't worth it. I'd put my head down and get through. I'd be a well-behaved, docile, practical girl. I'd make adults proud, and then I'd become an adult and I'd make myself proud. Sitting awake at night, staring at the cream-colored ceiling of my freshman year dorm room, I wondered when I'd feel certain—of my choices and my path and my independence. And I told myself a story to stay alive—that when I graduated college, just like I'd seen from movies and TV shows, from media and pop culture, all of this uncertainty and adolescence would simply fall away. Surely there was a day where you'd just start feeling like an adult—and I saw the light at the end of the tunnel at twenty-two. There'd be no more chubby cheeks and no more questioning—I'd be chiseled like a statue made of marble and be certain. I'd be mature and adult in the way twenty-two-year-olds seemed to be on Instagram. I'd be like my mom, who knows the answers to things without using Google. I could make peace with drowning in a river of uncertainty at eighteen, nineteen, twenty, and twenty-one if I sold myself the story that when you got to twenty-two, you had it all figured out. I couldn't make sense of the future otherwise. There had to be a point where you grew out of your childhood tastes and your childlike wanting and your big, lofty dreams and your adolescence, where young adulthood stopped and adulthood began. When, otherwise, did we grow out of our childhood tastes? When would we start feeling like an equal to the adults around us? When would we turn up our noses at the sight of sour gummy candies and know how to get any stain out of white pants? There had to be a moment where you ceased to be unsure and were reborn with a feeling that you had your shit together. Becoming an adult isn't like a birthday or a college graduation—there's no ceremony. Eventually it just is, and I had to hold out hope that the time of adult certainty was coming. I didn't feel like a sure-of-herself, put-together adult when I turned eighteen, so I assumed that it was like a delayed hit—your adult self took a while to come out, like a caterpillar in a cocoon waiting to be reborn a butterfly. I knew plenty of twenty-two-year-olds, and I saw them as sure and certain and fine. So I told myself a story of hope, because I couldn't stand the growing pains of the dark and foreboding unknown. I needed clear skies. No turbulence. A safe landing.

•

At twenty-one years old, sobbing into my best friend's knees, scared out of my mind—less than three months away from the coveted twenty-two years old—I felt much more like a helpless, timid little girl than a chiseled marble statue. I had no plan. And adults had plans. I still liked sour gummy candy and saw my passion for it going nowhere. I couldn't get most stains out of white pants. Sadie was organized and sure of herself in the way a lot of Sagittarian women are. She was going to move to San Francisco and take a job with the company she interned for the summer prior. I imagined her meeting a super-hot, super-mature older guy at a wine bar down the street from her well-decorated apartment. I imagined her getting a promotion. I imagined her getting a dog and going to spin classes and throwing her head back and laughing her sparkly laugh with a gaggle of new girlfriends who drank beers and said the right things. I imagined her leaving me in the dust. Not because she didn't love me, but because she'd graduated from adolescence and I was her friend from college, the girl who never figured it out. The girl who got caught up somewhere in the in-between.

I imagined myself nowhere. I didn't imagine myself moving back home, but I also didn't imagine myself in a swanky apartment with a charming view of Manhattan's jagged skyline. I didn't imagine myself with a super-hot, super-mature guy. I didn't imagine myself with new friends or promotions. I didn't imagine myself in shape or in style. And I definitely didn't imagine myself drinking beer. Not only did I not imagine this life, I couldn't. And that terrified me. Because even without my ability to picture the future, it hung in the distance, and I hoped I would make it. I knew I'd have to.

It was inevitable.

•

College was not the best four years of my life, but it was the most formative four years of my life. A lot of people go to college searching for answers, and I was one of those people. But instead of getting answers, I ended my four years with questions upon questions upon questions. It was a privilege to be educated—and to find myself with questions based on that education and experience—but back then I would rather have had a cheat sheet with all the answers.

One time my mom went to a psychic, and she was told that her daughter would never graduate from college. And while technically, I earned my degree, I never had a graduation—because my graduating year was 2020. My senior year was eclipsed by the pandemic, and I remember feeling nothing when we found out. We were at Chipotle stealing bottles of hot sauce to eat with our bowls when we got an email from the university telling us our graduation was canceled, the remainder of the semester would be online, and we should all go home. *Go home*—that part kind of got me. Was Ann Arbor not my home? The house with our neighbor's plastic beer pong table on the porch every other weekend (we shared it), a revolving door of bright adolescent faces, lecture halls and improv shows, the theater school's annual lingerie party, the corner liquor store, the way the sky got purple before it snowed, Sadie's organized closet, and telephone wires with tied pairs of sneakers pulling them down. I called New Jersey home in the way we all called the place we came from home, but it no longer held the sweet and heavy connotation of home. Nowhere did anymore. We all just sat in the hazy shift.

A week later, I'd said goodbye to my friends, packed up my house, rented a Mitsubishi Outlander to drive to New Jersey—and been accepted to Columbia University's graduate school of journalism. I picked up my brother and his bags from the apartment building of a girl he loved early one morning, and we half silently drove "home." I was lucky to have that physical home. Lucky to have my health. Lucky to have a brother in the passenger seat. I photoshopped a Columbia University logo onto a plain gray crewneck sweatshirt and uploaded the picture to Instagram. Grad school seemed like a cop-out and an avoidance and also my only real option. I submitted an application for student loans, and my heart and mind felt like they'd been rubbed with numbing cream and forced into silence.

Back in New Jersey again, I felt both eighteen and eighty years old. I was neither. I was twenty-one, unpacking squished boxes of memorabilia and full notebooks and hair tools and scarves. I was forced, in many ways, to unpack the duffel bags chockfull of emotion and unfinished thoughts, the emotional baggage I didn't want to sit with. In many ways, the solitude and isolation of spring 2020 forced a lot of us to reflect—on our wants and interests, our hopes and dreams, what we missed fiercely and what we could now do without, our habits and routines. I remember sitting in front of my laptop, staring at a blank document, willing a story to life—hating myself for not dedicating the time forced inside, isolated, to writing the great next American novel or working on my craft. Isn't this what every artist has ever wanted? Uninterrupted time to create?

Somehow March faded into April and April to May—my twenty-second birthday on the horizon. The clarity I craved had been replaced with further questions and concerns—am I just going to grad school to avoid the inevitable? Is this the right move? I always said I wanted to move away from New York—should I really move there?

And then, one night in the middle of May, I uploaded a video to TikTok (intended for friends only, but accidentally made public)—and everything changed. This part of the story is not relatable, nor is it universal, but I'm going to tie it into a lesson (and I beg you to stick around for this all to make sense). I always loved the word *serendipity*—meaning "happy accident," like running into a friend waiting for a table at your favorite restaurant, or booking the wrong train time and meeting the love of your life. My first rodeo with serendipity was on that May night—the seemingly insignificant mistake of posting a TikTok video to public was the start of my entire future, the reason I started to believe in myself, and the beginning of my eventual foray into becoming a professional artist, creative, and published author.

A mistake became the foundation. A faux pas became the future. A dream bloomed out of the sky like a puff of smoke swirling from a barely lit cigarette. There was, of course, over a decade of delusion involved as well. A girl who for some reason, even when she went off path, even when she tried to maintain practicality, never truly abandoned the dreams now actualizing right in front of her face. All of the tears shed on dream jobs, guys who'd never love me, and bygone opportunities felt so silly now.

I wish I could've gotten out of my own way at twenty-one—that I could've been wise or aware enough to understand what I know now. I wish it hadn't taken a TikTok video or superfluous vitality online to make me realize that what I feared more than failure was complacency—what I feared more than falling on my face was staying where I was—what I feared more than trying was not trying at all. But this isn't about the TikTok, and it isn't about social media, and it isn't about COVID. It isn't even about me. This is about our universal hatred of uncertainty. Our human, constant need for a plan. The myth that college is supposed to answer all your questions and be the best four years of your life. The pressure we put on eighteen-year-olds and then twenty-year-olds to snap into adulthood as though it's a seamless transition. This is about being pushed off the high dive and making the choice in midair that you're going to swim, not sink.

•

I now reflect on that day with my terrible play and the rejection email from the dream job and Sadie's words, and I wonder what my life would've looked like if I had been certain, if I'd had a plan. Sure, there's a chance I would've adored the fellowship at the *Journal*; maybe it would've turned into a full-time job. Maybe I would live in a studio apartment and own a lot of blazers. But I wouldn't be sitting on a plane coming from my boyfriend's hometown, flying back to our shared apartment, thinking of plans tomorrow with my friend from grad school. I wouldn't have worn pink shoes on the red carpet at the Tony Awards. I wouldn't have sat in the living room after busy days with my best friend from grad school, whom I went on to live with, Jen, and listened to her tell stories about college and her sister because I wouldn't know Jen. More importantly, I would absolutely not be writing this to you. Maybe one day there'd be a book deal; maybe one day there'd be a handful of readers or a different boyfriend and a different best friend. It is both heartbreaking and affirming to reflect on the lives we could've lived that we didn't choose. But I wouldn't be here, and we wouldn't be pulsing silently on this page together.

If I had never been uncertain, if I had never been the planless loser racking up rejections, if I had gotten that dream job, I wouldn't have been able to hold the hands of a girl with shiny hair at a theater in San Francisco when she told me that because of my journey, she started writing again. She saw that I believed I could and started believing she could too.

It was a gift to know so little back then.

What I'm trying to tell you is that you could see uncertainty as terrifying and terrible, or you could see it as an opportunity. Rejection and uncertainty are simply the universe's way of telling you what is meant for you is still yours to discover. Perhaps if you were sure, there'd be nothing more to learn. Perhaps the plan you craved would become a reality you loathed. Perhaps the certainty you desire would become a dead end. I thought the key was being overplanned and überpractical—but the truth is uncertainty is the best thing to ever happen to me. My dream was not something I conjured up; it was something that called me on the phone when I was ready to pick up. In the same way that you can tell yourself a story of a worst-case scenario, you can tell yourself the story of a best-case scenario—you're the storyteller, so tell yourself the one that keeps your nervous system regulated. To be unsure is not a bad thing; it is the very chance to embrace chaos and carve it into something that makes sense to you.

Uncertainty is not you failing; it is not you falling apart. It is the universe's way of saying that what is in store for you is something you haven't considered, something you don't even know exists, and the minute you meet this place or opportunity or person, it'll make sense. But of course, while we can train ourselves to redefine uncertainty, that doesn't mean it will automatically bring us joy and not fear. It can be terrifying and it can also be okay at the same time—two things can be true, and in this case, they will be. You're going to be anxious when you graduate from college and feel lost. You're going to be upset when you go through a breakup with a person you thought you'd be with forever and now won't be. You're going to be unnerved when you get rejected from the job that you thought was meant for you. But you're also going to be okay. Being lost is an opportunity to go out and find your way home—wherever home is, whatever home is. Four walls, or an art studio, the place down the street where you do yoga, the pair of hands washing dishes in the sink, the glossy eyes of your best friend waiting offstage for you to take your bow. You will come home, and that home will be something you built for yourself. And you'll be so grateful that you got lost, because of all the love and Polaroid pictures and people you collected along the way.

•

These days, I no longer refer to anything as my "dream"—not a job, not a person, not an opportunity, or a school. I could feel strongly about attending a school or applying to a job and have my fingers crossed that it would work out. I could meet a great guy and hope that he texts me and asks me on a date. But none of those things were my dream job or dream person. How would I know if my dream was that job before I even worked there? How could I know that guy was my dream guy before we'd even gone on a date? I couldn't. I could know I wanted those things. I could hope they worked out. But I'd have no idea if these specific roles and people were my dream. And if they didn't work out, I'd be shattered to miss out on what I was sure was my dream. Truthfully, I knew my dream was to be a writer because I'd written before and was addicted to it, attached to it, enamored by it. I knew my dream was to fall in love with a great person because I'd fallen in love before and prayed for the day I would again.

But if the object of my affection doesn't work out—if the opportunity falls through or the job says, "No thanks"—that is just as good an outcome as things going my way. Instead of seeing rejection as a failure or a stop sign, I see it now as a redirection. It is as though the wind has picked up, and the universe is whispering to me, "Not this one. Trust me. I don't want you to miss out on what's around the corner." With this new mindset, not only does rejection sting less, I see rejection as somehow equivalent to success—it isn't always a yes or a no; it's either a yes or a *something else is meant for you*. You can be sad when you get the rejection email or he never texts back—but you can't lose faith in yourself because the dreams you perceive yourself to have are smashed. What really happened? The road was closed, you could never have driven that way, you're getting a new set of directions, and you're taking the scenic route. I know you'll be glad the road was closed, despite the interruption and frustration, when you stop at the random diner you wouldn't have gone to otherwise and meet the love of your life.

•

On my twenty-second birthday, in July 2020, I did not feel certain, and I did not feel like an adult. I felt like the bicycle I'd been riding always had training wheels, and now I was expected to ride a two-wheel bike—no training, no extra help, no concerned parent making sure I didn't fall. I wish I had been brave enough to say, "Does anyone else feel this way?" or "Does anyone else have no plan?" instead of suffering in quiet silence, softening the blow with self-deprecating humor.

I knew nothing then, and I had a long way to go still. One day I'd be twenty-five and riding the subway, and I'd watch versions of myself at thirteen dance around me, wishing to be older. We'd always wish away the present with such intensity, such volume—we'd always wish away the uncertainty because we internalized it as fear. I wanted to stay on the subway forever, on the way to my friend's twenty-seventh birthday, a bottle of wine between my legs. I'd become the plastic seat, and I'd be the place people rested on their way to birthday parties and first dates and adolescent nights out and work. I'd soak up all the stories and fears like a sponge. I'd never have to face my own stories, my own fears.

On my twenty-second birthday, I didn't know that nobody would believe in me until I set the precedent that I believed in myself. I didn't know that being serious is a load of shit—because hardly any great genius or success story ever started with someone choosing the safe route. No great love story begins with staying home. You can't hit a home run from the bench. If you want to be a winner, you have to risk striking out. There's no other way. I didn't know that it is a great privilege to be a creative. I knew that art is as imperative to the world as oxygen, but I never believed I could be part of the people building the stories that sustain us like I was a gardener of prose planting trees in the form of essays. I knew that college was not the best four years of my life, but I didn't know that it was okay to feel that way—and that other people felt that way too.

And maybe this isn't practical advice, but don't take the world's word for it. You can listen, but the world doesn't know you. Only you know yourself well enough to choose. Being practical is bullshit. Being palatable for society is never where the magic happens. Art is serious and legitimate and real and vital. There is no one way to do anything—the right way is the way that is your own. Being lost is when you find the restaurant with the best burger you've ever had, the peaceful park with the flowers in full bloom, the overlook where you watch the sunset, and the girl in your passenger seat whom you never would've known had you always been so sure of yourself. You squeeze her hand, and you can't believe she is there. She is there because you got lost, not because you were safe or found.

•

Sometimes the only plan you'll have—for your whole life—is what you're doing later that night. And that's enough. Life is all one foot in front of the other, after all. As I stepped off the subway platform at West Seventy-Seventh Street and into the chilly January air, leaving my thirteen-year-old girl gang behind, my only plan was to go celebrate Lizzie's birthday. To knock on her door and fall into her familiar arms, the way she smells like flowers and her dusting of freckles and the way she'll always remind me how much she loves me. We'll toast to her, and we'll toast to having no clue, because having a plan is overrated anyway. Have an idea, have an inkling, have a sketch or a draft you wrote in pencil—but be brave enough to leave it all up to interpretation, to be surprised, to play Mad Libs with your next step and let the blanks fill themselves as you go. If I'd had a plan, I wouldn't be writing this, and your eyes wouldn't be following each word on this very page.

And I think that's a wonderful place to start.

Does Anyone Else Know WTF to Do About Imposter Syndrome?

I've only ever felt like I fully belonged anywhere when I was in utero. I suppose I don't fully know how I felt while I was a fetus twenty-six years ago, but I can assume that to be the last (and only) time I've fully felt at peace. Fully felt a sense of belonging. Fully felt like I was somewhere meant for me. Somewhere I belonged.

Of course I have belonged since, but it never felt natural. Never felt seamless to me. There has never been a room I've walked into and immediately, with a soft sigh, said, "This must be what it feels like to be at home." Call it anxiety, or being weird, or always feeling like you say the wrong things. First I feel like a misfit, and then I feel guilty for feeling that way. When I'm finally home alone, folding laundry and answering emails, I start to think about how misplaced I feel almost everywhere I go. Is this a me thing? Is this a them thing? Is this an us thing? Does anyone feel like they belong anywhere? Or am I just an aberration? Am I the only person in the world who feels out of place everywhere they go?

Enter: New York City. Fall 2020. A fantastic place to feel like you don't belong while everyone else is pretending as though they do.

•

My first New York City apartment was a fifth-story Upper West Side walk-up that my best friends from college already lived in (they'd graduated a year earlier). As far as fictional depictions of moving to New York City go, I was a regular Hannah Horvath from *Girls* (though I lusted after a Carrie Bradshaw closet with a Samantha Jones attitude and a Charlotte York apartment). If you haven't watched *Girls*, you can just picture a puffy, annoying freshly twenty-two-year-old transplant with larger-than-life artistic dreams who is prone to making terrible decisions. At this point in our story, I'd decided that Katie Couric should watch out, because I was going to become this world's next big female journalist.

A lot of times, according to my Twitter feed of fellow down-on-their-luck artists, when you're feeling lost or shit out of luck in your career, you go to grad school. I half fit that bill. I was certainly lost, but not necessarily shit out of luck in my career yet—I was only twenty-two years old, an infant in adult years. But I'd been accepted to Columbia University's masters in journalism program, and at this point I figured if I could become a lifestyle journalist or an essayist, I'd be in a decent position to eventually acquire a book deal—which was my Big Goal™. A Big Goal is so lofty, so elusive, so far-reaching that you cannot even fully grasp it yourself. When you have a Big Goal, you might be in the habit of setting smaller goals that *could* be stepping stones to achieving the big one. I applied for a loan, saved exactly enough money for a year of rent with a few thousand dollars in an emergency fund, packed my things, and got a ride from my mom to New York, New York, to move in. Everyone remembers the address of their first New York City apartment. It's like losing your virginity or celebrating your twenty-first birthday—a moment in time, seared inside the invisible locket you wear around your neck. That is one thing that'll always be yours. That address where you knew nothing about life and life knew nothing about you.

Our laundromat was conveniently located across the street, four of us shared one bathroom, and my room was nine hundred dollars a month. The only catch was my bedroom didn't have windows, but that was okay; my parents' old wooden desk fit perfectly in the spacious living room, between my roommate's guinea pig cage and Lizzie's crafting table. Lizzie and I did Beachbody at-home workouts in the living room before I went to school. We watched *SVU* on the couch at night. There was this place down the street that did gluten-free bagels pretty well. There was the walk to Columbia for classes, bags of salted almonds, Hinge matches to reply to, and orientations to attend. There was an eerie solitude to being so young in buildings so ancient and hulking, playing the part of the journalism student. I was used to playing a part—a career chameleon, ever changing to fit the season or the breeze in the air. I cycled through versions of myself until I was unsure where I began and where I ended, until I was unsure if I was truly me, or just playing the part of me.

I'd heard about *imposter syndrome* and I'd heard about *healing*. I'd heard about *growth*. I wasn't familiar with any of the three beyond just as buzzwords. I read a blog written by a former Columbia Journalism School student about imposter syndrome. She published it online—all her thoughts about feeling like a fraud and a phony, undeserving to be a student at a school so prestigious, in a program so renowned. I found this blog post midway into my first semester. A time where I was blind to who I was, scared to find out, and attempting to discover myself through missed attempts at personal style. And as I read, I realized I didn't really relate to her imposter syndrome about J school. I mean sure, the program was difficult and the classes were challenging, but I felt that I'd earned my spot and deserved it. But I read her words anyway and hyperfixated on a few sentences, thinking, *I don't feel this way about school. . . . I feel this way about everything.*

An imposter in my own life. The earth's greatest con artist. A charlatan in every room I entered, in every friendship I held, in my online dating profiles and across the table from the date. Of course I felt like an imposter in my reporting class, where half the students were far more accomplished and far more intelligent—or so it seemed. Of course I felt like an imposter walking through the well-kept campus toward the journalism building, a red leather crossbody bag slapping my thigh as I did. Of course I felt like an imposter lugging my video equipment to my video journalism class. And of course I felt like an imposter in a semicircle of my peers, waiting for class to begin. But that wasn't all. I felt like an imposter on the 1 train back downtown, entering my apartment and boiling water for pasta. I felt like an imposter at Planet Fitness, while standing in front of our foggy mirror brushing my hair, in the line at Trader Joe's and TJ Maxx, while ducking into a theater to watch my friend's play, or on a jog on the West Side Highway. Unless it was the middle of the night and I was cosplaying as the sexiest woman alive in some guy's bed, there was nowhere I could go, except perhaps my windowless bedroom, where I felt like anything other than an imposter. I didn't feel like me; I felt like a girl trying on versions of who she could be, hiding behind facades, in a desperate attempt to find an identity that might fit.

It's no wonder, then, that I felt like an imposter as I approached the Riverside Drive apartment of a girl I went to grad school with who was hosting a small Halloween gathering. I had made friends with one other girl in our first month of classes—a sunny blonde also from New Jersey. She had side messaged me on GroupMe when I'd introduced myself in the polite and awkward way we all do in new internet group messages. She was extroverted and beautiful without trying too hard, freckled and tanned, a runner and a surfer. She'd invited me to the party, because naturally she'd made friends with every other midtwenties girl in our program while I had only made one friend: her.

•

I've often felt misunderstood. I am chatty and outgoing but introverted and anxious—a mix that many people can't seem to understand. It feels like everyone wants you to pick a lane—be quiet, subdued, and introverted or chatty, outgoing, and extroverted. But to be both? It always feels like everyone is accusing you of lying about how you feel. In college I was constantly stuck in between—like I was on a perpetual train ride, and while other passengers boarded and exited with leisure whenever we arrived at their stop, my stop never quite came. I tried to get off the train a few times, but I wasn't welcome in those neighborhoods. So I'd get back on the train and stare straight ahead, wondering if I'd ever get where I was going, wondering how I'd ever know if we did.

I was too sorority girl for the theater kids and too theater kid for the sorority girls. Once the sorority girls stamped "arts kid" on my forehead, I sought comfort and familiarity and friendship with the art kids, but they had already clocked me as a vapid sorority girl. Sure, there was a bit of judging a book by its cover happening—but my entire freshman year of college caused me to wonder if I would ever find my footing anywhere. It was like other people made up their minds about me before I could make up my mind about myself. They diagnosed me, prescribed me, and sent me home before I could even really say hello. If someone had asked me, I would've said I was just Eli. A theater kid, a voracious reader, a passionate storyteller, an avid Sephora fan, a SoulCycle attendee—always wearing ten different patterns and colors, scribbling something down in a notebook—a forever flirt, overtalkative, and incredibly energized. Just eager to make and have friends.

Maybe you're sitting here reading this, eyes sipping words, thinking, *So what?* The "so what" is: Everyone deserves to feel like they belong, firstly. Secondly, I understand many of my privileges give me a universal feeling of belonging, and I cannot begin to fathom how isolated those without the same privileges may feel. And lastly, these uncomfortable sensations weren't unique to me, they were and are universal, though shockingly secret. Everyone just hides this feeling of not belonging away, with the monsters, under their bed.

What is wrong with me? I often wondered. *Should I discard the parts of myself that seem too artsy to fit in with the sorority girls? Should I adopt some stereotypical drama-kid styles and ways of life so they welcome me into their group?*

Trust me, I tried both. Freshman year I bought every crop top Urban Outfitters had to offer. It was 2017, and I learned how to do my eyeliner on YouTube and drank Svedka and blue Gatorade and racked up a lengthy list of fraternity boys whom I'd locked lips with in sweaty basements. I tried to be rah-rah sisterhood, and instead I was miserable. Oh, and still nobody liked me. Because now not only was I not sorority enough—I wasn't authentic either.

My second semester of freshman year, I chose to slowly distance myself from the sorority girl persona and be the arts kid. Inside, that's who I was anyway. I joined the newspaper and a few different theater orgs, started swapping my wardrobe of girly tops and expensive jeans for acid-wash denim with a lot of patches and pins. The following year, I sank into being theater-kid Eli 100 percent. That's when I met Lizzie, who adopted the lost baby me into her friend circle in the theater program. She started bringing me out to parties and would loop her arm through mine on our walk to classes. We sat in the lobby of the Walgreen Drama Center together and shared bags of chips and drank sodas and gossiped. The thing with Lizzie was, she saw through all of it. All of the attempts to make versions of myself fit. All of the forcing myself into costumes and styles and ways of life that weren't natural to me. She always just saw me. To be seen was a privilege, and it should be a right we are all afforded—to be seen and accepted as exactly who we are, even when we're in transit.

At some point, years past college, I was with my friend Bailey, whom I met at the school newspaper. She was one of the first people to be kind to me when I showed up on the first day alone, wearing a SIGMA KAPPA sweatshirt, knowing I wanted to be a writer and not knowing anything else about myself.

"I'm not going to lie," she said, "I judged you a little bit that first day. I was like, who is this sorority girl?"

We laughed about it.

I can laugh about it now too. Because Bailey chose to see

me just like Lizzie had. But it confirms exactly what I always thought: one group would look at me and say, "She already has a place in this world," without knowing the place they figured was mine didn't want me either.

Really, we should give eighteen-year-olds a little more space to breathe. Nobody knows who they are at eighteen, but for some reason we feel the need to pretend like we do. And when we all pretend to be something we're not, the pressure grows unbearable. The truth is, we're all just figuring it out. If we stopped pretending, we could commiserate and explore and find ourselves together. I wish more people were willing to be glaringly unknown, openly unfinished, presently confused—it takes far too much work to pretend you know who you are when you don't. Figuring out who you are is like the world's biggest open note test. You can read and learn and consume as much as you'd like in the process of working yourself out like an equation. Because you are just you. You already are you. And the only real way you can fail a test like this one is when you rush your answers or when you can't shut off the noise, so instead of sinking into yourself, you run from yourself. You run from the joy and the outstretched arms waiting for you around the bend.

It is brave to be yourself in this world. It shouldn't be that way.

•

As I approached this Halloween party, my own past licked like fire at my feet. It spread all around me and threatened to burn my flare bottom jeans. First impressions were everything, weren't they? And my track record with those was abysmal. The last time I was in this setting—new school, new friends, fresh opportunities—I'd felt so isolated . . . and was it me? Was I the problem? Was I a girl trying to do too many things, be too many things, all at once?

I shouldn't have eaten so much today, is what I'm thinking as the elevator climbs floor after floor, closer and closer. *I should text that guy, the one with the tiny bedroom*, is what I'm thinking as the elevator door opens and I bite my lip. *I should turn around and go back down the elevator, floor after floor, and I should call Lizzie and ask what she's doing.* (I already know where she is.) *I should've gone as something cooler—boring cool, like a cat—but only hot girls can get away with being boring and basic, otherwise it isn't cool, it's boring and basic*, I'm thinking as I stare at the door. *I should never have gone to a party at all if the host didn't invite me, which is a traditional and annoying thing to decide, like something Paris Geller would say*, I think as I hesitate before knocking. *Everyone will be disappointed in me (my mom, Lizzie) if I don't knock.*

Will there ever be an age when I don't overthink my Halloween costume? Will there ever be peace?

Behind the door are ten pairs of eyes. A girl whom I'd one day call a best friend. Bags of chips and someone smoking a weed pen in the corner. This is what I was so afraid of. Other human beings, daring to exist. And yet even if you had painted it that way. Even if you had lined up all their insecurities and made me say each out loud. Even if you had told me they were all just as scared, it wouldn't have mattered. There was no reasoning with me then, the unreasonable. We underestimate how terrifying it feels to introduce yourself to strangers when you don't know who it is you're introducing.

Maybe that's just anxiety making its way about the track of my body, settling in each crevice and taking up too much space. Or maybe that's how we all feel when we're invited to a party and we decide to actually go.

•

The internet tells me that imposter syndrome may be accompanied by consistent feelings of not being good enough, or feeling undeserving of or incompetent in a field, job, or opportunity. But nobody really talks about being twenty-two years old and feeling incompetent at everything—inadequate in each conversation or relationship—so much so that you begin to feel unworthy of the camaraderie and friendship and success of the people around you. Nobody talks about the way that imposter syndrome is weaponized against young people just trying to figure it out, to the tune of intense recruitment processes, toxic workplace environments, and a lack of entry-level positions that pay livable wages.

It is normal to not know who you are.

It is normal to not know who you are.

It is so beyond normal to not know who you are.

Imagine for a moment you were twenty-two years old or twenty-three years old or twenty-four years old and sure of yourself. Imagine how little there would be to explore because of how little space you'd have to grow. Now imagine someone else at twenty-two or twenty-three or twenty-four years old whom you perceive to be sure of themselves. Why do you see them that way? Is it their Instagram? Are they actually self-assured, or have they adopted the bravado of someone who is?

Every example I can come up with of a young person who seems 100 percent self-assured and authentic is someone I do not know, someone rich and/or famous, or someone who fits into the tight constraints of societal beauty standards. The truth is I don't know most of those people, and some of them are masking behind expensive travel or shoes or shiny hair.

It took getting through that first postgrad year for me to understand that it must be natural to feel like an imposter in the adult world. But still, in every dimly lit bar, at every twenty-fourth birthday party, work happy hour, and spin class, nobody is talking about it. Nobody is uttering a word. It's like we all silently agree to play a game of charades, and we hide our tired eyes behind a facade. For the previous twenty-one years, to some extent, I'd been slowly growing out of my naivete. Growing up feels like unlocking doors that have been padlocked to you for your entire life so far, discovering truths behind each. Every door unlocks a slew of information that you weren't allowed to have access to before. You break open so many doors, approaching so many locks, until tears are rolling softly down your cheeks; at first there's only a few, but the closer you get to the center, the closer you get to the truth—and the more pain and hurt you see. Growing up is to discover the pain and the hurt and the humanity in everything, everywhere—and be forced to carry on like nothing at all changed.

And then one day you graduate high school, or college, or turn twenty-one years old, and you're expected to transition seamlessly from adolescence to adulthood. You're expected to fully exist in adult form—when that has never truly been required of you before, and nobody ever told you how. Your only method of survival is playing the part. Wearing it like a costume, only allowing yourself to crack and crumble behind the closed door of your bedroom, terrified for anyone to see the breakdown, believing that nobody else feels this way. Believing that you have to hide it from the world, otherwise people would see you trying—people would see you clinging on for dear life—and what could be more mortifying than that? What would be more mortifying than to say, "Does anyone else feel this way?"

And be met with silence.

In the last twenty years, the transition from adolescence to adulthood has become unscripted and independent. The way we handle the transition, from child to adult, has changed dramatically in the last few generations—especially for non-men. In the 1990s, the median age to get married was below twenty-four years old for women and below twenty-six for men.* The transition from adolescence to adulthood was neatly defined—you'd meet someone, get married, move in together, start a life together, and have children. While this isn't what everyone was doing, nor was it the path to universal joy, it was certainly the average and certainly the "norm." Though I would not trade my reality for the realities many women felt coerced or forced into in decades past, and while I'm sure many of these people felt lost, alone, isolated, and unsure of themselves, their path was defined. In 2023, the median age for women to get married was 28.4 and the median age for men was 30.2. In the past twenty years, the zeitgeist has completely shifted—we are marrying older, if at all. We are choosing to live childfree, to live alone, to travel, to move in with our partners prior to marriage or engagement. And now Millennials and Gen Z are the first generations to truly sink into this new reality. To truly experience this strange, freeing, mystifying transition to adulthood.

To be clear, in no way am I saying this shift is a bad thing. In

---

* *Figure MS-2: Median age at first marriage: 1890 to present.* United States Census Bureau. (n.d.). https://www.census.gov/content/dam/Census/library/visualizations/time-series/demo/families-and-households/ms-2.pdf

fact, it's a wonderful thing. It is also just a very new thing, and one we don't have a lot of guidebooks for. Not only is society growing out of the idea that the heteronormative trope of marriage and the nuclear family do not suit everyone and should not be the universal standard—women of my generation are accomplishing things our grandmothers could never have dreamed of at our age. Owning property, having our own credit cards, prioritizing our careers, claiming leadership positions, and existing as full beings outside of the family and the home. Some of us are the first of our family lineage to live alone or with girlfriends or roommates. Some of us are the first of our family lineage to be above the age of twenty-five and remain single, unmarried. We've come so far, and we still have so far to go.

What I am trying to express is that somewhat recently, standards have shifted, norms have been erased and rewritten for our own benefit, for our own freedom. But when standards shift and norms are rewritten, there are going to be some growing pains. We have a blank canvas, and endless possibilities and opportunities. And this can be both wonderful and overwhelming simultaneously. Not only is it overwhelming to have so many options, but since Gen X, Millennials, and Gen Z are really the first generations to have so many options, so much mobility, we will also be the blueprint—we will be the example younger generations look to. Which leaves us with nowhere to really look—except to one another. And instead of asking one another for guidance or a shoulder to cry on, we've been conditioned by society to hold it all in. We see older generations "adulting" with perceived ease, and we mimic them, though realistically, our reality and their reality couldn't be more different.

The ability to make a choice about how you'd like to live your life is a privilege, but decision fatigue is also real. As a phenomenon, decision fatigue is when one grows physically, mentally, and emotionally depleted, the more decisions they have to make. The more options they have. Housewives of the 1950s were imprisoned by the decisions being made for them. Young people of the 2020s have the freedom to make decisions—about almost everything—and that is allowed to be overwhelming. We can be grateful to have the chance to choose for ourselves, and we can acknowledge that choosing for ourselves can come with brain fog, anxiety, and emotional turmoil.

Today young people mourn their college years while dealing with an infinite number of choices laid out before them, the expectation of adulthood looming like a storm cloud, and a deep uncertainty about themselves all at once. On top of this, conversations about this unique uncertainty are both abnormal and uncommon—so it's no wonder that I felt like an imposter in my own life at twenty-two years old.

•

I often felt like I was losing my sparkle in grad school—like instead of finding myself, I was losing touch with myself more and more. It was sticky and emotional to hide from the reality of feeling unsure of myself. Simultaneously, it was terrifying to wonder if I'd ever be sure of myself, because I'd never heard anyone try to put these uncomfortable emotions into words before. I'd never heard any other twenty-two-year-old say, "I am so proud to admit I do not know what I want out of life, I do not know who I am, I do not feel like an adult, and I don't know if I ever will." I saw endless photos of perfect lives on Instagram and job update after job update on LinkedIn. I saw happy relationships and vacations and new apartments with city skyline views. Thin limbs, clean bedrooms, aesthetic grocery hauls, and fancy office common rooms. There wasn't a social media app to share our deepest fears and everyday anxieties and the inner turmoil of such a rocky period.

I avoided instigating relationships because, in growing close to people, I was afraid that I'd be found out. It was easiest to be just an arm's length away from everyone in my life—don't let them close enough to read the fear on your face. I worried that if I made a close friend, they'd unearth those everyday anxieties and inner turmoil and think I was an enigma, a messy, unfinished creature they no longer wanted to share their lunch with or text memes and TikToks to in between classes or meetings. The minute I felt myself growing close to someone, I'd cut the night short, cancel the plans, or grow flaky or unreliable. It was never because I didn't want those friends; it was always because I feared if they got below the surface with me, they'd see who I truly was—they'd gaze into the murky, blurry contents of my soul and run for the hills. It would be far better to do the abandoning than be abandoned, I felt.

But here's the truth. While I was overanalyzing my frizzy hair or the sweater I loved that now seemed frumpy, while I was distancing myself from potential new friends because I thought they would read me as inauthentic and uncertain and scared and not want to be my friend anymore, while I was caught up in an endless cycle of fear over the perception others might have of me . . . people out there were looking at me, wondering how they could break in, wondering how they could be my friend.

My Art of the Profile classmates would always gather outside the journalism building on a patch of grass to chat and catch up before class. Afterward, we'd venture to a nearby student bar to have four p.m. drinks and talk about reporting and our pasts and our futures. The preclass gathering started one day when I was sitting on said patch of grass alone, engrossed in a podcast, scrolling on my phone, and one of my classmates took a seat on the chair next to me. That attracted the rest of the class, a chronically early bunch, and then from there, it sort of became a tradition. I had a habit of keeping mostly quiet at these gatherings, chiming in without commandeering the conversation, never letting anyone too close. That was until a smiley woman with dirty blond hair turned my way, mentioned she saw on Instagram that I liked astrology, and asked if I'd be open to reading her birth chart.

Four years have passed since I told her what it meant to be a Taurus. About a year into our friendship, she wound up admitting to me she'd been trying to find a way to be my friend since class started, but she was intimidated by me—didn't know how to break in. The whole time, I had been worried about befriending people who truly and deeply thought my fears were actually a sign that I didn't want to be their friend at all. I wish I could've assumed the best, instead of the worst, about her—about everyone—but I had my guard up far too high to even try.

•

Somewhere on Etsy you can buy a poster that reads some sickly-sweet phrase like "Be yourself, everyone else is taken!" And while you can acknowledge the sentiment as nice and well and good, none of us actually have any idea what the fuck that means.

I'd love to ask the poster maker how everyone else became taken. How everyone else melted into a version of themselves that felt comfortable and authentic. How everyone else became so glowy and joyful and light and free. I'd love to ask the poster maker on Etsy how they recommend we be ourselves in a world pushing aesthetics and eras and manufactured joy at us from every angle—TikTok For You pages, Target aisles, influencer Amazon Storefronts.

> Oh my god, if you're a coquette girlie you totally need this set of ballerina core Lana Del Rey bows from TikTok Shop. Okay calling all no-makeup makeup chill girls, you absolutely need this eye shadow palette to master the perfect lowkey smoky eye look. Where are all my coastal grandmothers? You need this set of gingham napkins for your perfect coastal gran kitchen aesthetic.

"Just be yourself!" they say, while my insides feel like the most uncomfortable, itchy sweater you've ever worn.

"Just be yourself!" they coo, while I wish to take my brain out from the inside of my head and let it dry out in a bowl of rice.

"Just be yourself!" they urge, and I don't know who the fuck that is.

•

Imposter syndrome at twenty-two felt like the smallest house atop the tallest mountain, far from anyone else, far from even a halfhearted idea of myself. It was so quiet there, so bitter cold and uncomfortably silent, so banal—with all blank walls, void of any sign of life or love or being. Imposter syndrome felt like the scariest thought in the world—that I'd keep pretending for the rest of my life. That I'd live a life of make-believe, that I'd let the minutes fall off the clock before ever feeling sure of my place in the world. Imposter syndrome made me feel like I didn't deserve the love pouring from the hearts of my friends. It made me feel like I could never ask for help, never admit that I wasn't okay. Imposter syndrome felt like the world was slowly closing in on me, and by the world, I mean an Etsy shop of quasi-motivational posters, prints, and T-shirts that I couldn't relate to.

But what was I really afraid of? Never finding myself? Or revealing who I was to the world, and the world turning in the other direction? Had I ever really lost myself, or did I just fear that who I was, who I knew I was, wasn't fabulous or fantastic or brilliant or bright enough? Was I ever afraid that I didn't know who I was, or was I really afraid of the perception others could have of who I was?

To be fair, it was a little bit of everything. I was still finding out who I was and who I wanted to be—and that's a very vulnerable and intimate thing to do. I do it at twenty-six, still, every day. At twenty-two, most of us are attempting to quickly figure out who we are while desperately trying to hide that fact from everyone else. Compounding the stress of feeling like you MUST figure out who you are is the very present anxiety that once you figure it out, other people will perceive you. And being seen is almost more terrifying than staying behind a closed door your entire life. Because when you unveil the truth in adulthood, behind one of those doors is you. Behind one of those closed doors, you find yourself, all weak and terrified, ready or not—about to meet the world. No wonder you feel uncomfortable everywhere you go. You're taking yourself out into the world for the first time, and it feels like some type of a grand reveal.

Let's get on the same page about one thing—it is very normal to have no idea who you are. You are having a normal reaction to an abnormal situation—the normal reaction is panic and anxiety and fear; the abnormal situation is the very sudden and sharp drop into adulthood. Figuring out who you are, deciding who you'd like to be, feels like a permanent series of decisions, but really this is something that is ever in flux. You will be morphing into versions of you for the rest of your life. Who you are is a fluid, amorphous, invisible thing. Lean into how weird and disjointed and strange that is. Lean into how universal that is. How every neighbor and loved one and stranger you will ever encounter is also always in limbo, always in flux. That is your norm. That is your ground. That is where your feet are.

All that matters is that you like yourself. All that matters is that you feel confident and comfortable in the skin you wear. Because you have always known who you are; you are just surrounded by a world trying to convince you otherwise. In order to like yourself and find yourself, you need to carve out a life that you like. Something you built all on your own.

You are Michelangelo, and you are your very own God. In your universe of one, you are everything. You are all your lovers. You are your best friend and your worst enemy. You are the cook, and you are the creator. You are cleaning up after yourself and tucking yourself into bed. You are the greatest entertainer, and you are a mother, and you are a fucking force. Why pretend to be just one thing? Why shove yourself into one tiny box when you are gigantic, containing multitudes, made up of cities and sights, places you've been, and dreams you'd like to see through? Society finds us most palatable when we are taking up no space at all. When even our thoughts are slimmed down to paper airplanes. When we fit an aesthetic or a box. When we are "that girl." The world finds you the most lovely when you inflate yourself to take up space—there are parts of the ocean we haven't yet explored, patches of land in Antarctica no human has ever stood upon. There is plenty of room for you to be yourself. There is plenty of room for me to be myself. Don't ever let the perception others may have of you (but likely do not) ruin or obfuscate your own perception of yourself. Because you are in charge of the country inside of you, you are the governor and you are the queen, you are your tough critic and you are your biggest ally. You are your favorites, all memorized like second nature—film and musician, pasta dish and coffee order. You are changing your mind. You are a muse, even if you've only ever had muses yourself, because you are the muse to the artist painting a mural in your soul. You are the smile that spreads across your face when you find something funny. You are your tears when your heart tugs in the wrong direction; you are the one breaking generational trauma and carrying it in your handbag; you are all your hobbies and quirks and the things someone will point out that they just love about you.

Holy fuck, you are so many things. Maybe you are an imposter too. Maybe you just feel like one. Well, you can't feel like an imposter, because imposter is not a feeling, it is a state of being. You can think you're an imposter. You can feel imposter syndrome, but a thought is not automatically the truth, and neither is a feeling. They are signals. Thoughts and feelings—signals that you are uncomfortable in a period of intense change, that you are cracking under the pressure that will eventually lead to the version of yourself you always hoped to become. If you were not ready for these opportunities—the cool friends knocking on your apartment door, the classes you daydream in, the job you applied for and are qualified for—those would not be your friends or your classes or your job.

•

I had a dream once when I was twenty-two. I was sitting on a cloud watching people walk down the street below. It was an overcast day, and the street I was looking down on was Church Street in Ann Arbor, Michigan—where I went to college. I was thinking about the students and professors below, watching their interactions, acknowledging the familiarity of the place and the nostalgia of not belonging there anymore. Suddenly, from the other end of the sidewalk, a girl started to approach me. She was alone, and she looked like a light beam. She was joyful and sunny—I could tell that from my spot on the cloud. She was pretty in a casual way, and as she started to come closer, I noticed her cool outfit, the way her hands hung by her sides in a self-assured manner. How she waved at passersby whom she knew and how she smiled at strangers. I started to feel jealous of her. How normal and well-liked she seemed. How simple yet beautiful, unique, and interesting she seemed. And I let myself steep like a bag of tea in this jealousy like it was hot water until she got close enough that I could really see her face and I realized that the girl was me.

And it started to rain then. On the Ann Arbor street, but not on me, because I was above it, in the clouds. She ducked and took cover inside a building I recognized as my freshman year dorm room, and then that was the end of the dream.

I could be the best writer in the world, and I would still fear how my words were perceived.

I could be the most beautiful woman in the world, and I would still find something wrong with my reflection in the mirror.

I could be the most certain person on the face of the earth, about where I'm headed and who I am, and still have questions.

And maybe if I felt like I belonged everywhere I went, there would be no growth to be had. Maybe if I belonged everywhere, it would really mean I belonged nowhere. And maybe if I felt like everyone in the world liked me and perceived me as beautiful and sunny and fine, I wouldn't want to have any friends at all, because it wasn't like anyone chose to love *me* specifically. And maybe if I had never felt like an imposter entering rooms and applying for jobs and pulling strings and making friends, I never would've pulled myself out of a hat like a magician doing a trick. Maybe then I'd never be this very version of me.

Sit with the uncomfortable things and listen to the noise before you decide what you'd like to mute. Be twenty-two years old and be unsure and then be twenty-three years old and be unsure. Find yourself in the dregs of the coffee shared with a lover or a friend. Find yourself in the theater where you saw a play on a whim, the concert you went to with a best friend, the difficult conversation you had with an ex. The moments you are proud of yourself and the moments you feel like you can breathe. Find yourself through the jobs you choose to quit and walk away from; find yourself in your pretty gaze above the leaky bathroom sink.

Nobody is looking for you. Nobody is hunting you down. Everybody is searching for themselves. You get to claim your place; you get to pin it on the map. To be so in control is wildly underrated and genuinely terrifying. But to be so in command of your own life, of your own being, is also what it is to be alive. Do not miss the stop signs begging you to sit in this discomfort and allow it to be the invisible string leading you to yourself.

Does Anyone Else Feel Like a Faux Adult?

I am twenty years old and riding the Staten Island Ferry with my then boyfriend. We stand on the boat's front deck, like an off-brand Rose and Jack, letting the wind mess up our hair and peel tears from our eyes. He holds a beer in a brown paper bag, and we sit with our backs up against the wall, our legs outstretched in front of us. He is handsome, and I know he isn't forever. I am young and pink and hot tempered. It's his idea for us each to pull out our phone and make a list of five goals we'd like to achieve by the time we turn twenty-seven. Seven years seems so far away, and I marvel at the idea that we could be anywhere or anyone in seven years. I feel like we both know we won't be together and that's why it's fun. The idea that what we have now is just for now, the idea that we have somewhere to grow. The idea that we will both cry on the phone when we end it. The idea that I know we'll be fond of these memories forever, because there was never any bad blood. We were best friends who tried something and lost each other in the process. We will look back on these goals as we look back on each other. We are similar, and we like the idea of making goals for our future selves. Our *adult* selves. I notice how easy it is to come up with five things I want to achieve by the time I turn twenty-seven. I know what I want, both to my own detriment and to my own chagrin. One of mine was "don't have a desk job or a conventional job unless it deeply creatively fulfills you." Another one of mine was to be in love. "Maybe with a person, maybe with life." We shout our goals out loud to each other over the warm, misty breeze. I remember us pinky promising we'd make them come true. Our fingers interlock to seal the promise. Even if we are pulled apart by some twist of fate. Even if we never speak again. Even if he moves to California and I move to New York and he tries to become an actor and I try to become a writer—which is exactly what happened, and I could've predicted it for you then. These goals would serve as a silent guidance counselor, tugging us along through our early and midtwenties. My third goal was to get a book deal—and I wrote down the exact dollar amount I hoped to get from the advance too.

I hate to do this again, lament about a memory with a man. And I hate myself for being so sickeningly nostalgic and so much of a try-hard. In many ways, I have grown. In many ways, I am still both.

Two years later, sitting on my bed in my Upper West Side sublet apartment on the same duvet cover he and I napped on top of in the middle of unbearable August heat, I revisit the goals list. I am a few months shy of twenty-three. I have recently graduated from grad school. I have a new boyfriend, and we have just gotten in our first fight, and I am afraid he doesn't love me back. I am going to start a nine-to-five job working in insurance journalism in a week. I have loans, rent to pay, things to prove to myself— the job is safe, secure. And besides, what else would a people pleaser like me do? Go against the grain? Figure I know better? Tell the establishment to go fuck itself?

I have four years to get those five things. The love, the passion, the joy, the spark back in my eyes, to not look so pale and bloated by desperation and loathing and fear. It feels as though I've made no progress, have figured nothing out. I live with two girls in business school who are very adultlike. I wonder how they see me—the little girl down the hall. They seem to have it all figured out. Serious boyfriends, serious jobs—serious. I do not feel like them. I do not appear like them. I can't even figure out what I want to have for dinner, let alone where I want to end up, what I'm doing with my life.

I am scared, and I don't know what feels worse: selling out and taking the sensible route or taking the risk. I read the five goals, the words glaring up at me stubbornly like an unfinished promise. I am exactly halfway through the timeline—perhaps slightly closer to the finish line than the starting line. I wonder if the guy from the ferry achieved any of his. My cheeks feel that strange heat that is so warm it turns cold. I start the desk job in a week, and there is no book deal. There is no whisper of creating anything that is just mine in sight. And my life is fine. It feels like it starts over again every single morning. I never feel like I build on the day prior. But I have everything I need, and that is more than most can say. I feel as though I am not living. I am getting by, under the assumption that unless you *have it all figured out*, you are unable to truly live.

I feel stuck somewhere between childhood and adulthood. I feel like college and subsequently grad school, interrupted by the pandemic, staved off the transition forever. Does anyone feel like an adult? Or do we all feel like overgrown children playing dress-up in adults' clothes? Trying to find something that fits at a shop that doesn't carry our size?

It is a month later. I am in the conference room of the office building where I spend the better part of each week, toying with an idea for a short story I want to write but haven't quite figured out yet. I am wearing suit pants and an appropriate blouse and shoes that pinch my toes. I am not doing the work I was hired for, and I am not doing the work I am paid for. That's because I already finished every task my boss gave me in an unfulfilled yet focused haze over the course of a few hours.

And this is how it always goes at work. I wasn't very good at the job, but it didn't seem to bother anyone. There were a lot of fluorescent lights and editorial meetings, eating lunch at our desks and marveling over the new espresso machine. Over the weekend I will see my friends, and we will wear short skirts and trendy jeans. We will sing the songs we know the words to at the bar and go home and prepare to remember again—life is not the sparkling Saturday night of each week. How unfortunate, how grim, that we cannot spend all of our days as the girls we know one another to be, drunk and twirling, twirling, twirling. We do not know how to cope and we do not know how to get by without "having it all figured out."

I remember sitting up in my bed the night after my first day at work, choking on my tears. I ignored the urge to analyze the bout of emotion because facing it would require an admission that I wasn't yet ready to share, not even with myself. I feared the choices I had made, I feared the path I'd gone down, and most of all I feared that adulthood would always feel this abstract and detached. *It's time to grow up*, I told myself, bunching up a tissue in my fist. *It's time to be in control*. It was time to have it all figured out, I assumed. I was on the verge of twenty-three years old, and surely I needed structure. I needed the strange isolation of working a job where nobody was passionate, and nobody wanted to be there, and nobody really spoke to one another. I needed a shock to the system—a metaphorical cold plunge. I needed to woman up and become an adult.

And what was more adult than being prepared for life's various yet ambiguous milestones? What was more adult than business professional attire, the commute to Midtown, the conference room where I spent most of my time? What was more adult than paying my own phone bill? Living in my own apartment with quasi strangers right down the hall? Not having to tell my mom when I was leaving or when I was coming home?

You're so young, my boss would say, and it came off as slightly inappropriate, if I'm being honest. Simultaneously, twelve-year-olds on TikTok called me Grandma (and this wasn't intended as a compliment).

Am I young, or am I old? Is it too early or too late? Will I ever stop feeling like a giant baby? An overgrown child? How can I be so emotionally mature, yet so lonely? So needy? Will I ever feel adult enough? Will I ever figure it all out? Why does being five feet three make me feel like I'll never be a real adult? (I always thought it would be easier if I was five feet seven. My tall friends tell me it is not.)

How come everyone else who seems to have figured it out won't share the steps it took to get there? I scroll by them on Instagram; I walk past them outside the subway station, smelling their perfume and validity; I make small talk with them at events for work that always make me feel like my chest is full of cotton balls and I can't form a cohesive sentence. The beauty queens, the not-one-hair-out-of-place twenty-three-year-olds, the adults who seem comfortable in the title, the people who have it all figured out.

And then there's me. Trembling and always in between the two places I need to be. Always fifteen minutes early or five minutes late, but never on time. I should get a watch, so I do, but then it breaks, and I never have an hour to spare to get it fixed.

•

I am taking a personal essay class, and it is my senior year of college. Heartbroken and confused, pissed off and uncomfortable, I feel peace here and only here. The university's old buildings are built like apples, and the English department hosts classes inside the fleshy core. I am excavating my short life for this class, and I love to write. Sometimes the professor invites a guest speaker, and this guest is always someone who has it all figured out. They are smart and poised, and I can never tell how old they are. They have a bio with a lengthy list of accolades—bestselling author of such and such, executive editor for such and such. The story they tell is always the same story in a different city with a different editor and a different good luck charm. Each untouchable, prosperous person in well-pressed clothes stands before us to tell us their winding story to success and offer us advice, and they all have the same thing to say. Not one fable of the unbeatable success that I so craved seemed to provide answers on how to get there—or where to begin—or what I had to do to have the same things.

"Keep believing in yourself," they said, and I found myself metaphorically rolling my eyes. Believing in oneself wasn't enough to build a bridge from the little kid I felt like to the successful young adult I needed to become. "Don't take no for an answer, keep pushing," they said, and I wanted to laugh at how annoying it would be to pose as someone who never took no for an answer. "You never know what door will open that will be the one you've been waiting for," they lectured, and it felt like they were just stringing affirmative words together in sentences that seemed well balanced. I was jealous of them. Wanted to be just like them—the way they moved their hands, so dignified and polished. The way their phones would beep midway through the discussion and they'd politely step out—so busy, so fulfilled. The way they were on their way, in tall shoes with four-digit price tags, to do something fabulous, and our class was just something else they'd thrown in—or an assistant had thrown in—to their never-ending schedule.

So adult they were. So put together. Classy, sharp, and fine. I wanted to be them, and I wanted them to die in the heat of my petty jealousy. I remember standing in the elevator after yet another class where I'd felt my dreams freeze up. I remember thinking I'd love to be a guest speaker, love to be revisiting Michigan one day—shiny hair, sheer tights, a well-tailored suit, expensive shoes, and a knowing look in my eye. And then I remember stopping myself from falling victim to such an irresponsible daydream.

You're never going to get that lucky, I remember thinking. Because that was what it felt like—hard work and being in the right place at the right time. Relentlessness and some twist of fate—the random job they took that turned into their big break, the person they accidentally met, the connection they never gave up on, for whatever reason. I put my realism goggles back on and returned to the adolescent world outside.

•

I tirelessly set overzealous goals for myself—*When you do X, you'll have it all figured out*. I worked against a clock I set to 3x speed—I needed to connect to every famous journalist. To cold email until something felt warm. I needed to write everything and submit everything everywhere. I needed to beg people to listen. To keep going. Keep going. Keep going. Write. Submit. Edit. And with each rejection, try again and again and again. I don't even know who lit the fire that was torching my ass, but whoever it was also added kindling with a fury. I think that person was me. I just don't ever remember starting the engine, just adjusting to the speed we were going.

When you get into grad school—you'll have it all figured out, I told myself. *When you get your first job—you'll have it all figured out. When you get into a serious relationship—you'll have it all figured out.* And when I did that arbitrary thing, when I achieved that difficult, far-off task, when I attained the goal, I changed my target. Because surely if I could get something that I figured would give me that reassured feeling and then that feeling never came, there was something else I needed. Something else that could bring me to the holy land of other adults who knew what they wanted. Something else to make me whole and complete. I needed to get my eyebrows done and my nails done. I needed to stop being such a baby and just go get the Brazilian wax. I needed to say "I am sorry" and clear the air. I needed to start dressing better, to listen to more interesting music, and to have something better to say when there was an awkward pause in conversation. I needed to be less reliant on my mother, I needed more friends, I needed to get really good at sex and then start having less of it. I needed to open a credit card, get a good credit score. All the things I did to try to feel like an adult and have it all figured out. All the ways I twisted up my emotions. All the ways I drove myself insane. On a highway to the loneliest town in the world—where you have everything you think you need and nothing you actually want.

I'd spent a year of my life trying to *have it all figured out*, trying to pantomime adulthood, trying to squeeze the me out of everything in my life and fit an ambiguous mold instead. I never once paused to wonder what it meant, what it would mean or look like to *have it all figured out*. I never once halted my marathon of meandering thoughts to think about what such a state of being would look like. I never once pressed pause and asked myself what it would be to live a joyful life. I wanted to live the life of someone who, from the outside, was doing amazing, and from the inside felt like it too. Looking back now, I suppose I wanted to put an end to an ever-longing, uncertain feeling I had in the back of my throat all the time. I wanted to feel like I was among peers when I stood among other twenty-three-year-olds. I wanted to feel like the adult I was perceived as when I didn't get carded at the bar. I wanted to see myself from a third-person POV and like what I saw.

But I know now to pause. Even if no thoughts fill the stale air—just pause. Maybe think of nothing at all. Maybe consider my own why—what was feeding these zany thoughts if not for me? Why did I not feel like enough? Why did I need to *feel* like an adult—what if I was one, and this was what it was? What did I really want after all?

We should start with the word *feel*, because it is one of the most misused words in the English language. You cannot feel like an adult, because feeling like an adult would insinuate "adult" is an emotion, which it isn't (although perhaps it should be). We do this all the time with the word *feel*. We say we "feel" like a failure, when we mean we *think* we are a failure. We say we *feel* like we will never find love, when realistically we mean we *think* we will never find love. And for some reason it sounds so much more silly to say *I think I am a failure.* Because we can all agree that our thoughts, for the most part, are not automatically facts. Our thoughts are questions, truly—little bones we dig up inside the forest of our minds, pieces of history to investigate, observations to lean on or wonder about. We cannot help our feelings, and our feelings, the inner stirrings of our hearts and souls, aren't up for question in the way that thoughts are.

So saying "I don't feel like an adult" or "I don't feel like I have anything figured out," didn't make sense. Instead, I should've been saying—"I don't think I'm an adult" or "I don't think I have anything figured out." I was an adult. I am an adult. My teenage years are the dregs at the bottom of the bottle, poured down the drain, moments I've made peace with. There is no one feeling that can accompany adulthood. In the same way that there was no feeling that could accompany teenagerhood. There was no one way to feel like a teenager or feel like an adult, because that would mean every single teenager and adult is moving through the world with the same set of circumstances and the same heavy heart.

I spent time doing a list of things adults did, and I checked in to see if the feeling of adulthood ever accompanied these actions. It never did. I thought I was a faux adult, dressed up in my mom's heels, three sizes too big, with a wide, goofy smile plastered on my face. I thought one day there'd be a clarity, an assuredness, a put togetherness, some adulty feeling I hadn't yet encountered. I thought one day I'd feel that I had it all together, all set, all organized. I had an obsession with certainty. An obsession with knowing. It was sharp like the back of an earring pinching your flesh. It was dull in the way a bad kitchen knife is, one that'll really hurt you when you slice yourself.

In the morning, I thought about all of it while I brushed my teeth and picked out a pair of pants to wear. In the evening, I thought about it again, as I collapsed on the couch in our living room, next to my roommate Jen, and asked her to tell me a story—a story about anything—because she tells the best stories, and I needed to be distracted. But during the day I masked so brilliantly this crippling fear, this lingering anxiety, this awkward tension I had with myself. I felt crazy, but I didn't want to tell anyone that either. Being the eldest daughter of three kids, being the caretaker of everyone in my life—I thought no one should spare their worries on the girl who usually worried about them. If there had been one person, one whisper, one internet star or celebrity's daughter or random acquaintance willing to share that they didn't have it all together, that they had no idea what the fuck was going on, that they didn't feel figured out, or sure of themselves, or clearheaded, or flawless, or supreme—I would've built a house out of our mutual fears and felt so much better when I put down the hammer and added a fresh coat of paint. But there was never a soul willing to say a word. Never someone willing to admit to such a vulnerable state of existence—and for so long, I was the same. I figured nobody would relate. I thought about how horrified and shocked and blindsided people in my life would feel—the girl who is always fine, now like a spinning top, threatening to go over on my side.

On Instagram my peers posted photos of glow ups. They were holding hands in Terminal A of Newark airport, returning from a trip where they got engaged. They were getting promotions, starting businesses, and upgrading from studio apartments to one bedrooms. I sat in my bedroom on my bed without a bed frame, and I projected my own idea of their clarity onto each profile. *She has it all figured out*, I'd think. *He knows what's next for him, he has a plan*, I'd decide. *She seems like an adult, like she mastered the transition*, I'd diagnose. Today I look back on that person—so desperate—and I recognize that scrolling and assigning as an act of projection. I projected onto my peers—the ideas I had of their lives and their fears, their mental states and emotions—when I had no real idea how they felt, no real concept of well-being or certainty or adulthood. And perhaps in many ways, there was someone else sitting on their bed, projecting onto me. It was hard to picture then, but now I see it so clearly—that's what the internet does to us. We are really all just projecting onto one another, filling in the blanks about someone else, creating a story for them that confirms the anxieties we have, and then they do the same for us too. There is no oxygen on Instagram. We cannot breathe there. We are not real there. We are all making assumptions about one another, that we must have it all figured out. I was making assumptions about people who didn't have it all figured out based on the 1 percent of their life they were choosing to show me, in a fake place with no air.

The truth is that nobody has it all figured out. It is impossible and boring. And nobody ever will.

The second truth is that if we had it all figured out, we'd be miserable. Nobody wants that, no matter how much they think they do. I promise you. Walk with me.

•

The race was unbearable to run—the one against only me, in this weird competition to figure out my entire life, to feel sure, to feel like an adult. It got hot and my lungs burned and my legs went numb. I had to stop running to save myself. Stop running from myself, stop running toward the thing I thought could save me.

Why would I want to have it all figured out? I love to learn. I love to read. I love to discover something I didn't know about before, and that's the thing—in order to be a curious person, there has to be so much life you are uncertain about, so much you don't know. You cannot be a learner of this world, you cannot be curious, and also be certain about everything. You cannot have both. "Having it all figured out" insinuates that it's possible to outsmart fate. It insinuates that it's possible to avoid a mess that only you can clean up. It is impossible. Because so is perfection—objectively. You will call something perfect and your next-door neighbor will call its opposite perfect. There is no such umbrella perfection. Being perfect would leave you no room to try and to learn, to grow and to mold, to course correct, to find serendipity and encounter those once-in-a-lifetime sunrises that you didn't plan on being awake for.

These thoughts I was having, their dizzying accompanying emotions, were coming from somewhere. They were not random, and many people felt them in tandem. We put an unearthly amount of pressure on women specifically to "have it all figured out," because in many ways "having it all figured out" means being palatable to society in a way that it can handle. The opposite of having it all figured out is having nothing figured out—which is accompanied by trial and error and wanting. Filling rooms, growing, molding, and changing. It is accompanied by curiosity and opportunity, and that means girls would grow into women who take up space. They don't want us asking questions. They don't want us following the tree-lined road of curiosity. They don't want us writing our own scripts or rewriting theirs. They told us what we should want—they told us what they want us to want—and we're not meant to want for anything different, or anything more.

Do not let them box you in. Do not let them discourage you from following your senses. Having it all figured out would mean I had nothing to learn. It would very likely mean I was at home, with a magazine-perfect, white-picket-fence life that I simply do not want. In no way could life leave a welcome surprise on my doorstep. There would be no shades of gray—the moments we live in so deeply and so intimately and feel so grateful for on the other side. The uncertainty has to be spoken about out loud because we have to decide, together, to embrace it. To see it as an opportunity, not a nightmare.

•

I am twenty-five years old, and the University of Michigan alumni center is hosting me as a guest speaker. Instead of at a building like an apple with a deep core, I meet them at the fancy building with the wide steps and the view out toward the rest of campus. I will talk to two hundred students about my career. I will talk to them about my book. I will tell them the winding story, the one that got me from Michigan to a book deal to hundreds of thousands of strangers' profiles at home on my TikTok app.

I am twenty-five years old. I have the expensive high-heeled shoes. My suit pants are tailored, because my mom said you have to tailor your clothes when you have professional engagements, but I wear her blazer with them, because she is a part of all of this, through my DNA. I also wear a T-shirt that says IT'S NOT ME, IT'S YOU, because I have not become a woman who wears tailored suits and thinks very carefully before she speaks. So much has changed since twenty-three and so much has changed since twenty-one, when, on a cool March day, I said goodbye to campus and drove away from it for the last time as a student. Four years is a blip and it is a lifetime. I am touching up my makeup in the bathroom and trying to feel just one thing—but there is a torrent of joy and sadness and pain, celebration and luck and fervor and bliss making a racket inside of me. And I wonder if this feeling is the one I was always racing toward, the one I never found, the one I still haven't ever come across.

I am the guest I used to threaten with my inner envy, and I have no idea what I'm doing. I do not have it all figured out. I look in the mirror and feel like I'm looking through myself. I'm so familiar with my nose and my gaze, I can't imagine what I must look like to someone else. And for some reason, that's fine. I am lucky. Lucky. So unbelievably lucky. And I have been on the highway toward this moment for a lifetime, only I never knew it. And in twenty minutes, they announce my name and everyone cheers and it makes me sick to think that all these girls with their bright eyes and murky minds could look at me as someone who has her shit together. So I grab the hand of my inner teenage girl and I drift on their applause to the cushy chair in the front of the auditorium and I answer their questions for real. I share with them my fear, my confession that I still do not have it figured out and never will, my desire for them to create something and to share it with the world.

If I'd had it all figured out when I graduated college, or when I graduated grad school, or when I started my first job, or even last week—I wouldn't be sitting here in front of all of you, right now, is what I say, and I mean it. Every word.

•

Not even the adults feel like adults. We're all cosplaying adulthood until we realize that the effort is too much and it would be better to just be the adult you are. The person you are. Be your name, your heritage, where your feet are planted. The twenty-five-year-old or twenty-four-year-old or twenty-three-year-old you are today. Be her and just live. Take off the costume and find a pair of pants that fit. It strikes me as fascinating that when I am all alone, at home—doing my laundry, refilling my prescription online, calling my insurance company, making myself a balanced dinner—I feel just fine. I am doing a good job. I am an adult and I am taking care of myself. But then when the curtain falls and I have to go out into the world, I am met with a deep desire to cover myself up, to play pretend, to overcompensate. I am met with the feeling that I am doing a terrible job, that I am an overgrown child, that I need to figure everything out. It is not so much that I am not an adult, or that I am doing a bad job at being one. It is that the world makes me feel that way. I will not let it anymore.

Life is not a game to be played. It is not a contest to be won. It is not a test to be aced. It is an opportunity to be alive and to love. That is all. It is an opportunity to create your own joy and your own miracles and to not know and to fuck up and to try again. Life does not want to be figured out and has banned us from figuring her out successfully anyway. You might as well build a life for yourself that feels joyful and freeing and exactly like the one you want to be inside.

When I was twenty years old on the Staten Island Ferry, I knew exactly what I wanted. And it was so easy to tell my notes app and my ex-lover. It felt like second nature, like a laugh you can't stop from coming out even when you're trying to stuff it back inside. I was younger then, but I was somehow wiser, in the same way children are raw and honest. I wanted to grow up to be an adult who says what she means. I wanted to grow up to be an adult who follows what she wants. I wanted to grow up to be an adult who loves in a way that is ravenous and all-consuming. And having wants is the beginning of the construction of a life. Child you probably knew better. She was unafraid. She was unscarred by the hurt and pain of everything outside.

The transition from teenage girl to young adult to twenty-three years old is harsh and moody and tender. It feels like being embarrassed about nothing and everything at the same time. But there is no need to figure anything out—not only is it not possible; it is going to ruin your chances of living if you're constantly searching for a manual on how to live. There are some things you need to do, and these I will share with you.

You need to be kind. Not nice, but kind. You need to change your sheets every week. You need to call whoever is home to you and check in. There will be bills, there will be rent, there will be tests and obligations and days you work too hard. There should also be fun, there should be curiosity—and you should never allow anyone to mislabel you as distracted. You will have opinions, and you will change them. This experience is beautiful. You are too old for so many things and too young for so many others. Acting your age sounds dismissive and rude, but really it means honoring the chapter you're in—and being okay with it. We are all the little-kid versions of ourselves, in grown-up bodies with curves, and grown-up minds with trauma and knowledge. Sometimes I think letting someone in means letting them get to know the child you were, the person you always will be—the mind and the heart before either was ever brushed with the strokes of a lover gone wrong or an experience that changed everything for good.

Knowing so little about what's next allows me to be open to attracting greatness and gold. A job doesn't do that. Grad school doesn't do that. Being in love doesn't fix things. You don't automatically feel whole, feel complete when you win an award that says you're good at something or when you attain a goal you've been working toward. I don't remember what it was like to be in high school and feel so dramatic over boys my friends and I had all kissed, but I remember what it taught me about feeling and about friendship. I don't remember what it was like to be in college and to want to steal the lives of guest speakers passing through prestigious hallways, but I remember what it taught me about wanting and achieving. I remember the time I wasted trying to domesticate a life that would never be tamed, never be caged—a life that wanted the freedom to become whatever it wanted, as it got wind in its sails and I did my best to avoid the choppy seas.

You do not need to have it all figured out. You do not have to know what you want. You are an adult by age, and you are a child forever because we all are. You are every version of you you've ever tucked into bed at night, every terrifying thought and silly journey you took to go after your own joy. You are in control even when you feel like you are in the eye of the hurricane. And from where I sit, unsure and reveling in the moments that not knowing will bring, like the lightning strike of a lesson learned, I feel sort of light.

Because when I let go of my need to know, I gained my whole world.

Does Anyone Else Feel Like Relationships Take Work?

When I was twenty-two, I spent eight months nannying four times a week for a family on the Upper West Side. They had one baby, who was six months old when I started. Looking back now, I sort of feel like we grew up together over the course of those eight months. She went from sleepy and still to walking and babbling, and I felt newly actualized—as though I was relearning everything I'd ever known as I watched her take the world in for the first time. Her parents worked from home. They were adorable and friendly New York City transplants from the Midwest, just shy of their thirties. We were too close in age for them to feel like my elders but also immersed in immensely different chapters of life—and that was both comforting and unfamiliar.

I remember singing the baby "You Are My Sunshine" every day as she fell asleep. Playing with her on the floor, feeding her bottles and, eventually, a variety of colorful mush. And I remember a conversation with her mom after I'd commented on the variety of wedding invitations and baby announcements tacked on their fridge. It all felt vaguely overwhelming and intensely celebratory.

"We're at the tail end of the wedding thing now," I remember her saying.

"Are you in wedding season yet? You know, when everyone is just getting married one after another?" she asked. And I laughed a little because I'd never heard of *wedding season*. I didn't know anyone getting married. I didn't have any friends who even had weddings in their periphery.

"No, not really. I mean, I'm twenty-two, so . . . none of my friends are really getting married yet," I said.

"Oh yeah, it's a little early then, but once you turn twenty-five . . . twenty-six . . . it'll start. It'll be everyone, one after another, it's crazy." She slipped back into their home office, and I was left a little speechless. Of course she didn't mean to shock me—after all, writing this now, nearly four years later, I know she's right. I've been invited to five weddings this year alone, have already been to one, and have others pending.

But at the age of twenty-two, in a sweatshirt stained with someone else's baby's puke, writing my thesis on a couch that wasn't mine, I hardly felt like a fully functioning person, let alone a person who knows people who are getting married. I didn't feel capable of making the commitment to meet someone else for dinner, let alone lifelong partnership and devotion.

Though they were only seven years my senior and only lived a few blocks away, the couple whom I nannied for felt like they existed in an entirely different universe than mine. One with weddings and newborn babies. One that I could not imagine myself making it to in just five to seven years. Did good things really take time? Would time *fly* while I was having fun? What would two years bring—let alone five?

In tandem with the development of my prefrontal cortex in my midtwenties came the realization that the very nature of our relationships changes—and that makes sense. As we change, our relationships, and how we behave within them, do too. I like to think of this shift as the Metamorphosis—because the phrase "the development of the prefrontal cortex" is very clunky and unattractive.

I see the Metamorphosis as the passageway between childhood and adulthood. A time that strikes at different points for everyone and manifests in different ways. The common thread of this time of change is just that—it is a time where you will change, and with you, your relationships to the people in your life will shift as well. One that you will handle in your very own way given your very own circumstances.

With the development of the prefrontal cortex (in our midtwenties, around twenty-five), decision making technically becomes easier, but the clarity that accompanies this new development makes many other things more complicated. When a fog lifts, it should be easier to see. But the world is far more digestible in the fog, and it is far less profuse, far less abundant. There is less to handle and manage when there is less to know and understand. When your vision only extends a few feet in front of you, the world feels controllable and easy to manage. Allow me to put it like this—choosing between three things would be far easier than having infinite choices. Even if we'd rather have infinite choices, we can recognize how the lack of walls around us can be a massively isolating feeling. Kylie Jenner once said she spent a year with her friends "realizing things," and everyone made fun of her on Twitter, but I kind of understood just what she was trying to say. At twenty-four, and even more so at twenty-five, I felt like the rose-colored glasses were smashed in front of me and I saw the world for what it is—every day, opinions molded and shifted, lessons were learned at a speed so intense, realizations were had that I never considered prior. They say ignorance is bliss, and idioms like that one have been said for ages by our grandmothers for a reason—there is some truth to them. The world was easier to digest when I understood it less.

There are many ways the Metamorphosis impacts us, but here I want to focus specifically on how it impacts our relationships.

•

Today I'm twenty-five years old, writing a book on a couch that is mine, and my friends are getting married. Well, some of them. Family friends and cousins—people who have always been just a couple steps ahead of me, friends in their late twenties—are certainly getting married. And every time I open Instagram, someone I know is engaged. Sometimes they're younger than me—twenty-four or even twenty-three. The save-the-dates come in thick, expensive envelopes, and they're typed out in an impossible-to-read script, and they all kind of look the same (sorry, it's true). Sometimes they have a QR code that leads to a website full of rules and details and registries, which feels very advanced and very technologically savvy. I write the dates to save in the shared calendar I have with my boyfriend, and then I recycle the save-the-dates because I have enough clutter in my life as it is. I am not the type of person who tacks up save-the-dates on the fridge. I wish I was sometimes. I comment on another Instagram of a sparkly diamond ring and elated expressions, and I marvel how we so quickly zipped from fraternity basements to *I do*s. I cannot believe I am the same age my mother was when she was pregnant with me. I cannot believe my best friend went ring shopping with her boyfriend. I cannot believe that this is what it feels like to be twenty-five. And this is in no way a bad thing—we can chalk it up to the circle of life, but admittedly, it also feels very strange. When you are twenty-one, you look up to twenty-five and think they seem so adult, so mature, until you become them. You look back on twenty-one and think they seem so young, so childish—and surely, you think, you didn't appear that way then.

I am no longer nineteen. I am closer to thirty than I am to thirteen. It was incomprehensible at the age of twenty-two that people around me would be getting married—that we'd be mature enough to say "I do." But then I experienced my own Metamorphosis, and now I have landed in a universe where my friends are getting married. And it's beautiful and sorrowful and sweet to get all dressed up just to celebrate a bond that everyone in the room hopes will last till forever. I love weddings. I also sometimes wonder if there is ever a time in a person's adult life where they can be celebrated for something other than a wedding or a baby. Because if someone chooses to do neither, the world seems disparaging and cold. It strikes me as interesting that there are internet threads a mile long with parents anonymously lamenting that they regret having children or adults sharing that they regret tying the knot—but not nearly as many threads full of people who regret staying unmarried or not having children. It feels as though the people criticizing those who choose to remain unmarried or childfree are secretly envious of those bold enough to make a choice for themselves, to dictate their own happiness. It is one massive projection of idle insecurities and phony superiority. Just let people do whatever they'd like to do, especially if it does not impact you, or anyone else, negatively.

At the wedding of my boyfriend's friend from high school, people elbowed us in the ribs and told us we were next. That's what people do at weddings. We all get high on wedding air—the fundamentally lovely idea of a forever bond, the romance of a white princess dress and the same thirty songs, an open bar. Everyone looks around for the most committed unmarried couple in the room and tosses them the metaphorical bouquet. It is strange, the way some people just assume everyone around them wants the same white-veiled traditions.

Maybe we are next—it's been a year, and nobody else in the friend group has been engaged since. Only time will tell. Plenty of people want to get married, and I'm at a place where I want that too. But I wasn't always so sure, and that's okay. When I was a child, without a shadow of any doubt, I wanted to get married. But something shifted at some point in my teens, and I realized the only reason I wanted to get married was because I thought that was what I was supposed to do. And when I was small, I viewed getting married as a box to check—one of those things I'd do because . . . that's what people do, right? It was a milestone I'd inevitably reach because I was told that's what good girls do. That's what nice girls do. That's what quiet, pretty girls do. There didn't seem to be many other paths. I didn't really know what funny, outspoken, messy girls did, and my entire life most people silently cautioned me not to find out.

But not all of us have the same desires. Outspoken, messy, funny girls can get married if they want to. Quiet girls don't have to get married if they don't want to. It shouldn't be a privilege, but somehow it is—I'd like to take a second to remind you that you have a choice. And your choice is just that—yours. It is not your mother's choice, it is not your friend's choice, it is not the world's choice. It is your choice. Because at the end of the road, all you will have are the choices you made—the noise will not matter, the people who cautioned you against it or told you to go for it won't matter. You will not waste your last thought on what people said about you. It will just be you, reflecting on the risks you took and how they played out. And I want you to be proud of yourself when you look back on it all.

Adolescence eventually faded, and I realized I didn't know if I ever wanted to get married or if I just wanted to fit in, just wanted to do what I perceived was right, just felt so goddamn pressured to be the good, nice girl. So instead I decided I just wanted to be happy—and if I met someone whom I wanted to be with into the future, who appreciated the funny, loud girl I am at heart, at a time in our lives when it made sense, then I'd like to get married. And so much of Gen Z mimics this style of thinking—prioritizing financial independence, career, and personal joy above the need for long-term partnership. Sure, many of us want long-term partnership, but we are also freckled with so many other wants. Plenty of people in lasting relationships also opt out of marriage—fatigued by the concept or wary of the rate of success. Marriage isn't the answer to everything. It is, in fact, not an answer at all. It is a choice you and your partner make for your lives together. That is it. It cannot fix anything that is broken; it will not magically erase anything that has gone wrong.

And when you crawl into your midtwenties, you begin to realize that relationships of all kinds—the ones you have with everyone, from your coworkers to your lovers—are not fairy tales. They do not exist always, no matter what. They will shift, and they will change. Your concept of what you want from these relationships will change. The very nature by which we love and receive love shifts. The wounds deepen and the knives sharpen and the stakes rise. Relationships grow more difficult, and subsequently they also grow broader and better. The Metamorphosis opens you up—and that opening, that blossoming causes you to confront more love, more hurt, more pain, and more desire than you ever experienced before.

•

As a child and even as a young adult, you have the privilege of time and naivete on your side. Perhaps someone else handled the "adult things" in your life—like bills and rent, appointments and arrangements—and you had the ability to fill your days with hobbies and activities galore. In fact, children and young adults are effectively *criticized* if they don't have hobbies—our first résumés are effectively just a list of hobbies. Hobbies and activities build community, and community builds and fosters relationships. As a twenty-three-year-old, I quickly perceived that hobbies and activities for adults are viewed as distractions—and community was also no longer meant to be a priority. You have to work, and you have to figure out how to adult (which is eerily similar to figuring out how to ride a bike with no practice and no training wheels). You have to care for yourself and pay the bills and stay on top of the rent and make your appointments, AND you have to manage to fit in fostering, maintaining, and watering your relationships on top of that. Adulthood seems to steal our time from us, in a way we were remarkably unprepared for, while simultaneously upholding the idea that we should all have sparkling, wonderful social lives—friendships and romantic relationships and familial relationships too.

If you counted the number of hours in the day and built in eight hours for work, eight hours for sleep (if you're lucky), an hour to exercise, an hour to commute, an hour to cook meals and feed yourself, an hour to clean and do laundry, an hour to shower, you're already at twenty-one hours down the drain. And with the remaining three you're supposed to go to weekly therapy, have a thriving social life, go on dates, pick up prescriptions, keep appointments, develop "personal style" (whatever that means; I'm still trying to figure it out), have a cool hobby—it is nearly impossible to keep up with it all, especially when so many of us transition to this type of schedule from college, where socialization and friendship are at the top of the pyramid.

There is somewhat of an argument in the media these days over whether adult relationships should be work. One side of the argument insists that relationships should not be difficult, should not take work, and it is a red flag if they do. And I, on the other side, firmly believe that relationships are work—full stop. It is not a matter of whether or not they should be work; it is a matter of whether or not you'd like to put in the work, effort, and energy required to maintain said relationships. Even the people who are claiming that adult relationships aren't work are putting time, effort, and energy into them—which is work, and is difficult given the aforementioned circumstances of adulting. Relationships are hard in the same way a workout class is hard—you push yourself because you know overall that it is good for you and you know that by exerting the effort and energy required, you earn the inevitable endorphins, the physical and emotional health benefits, on the other side. You are there because you want the good parts. Relationships are not meant to be hard like grief or tedious like trying to undo a series of knots in a dainty necklace chain. They challenge us in a *good* way. And I just wish someone had prepared me for the uneasy shift relationships take in adulthood.

•

The woes of my college relationships pale in comparison to the challenges I've inevitably had to tackle in adult romantic relationships. This is not a bad thing. It is a gift that my partner and I have grown close enough to each other that we have had the privilege to tackle challenges together, to have hard conversations, to consider what it looks like to blend two lives into one. This is also not meant to say that eighteen-year-olds cannot tackle challenges in their relationships, or that college relationships cannot be deep, long-lasting, or turn into a forever. But as I've grown, I've grown to understand and realize what people were trying to tell me when they said that relationships take work. Adult relationships are met with adult issues and adult schedules and adult clarity that simply don't exist in college life at the volume they do in adult life. Again, this is not to say that college relationships cannot be complicated or challenging—just that when life's training wheels come off, it is much more difficult to balance well, to ride the bike.

Going through the Metamorphosis with a serious romantic partner or while dating is difficult. Going through these shifts single is difficult too. Not difficult like taking the SAT, but difficult like running a marathon when you are well trained—a good challenge. But one we should acknowledge nonetheless, because I haven't ever heard anyone attempt to make sense of the gray space before.

Everyone wants to talk about "growth" these days as it relates to our ability to mentally, emotionally, and spiritually mature and improve. I was familiar with the term on a surface level for most of my life until my midtwenties, when I had no choice but to grow. There was a certain clarity to the blue of the sky, the expressions painted on the face of a stranger I could now read, the heaviness of the earth's sorrow filling me up. And the experience of growing up in your midtwenties in tandem with someone else—in a relationship we began at the happy-go-lucky age of twenty-two, which I am still in today—is an undertaking.

After I turned twenty-five, my priorities shifted radically. I grew more sentimental, sharper, and wiser. I can only describe the development of the prefrontal cortex like I was tasting everything at 50 percent before, and one day I woke up with the ability to taste at 100 percent. I was ingesting the world like it was a diet soda and I didn't even know the real version existed. I have never felt deeper about my boyfriend, Noah, and also everything in my entire life than I have in the past year. It feels like I've been prescribed a pair of prescription glasses for an eyesight problem I never noticed until now, and I can finally see clearly.

You learn so much as you love during a time of shift, where your inner tectonic plates rumble with knowledge and breakthroughs. Communication is more integral than ever—something I always knew but never truly practiced. I used to let things go unsaid in my relationships, in hopes that they'd resolve themselves or in fear that saying them would cause the person receiving my words to change their mind or abandon me. But if telling my truth, sharing the bits eating me from the inside, asking for what I need, is going to cause someone on the other side of my honesty to abandon me or change their mind, they would have abandoned me or changed their mind regardless. You must find it inside yourself to say things out loud. See how they settle in space. This is true both when you are in a difficult conversation with someone you love and when you are just living your life in tandem with theirs and something itches at you. How you feel is never stupid or silly. It is how you feel. And your feelings deserve a life outside of yourself—and they are born when you share them.

My adolescent relationships were freckled with petty fights—arguments about guys before him, spats about the girl he was in a group project with. They were punctured by my relative unwillingness to communicate openly—fearing that it would leave me all alone if I was just open, if I was just myself. If I just said what was on my mind or what I was feeling. Instead, I was prone to burying things I wanted to say, choosing instead to lash out over something silly or inconsequential. Together, we have learned to communicate. Together, we have grown comfortable sharing how we feel. Together, we have learned to not take these honest truths personally, that by sharing our individual thoughts and feelings, we opt in to strengthening our relationship.

Prior to my moving in with Noah, we made it a point to discuss everything—what we'd do if things weren't working out, how we'd handle rent and bills, what we feared and what we were excited about, what we needed from each other, how we could work together to succeed. We've been living together for a year now, and I have both loved and learned more than ever before. We do not resort to bickering when something bothers or upsets one or both of us. We talk like two people on the same team who both can agree to one thing—we love each other, and want to work through whatever is coming up against us. And sometimes a conversation goes nowhere, and sometimes it goes somewhere. Sometimes it builds off a past conversation, and sometimes it warrants another later on. The work we put in—the effort and the energy—is what makes loving him so easy. The communication we center, the honesty we treasure, the difficulties we walk into hand in hand, that is the work. It is not easy, but it is worth it. I believe, fundamentally, that you should always be getting more out of a romantic relationship than you are putting in. Love is not supposed to be hard. That is the easy part. Love is the endorphins that come at the end of the race. We love each other in the ever-hungry and grand way only two people learning about themselves and making their way in the world for the first time can. It is the privilege of my life to love someone who has never feared sharing his vulnerable shadow with me. It is terrifying and gratifying to start building a life with someone, one where we are choosing each other—choosing to knit our souls together, while we admire each other for the individuals we continuously become. Because love begins as a fall, and it becomes a choice.

But as we experience the Metamorphosis, we grow, and thus, we inevitably change. We cannot halt the way our newfound understanding of the world will cause us to change, to grow, and to adapt. Our opinions shift when there is more to see, we choose differently when there is more to choose, we understand each other in a different way when we see them clearly. Sometimes we change in the same direction of our romantic partners, sometimes we change in opposite directions, sometimes we change into versions of ourselves that will no longer fit together. This is inevitable and a part of the gamble of love in adulthood, I've found. To love someone as they change, to change in the same direction as someone, is to deepen a bond that is meant to move with you into your next chapter. But it is equally okay if you change in the opposite direction from someone whom the prior version of you loved very deeply. It is okay if, in growing, you realize you've grown out of a relationship. This is as important to our becoming as changing in tandem with the person you love.

You should feel free to change. Don't fear falling apart from someone while you become the version of yourself you have been working toward every moment so far. Because it is integral that you make yourself at home in your own body, with your mind and your scripture, before you make a sacrifice for someone else. It is important for you to share your inner troubles and feelings with a romantic partner in lieu of hiding them away because you fear the loss of them. One thing I know for sure: there will be someone who fits the version of you that you've grown into and who can stick with you through all of the future mutations you will experience. Sometimes our idea of forever changes. Sometimes our morals and values, priorities and needs, morph when we were so confident about them before.

We need to be open to the gift that it is to bloom, to swell and expand, to be our own snowball effect. Of course it is scary, the idea that you could lose someone when you find yourself. Of course it is trying, the idea that you could grow into a version of yourself that would be unrecognizable from the one you live with now.

But it is inevitable, this expansion and cultivation. And each version of you that ever walked a day in your shoes will nestle inside of you like a nesting doll, one inside of another. You never lose that version of you or the memories or the lessons that accompanied it. You grow into a version of yourself ready to build upon everything that came before. And sometimes that means losing what you know.

I hate writing about the idea of losing Noah, because even the acknowledgment of the possibility makes me sick. But I know, for a fact, that there is always a chance we will grow apart. I am trying to find comfort in the endless possibilities for my life. And if we did end up growing apart, I would not regret a single second of loving him and how it made me feel to be loved by him. I would understand, eventually, why it had to become a finished chapter and not one I am still working on. The lesson of his love is something that should be written about in academic texts and PhD theses. He is my magnum opus in so many ways, and I am breathlessly proud of the sapling we have grown into a healthy plant, turned toward the sun. The versions of me that have experienced his love will always feel it back, but if there comes a day that there are versions of us in this world who no longer love each other, I will simply be grateful for the versions of him who loved me as deeply as they did. It has taken me twenty-five years to realize that there is a reason we all want to believe in "meant to be."

Maybe that is more realistic than it is romantic. I find it a best practice to hold both, romance and realism, close at all times. You should get your hopes up because that is sometimes all we can do, but you should also learn how to cushion the fallout from your hopes, if things don't go the way you planned. While romantic relationships grow inherently trickier with the complications of adulthood, they also grow inherently better. With our clearer, more complex minds, we can dig deeper with each other—what was once able to go only five feet below the surface can now go fifty feet down. This depth can be both complex and also comforting. We can strike gold there.

Eventually, we all will.

•

There is, of course, no right way to experience the Metamorphosis. Some of us will do it single, some of us will do it dating, some of us will do it in a relationship or while going through a breakup, and some of us will even do it engaged or married. I believe you can, absolutely, experience growth while you are in a romantic relationship—and any relationship that makes you feel as though you cannot grow as an individual is one that isn't worth being in. The idea that people could be together for ten, twenty, or thirty years without ever experiencing individual growth or change is not realistic and also sounds miserable. I cannot imagine still being who I was at twenty-two, let alone fifteen—and both change and growth have allowed me to bloom into the version of myself I am today.

It can be lucrative to experience growth as a single person—and can be affirming to date while in a period of growth and change. There is no right way to grow. There is no one perfect way to self-actualize or make your way in the world. You can experience personal growth with a new sexual partner every weekend, in a serious relationship, or while not dating at all, with no desire to. Where you lay your head at night, and whom you choose to lie next to (if anyone), does not change the fact that you are a caterpillar that is becoming a butterfly. You will change regardless—this is out of your control. However, the circumstance and the environment around you while you change are what you can control. Perhaps you are single, and you are going through your great Metamorphosis as you read this. Perhaps you feel some intrinsic pressure to be actively dating at all times, to be in pursuit of "finding someone." Perhaps the world has made you feel like this is required of you, being in your mid-twenties. Allow me to tell the world (proudly) to fuck off. You do not need to be actively dating at all times, and actively dating will not serve you at all times. Dating takes time, energy, and effort. There is a world where you have that time, energy, and effort and simply do not want to use it on dating. That is valid. There is a world where you have made a long list of your priorities, and dating has not even been a consideration. It is frightening and freeing to realize that nobody can make the choice for you; it is yours to make and then embrace alone. Your only job, as you go through your own Metamorphosis, is to make yourself as comfortable as possible and construct the circumstances for you to feel as joyful as possible. If dating is not a part of these circumstances, then dating is not a part of these circumstances.

Conversely, it is 100 percent possible to start dating in pursuit of long-term partnership (or short-term for that matter) while you are experiencing your own Metamorphosis. The fact that you are changing and growing does not automatically mean you cannot share yourself and your life with someone else. Putting yourself out there may feel more vulnerable considering the clarity we've gained trickles into all areas of our lives. For some, the proliferation of options makes it easier to know exactly what we want, exactly what we're looking for. For others, what we thought we wanted or what we thought we were looking for changes overnight. I cannot tell you what this Metamorphosis will look and feel like to you. I cannot prescribe you the perfect array of remedies to alleviate the stress.

All I can do is remind you that you are in control. Even when it feels like you can't reach the brake pedal and you can't accelerate. You are in control. This is your car; you are driving. You have the ability to choose. To date or not to date. To flirt or not to flirt. What works for you isn't necessarily going to work for your best friend or your coworker or your roommate, but don't let that sway you from choosing the path that suits you best. Remember—the people who truly love you, who are worth loving, are going to celebrate you for making a choice in pursuit of your own happiness, even if that isn't the same choice they would've made.

In many ways I didn't choose to experience my own Metamorphosis while dating Noah; rather, I was dating Noah, and we both started to experience a shift, and we made it through together. The entire time, though, I was in control of how I was reacting to the inevitable. We grew together, and that is a gift. But there is a world where we didn't make it through together. There is a world where we ended things before the shift even began. These are lives I won't live and worlds I won't harp on, but I acknowledge and mourn them nonetheless. I have friends who began this time in their lives in a serious relationship and came out the other side having shed that relationship. I have friends who steadily dated throughout this time in their lives; I have friends who stayed single too.

What I'm trying to say is this: love is easy, but relationships take work. And as we transition into these adult versions of ourselves, dating will transition too. It will be less adolescent, with fewer games, and in many ways, it will be better. It will be overwhelming to feel with the sparkling clarity of a fully developed frontal lobe, but that doesn't mean it will be bad. It is innately complicated to undo yourself in front of another person and ask them to do the same, in the name of devotion. It is also beautiful and maddening. The gift of understanding another person, all the way to their core, is something I marvel about today in a way I wouldn't have at twenty-two. Things are deeper; they will be deeper yet, and we will be okay.

It made me feel insane, as though everyone was ogling at me like I was a part of the circus, to keep all of this inside. I started to feel better when I reached out to say: Does anyone else feel this way?

•

I choose not to view romantic relationships as superior to my friendships, my familial relationships, and the relationship I have to myself. I find that, in experiencing romantic love and heartbreak, the love in your life is elevated overall when you treat all your relationships as though they are equals. Surely, at times, certain relationships in your life will require more energy, effort, and work than others. But if you had four plants, each representing a type of relationship you have in your life (familial/chosen family, romantic, platonic, and self), and you chose to only water one of the plants, the others would eventually die. For your survival, it is necessary to keep all your plants alive. They give you oxygen; they help you breathe. Sometimes one will wilt, and you will realize you need to give it more attention. Sometimes one will need extra care, and you will make the decision to focus on it for a while—and that is okay. Society has attempted to value romantic relationships as superior to friendship, familial relationships, relationships to chosen family and community, and our relationship to ourselves. There is such a heightened pressure to find a romantic partner, but not to find oneself or to find good friends. I believe deeply that all our relationships are equal. The idea that romantic relationships are superior is a falsehood created to push the heteronormative American dream of the nuclear family. In tandem is a societal fear that adults in community with one another could actually dismantle the structure wherein women and men have roles in society, which, when obeyed, makes it easier for us (women) to be managed and controlled. Romantic relationships are no more important than all the other types of relationships we form throughout our lives.

And just like romantic relationships, the relationships you have to other people in your life will change, grow more challenging, and take on new life in your time of Metamorphosis.

You will wake up and realize your mom was also just a girl once, who had a whole life of wanting and living before she made you. You will see her for her flaws, and you will see her for her fears. Maybe she has told you, for your whole life, that everything is going to be okay. Maybe now you look at her and realize she didn't really know, but she just wanted you to feel settled and calm—and would do everything in her power to try to make "okay" come true.

You might evolve into a version of yourself that recognizes that your given family, by DNA, is not the family that serves you. Your shift may cause you to set boundaries, draw lines in the sand, and take a step toward protecting your peace that you never felt brave enough to take. It is never too late to do this, and you are not a failure for not taking the steps to protect yourself sooner. You might evolve into a version of yourself that chooses to forgive someone from the past. You might evolve into a version of yourself that realizes you were hurt by someone who was meant to protect you.

The only universal fact is that when you enter adulthood, you open the door to the party and step in among the adults you've known your entire life. And you see them bare and as humans, not as hulking giants or disciplinary beasts. It's as though they've been stripped of their adult costumes and are the same shade of human as you are—you see them as just people for the first time, like seeing a teacher outside of school. And inevitably, your relationship to these adults in your life will shift. One day you will be wearing your own adult costume, and some young person will be looking up at you like you are God. Then eventually they will gain a set of keys to the adult party and realize that we are all just people. And most of us are just doing our best.

My mom has been sick with Ménière's disease since I was fifteen. And when I was fifteen and sixteen and seventeen years old and I was terrified when her illness took her through bouts of weakness—I looked to her for reassurance that she was okay. That she was not scared. If she wasn't scared, surely I didn't have to be scared, I reasoned. And she would always tell me she wasn't afraid. She would always tell me everything was fine. And then I grew up, and I turned twenty-five, and it became clear that she is just a person, just like me. And we were both scared back then. And sometimes we are both scared today. She just told me otherwise. My mother is not exempt from the feeling of fear just because it is her job to protect and water me. It was her job to shield me from the worst-case scenarios, and I am lucky enough to say I was once a child who was always protected by the adults in my life. I know not everyone can say the same. This awareness, seeing her as I do now, has changed the way we move together through the world.

It has brought us closer—and in the end, it has been a positive. But there is a level of mourning too. Mourning the relationship I had with my mom when I truly believed she was my untouchable superhero, exempt from feeling afraid. I am so lucky to be close to her. I am so lucky we get to grow up together. I am so lucky to have her hand in mine as I navigate the seas of life that she has seen before. But there is a silent heartbreak in discarding what it was to be a girl and have her just be my mom. It is okay to feel sad and grateful at the same time. You don't have to pick one way to feel about each and every movement of life.

This is not easy. Growing up, getting older, starting to truly live in a way that nobody properly prepares you for. It is not easy, the shifts in our relationships to friends and mothers and lovers and ourselves. In writing this, I have realized that while a manual or a heads-up would've been helpful, the way this Metamorphosis impacts our relationships is also so undeniably hard to put into words. And it wouldn't be right to steal away the thrill of childhood with the heavy acknowledgment that things will get harder but also greater as well.

It has always helped to reach out my hand, to look up and be brave enough to ask: Does anyone else feel this way? And find that, in fact, so many thousands of people feel the same feelings in their very own way.

I cherish the friendships that have lasted through the turbulence of this Metamorphosis. The girls I can hold hands with, share clothes with, tell my fears to and never fear their reaction. The people I have weathered storms with for years, and those I have collected in this new chapter, and those I have collected in spite of it.

Sometimes you just need to go out to dinner with the girl who always wants to split a bottle of wine. And you both order pasta and you start out by talking about the bad sex she had with her ex the week before and then all of a sudden you both have tears in your eyes while you spill your deepest fears out on the tomato sauce–stained tablecloth. And then you get up and you walk to your subway stop and you marvel at the fact that you feel like a boulder has been rolled off your chest. All because you said, "I'm not really okay, but I trust you enough to ask you—are you?"

•

I watched two people embrace on the corner of Houston and Lafayette the other day. They were looking for each other, and had chosen this as a meeting spot. And I watched the way they lost control over themselves the moment they caught each other's gaze. I wondered how long it must've been since they looked for each other in a crowd last. Maybe it was just the other day, or maybe it had been years. I marveled at the way they laughed and shrieked and jumped toward each other like they were no longer adult people trying to maintain some sense of cool. That is what deep love does to us. It causes us to lose sense of how we look to everyone else. It causes us to flail our arms and yell and embrace in the middle of a crowded street, unbothered by the pissed-off New Yorkers in our path.

They could've met last year or ten years ago. They could've been childhood best friends, cousins, or former coworkers. They could've been anyone to each other. They could've been you and me.

But the thing about their interaction—as unfettered and unapologetic as can be—is that it was the most universal thing in the world. The delight that spreads through you the second you find the person you were looking for in a crowd, a person you love, who loves you back—for no reason other than the sheer fact that you are you. And for them, that is enough. Maybe you will not always be you to them; maybe they will not always be them to you. Hold it in your hands for right now. We only really have today, after all.

The reason it is so good—to find the person you were looking for in the crowd, to catch their eye and see familiarity and knowing staring back at you—is because it takes work. Because you've put in the energy to create something worth falling in love with, worth losing control for.

All of this growing-up stuff is mostly bullshit and growing pains, and it feels like riding a roller coaster without a seat belt while holding on for dear life. You are unprepared, you are afraid, you are shocked when you've been waiting in line to get onto the ride and you're finally allowed to step on and no one has seat belts and it looks slightly shittier than you imagined.

Our relationships are what save us. I have found that relationships have made it all worth it. I have found that loving has made it all worth it. Loving my friends even as I've lost some of them, even as we've grown apart. Loving the friends I have made as our Metamorphoses have reestablished what is important to us. Loving the people who have bobbed and weaved through my life. Loving my mom for her personhood, because it is so unbelievably bold of her to have been human all along. Loving my brothers even as they become people who no longer need me in the way they once did. Loving the bests and the worsts of the people who come my way. Loving the living hell out of the person next to me in bed, who is whispering into my hair, telling me I am worth it. I am worth it. I am worth it.

That is today. I have changed—in style, in thought, in many ways. But I have the same heart, and everyone I love is trapped somewhere inside of it, for all eternity. It is hard putting yourself out there. It is work, like building something that you will one day call your own. It is the only way we make sense of all of this—the people who catch us in all our unfinishedness and help us make our way, the "text me when you get home" and the promises really kept.

We need each other. And your people need you. Especially when we are twenty-five years old and have no fucking idea where we're going or what will startle us next. You don't have to be sure, and you don't have to be clear—but you do have to change; you cannot stay eighteen forever. On the other side of the shift, you will laugh and cry about it, and you will just be grateful to have one person or three people or ten people who take you in their arms and say they are proud.

Does Anyone Else Feel Like They're Having a Quarter-Life Crisis?

I am thirteen years old, but I wish I was twenty-three. When my mom was twenty-three, she got engaged to my dad in Nantucket. They'd only been dating for nine months. There's a picture of them in the bathroom of my childhood home, both wearing sweatshirts and staring down at her hand like they are the only people in the whole world to ever be in love before. I love that photo.

I am thirteen years old, and I just got my braces off, and I feel like my teeth are too small. I want to be the student council vice president my freshman year of high school, but I know I can't run because none of the boys would vote for me. I want to press fast-forward and be twenty-five years old and married, grown. It must be easier to be a grown-up, I figure at thirteen years old. You don't have to worry about how small your teeth are, or if none of the boys will vote for you in the student council election. You don't have to worry about being bullied for being in the drama club even though it's the only place you ever feel like you belong.

I am thirteen years old and obsessed with growing up. My friends and I are addicted to romanticizing and discussing our future lives—where we will live and with whom, when we will marry and have children, what kinds of jobs we will have, and what kinds of cars we will drive. We are thirteen, desperate for thirty—or maybe desperate for twenty-three (back then, I think we viewed thirty as old). We all want to marry our classroom crushes by the age of twenty-two. We all want to plan out our pregnancies at the age of twenty-four so that we can have children that are the same age. We spend hours looking up to these dreamy, expanded versions of ourselves—painting pictures of who we wish to become in our minds. My childhood best friend and I begged her mother to let us use her desktop computer to do research on future wedding venues. We'd each have a mansion and a guy, a perfect wedding and two babies—a boy first and then a girl—our lives all figured out before the age of twenty-six. Being a grown-up means we get the inside scoop and nobody can tell us no. We never think much of what could happen after all that—our minds can only think so far ahead. We can't see very far beyond the boundary lines of our small town. We just want to summer in the light of having no rules. We just want to be the type of women girls are supposed to grow up and be. Of course that's what we want. The world makes it look so shiny and comfortable. We're in between the fictional stories of Disney princesses and *Gossip Girl*—but even as we transition to more scandalous source material, we are sold the same message about who we should become. And we etch our timelines into the sand of our minds, and the tide never comes up to wash them away. Find the guy, have the baby, live the dream.

    That's what we thought we were supposed to do.

It's been thirteen years since I was thirteen years old. My childhood best friend is not married, but she is engaged, and I won't be invited to the wedding. We're not in each other's lives anymore. Back then, we wore matching outfits and combined our names into one long name that we requested everyone call us by. If you had told us then that we'd turn twenty-five and live just miles from each other and never talk, I think our shared world would've ended. I still have her phone number memorized anyway. Because time passes. And those little moments tend to stick around. But even though we spent all of high school attached at the hip and all of college on long-distance phone calls, our friendship dissolved in adulthood. We are no longer a duo, just two different girls with memories and happy birthday texts back and forth. And those timelines we made up together, of how our lives would be, looming somewhere near.

Thirteen fades, and you fall in love with eighteen and your first licks of freedom—you are alone and adolescent and burning hot. You hardly require sleep, blindly trust the girl down the hall, never get hungover, and for the first time feel sort of cool.

The five years between thirteen and eighteen don't offer a single pause. Growing up and the need to be adored take up all of your energy and attention—and for a minute, you may have forgotten about the preplanned wedding day at twenty-two and the family at twenty-four. But the timeline never went anywhere. You are still the little girl who wants a big, magical life for yourself, even if you've since changed your mind about what that looks like. We often forget that we are still the girl we were at thirteen, pining after what's-his-name, wishing for a happily ever after. But now you're eighteen and the wedding you planned for yourself at thirteen is only four years away. The baby whose name you already picked out is now only six years away. You recall that adolescent timeline of dreams and start working backward. If you want to date someone for a few years before getting engaged, you would need to have found them yesterday. And here you are, surrounded by your dorm room mess, which your mom would scold you for, pouring Blue Raspberry Svedka into a half-empty bottle of blue Gatorade, wearing jagged lines of black eyeliner on your eyelids and your shortest skirt, wondering if you can really find the love of your life in the Phi Delt basement.

Was I wrong about what I wanted back then? you wonder, and you think of the version of yourself with braces and Converse sneakers and puffier cheeks, wishing and wanting, desperate for tomorrow and the next day and the next. *Am I wrong for not knowing what I want now?* You think of the version of yourself in the dorm room with the situationship across town who has no plans to give you the world, and the card that you swipe to get into the dining hall. You push off the thoughts of existentialism and wants for the night—but you can't shake how easy it was to plan out your life when you were thirteen and how much harder it feels to do the same five years later.

It is an ache to break a promise you made with the you that you were at the age of thirteen. Whether or not she was right, that is what she wanted. And you will not give it to her. You cannot give it to her. You should not give it to her. She did not know any better. But what she wanted was still what she wanted. You hope that if you had told her then where you'd be at twenty-two, she'd have been all right with it. That she'd have forgiven you.

Maybe I can compromise with her? you think, and you wonder if you can push the timeline back just a little bit, allow yourself some room to breathe, a second to have fun before you get to work. Maybe you marry at twenty-four and the family comes at twenty-six. The desire to compromise is born of nostalgia and commitment—if this was always the timeline, how could you just let it wash away now?

I just wanted to give her the world she craved. I hope she will forgive me when I do not.

•

It is May, and it is the year 2024. I am well past twenty-two and almost two years past twenty-four. I am unmarried and childless, and the vast majority of people around me think this is actually quite normal. I do not foresee myself having children anytime soon, and I am okay with that. I am career focused and starved for success. The conversation surrounding futures and timelines, specifically as women, has shifted since I was thirteen. People want to make fun of Millennials for their occasional cringiness, but their ambition and prioritization of self-development have been integral to this shift in the zeitgeist. They have taught us to be intentionally selfish in a way I find really critical to our midtwenties self-actualization. My mom was engaged when she was twenty-three, and when I was twenty-three, I still had last night staining my eyes as I tried to figure out how in the world to be an adult and who in the world I wanted to be. There is nothing wrong with being engaged whenever you are ready to be engaged—I am just telling you that at twenty-three, I had not become the person I thought I'd be when I was thirteen. I did not follow the timeline I made for myself, one that I think, albeit differently, we all craft for ourselves at one point in our adolescence and leave hanging in the closet in the back of our minds.

When I was thirteen years old, I thought I'd be twenty-five and a homeowner (not sure where I got the idea I'd be able to afford a home, but I digress)—with a diamond ring and a framed photo of my wedding day in the living room. At twenty-five, the closest thing I own to a home is my mind. I am pleased to say that I got the blond hair dye out of my hair (after three years of growing it out and cutting it), and I wake up with an uncertainty sitting in my chest that I worry my seventh-grade self would be disappointed by. I am trying my best to make her proud and to mourn the life she wished we had—because at the very least, this is what she deserves.

The timeline is something I eventually had to abandon, and though the life I am presently living is the one I'd like to live, it is still bittersweet. For Gen Z and Millennials, I think most of us had some type of invisible timeline we abandoned once we reached our midtwenties and realized it just wasn't going to happen how we thought it would. In 1960, the median age for women to marry was twenty-one, and for men it was twenty-three. It is no wonder we made ourselves invisible timelines that saw us marrying and having children at such a young age—it is what we were familiar with, both through society and in popular culture and media. It was hard to find fiercely independent, unmarried, childless, successful women to look up to in the shows I watched with my friends and the movies we went to see. I found those women in books, but it felt like they never actually existed in the real world. Of course they did exist—but they weren't as easy to find. Jo March was a figment of Louisa May Alcott's mind, and that's where she lived. I could never actually be her, I figured. I had no idea how. In fact, I had no idea how to be much of anyone, and this became incredibly clear to me when I turned twenty-five and I had officially surpassed any chance of that now-ancient timeline. When the timeline went out the door, the quarter-life crisis turned the knob and weaseled her way in.

What am I supposed to be if not the woman the girl inside me so desperately wished I'd become?

I am not upset that I did not stick to my long-gone timeline. I am bewildered that it is such a universal experience to make these invisible checklists for yourself, and grieve them when they do not happen, even if you're happier without them.

Nobody prepares you for being twenty-five years old. Nobody prepares you for the quarter-life crisis. Perhaps because they do not know what to say. I would've liked a bit of a warning, and perhaps it would have looked something like this:

"Buckle up and welcome to twenty-five! You're going to be mourning the lives you dreamed of living, even though you don't want to live those lives anymore—while simultaneously attempting to navigate the type of life you do want to live, terrified of taking risks but also terrified of planting roots in the wrong place. Oh, and on top of it, you will experience a period of insecurity, uncertainty, and doubt about pretty much everything! You will feel like you've abandoned yourself, you'll also feel like you've found yourself, but the version of yourself you find will be unfamiliar to you. Everything you thought you knew is wrong, and it's time to make big decisions about your life! Also remember this is the youngest you'll ever be, so if you're not living your life to the fullest, you're wasting it! But also remember this time in your life is crucial for laying the foundation for the rest of your life too! Presidential candidates will use empowered, single, childless young women as the butt of the joke, and corporate America still clandestinely punishes women who want to prioritize both career and motherhood. But don't forget you're supposed to be both a girlboss and a baby-making machine. . . . Enjoy!"

People will tell you it's a quarter-life crisis, but nobody will advise you on how to get past it. Though the brutal honesty might've come as a shock, I prefer the above honesty to what we do hear about our midtwenties and the quarter-life crisis—"You should want to stay young forever!" and "Enjoy college, it's the best four years of your life!" and "Getting older sucks!"

I don't think any of those statements are true, but older generations, society, and the media use them in place of any sort of guidance for young people navigating that so-called quarter-life crisis. Perhaps this is because older generations were taught to bury their emotions and ignore their discomfort, and our generation is a generation of feelers—we cannot help but want to make sense of the intensity of the things that we feel. Perhaps because it is hard, and we fear speaking about the discomfort. Perhaps it is because we don't understand how to make peace with the fact that it is so impossible to plan a life—and this is our first taste of that heavy truth.

The term "quarter-life crisis" sounds dramatic, but I think it perfectly encapsulates the time period of change we encounter when we settle into our midtwenties. Not only is the temporary grace period of the postgrad transition period no longer granted, but we now have supposedly had plenty of time to settle into adult life and are expected to proceed as such. We are also at an "appropriate age" for major life milestones to ensue—people start getting engaged, having children, buying homes, changing careers, getting promotions, moving cities, and building the foundation for the life they want to live. We are taught to celebrate those things—and we abide by tradition as though there's some invisible rule maker keeping us in check. People start checking off the milestones on our forgotten timelines, and we're sitting at those celebrations in pretty dresses and are reminded of the longing we once had to live a life that we're not living at all.

The tide finally reaches the timeline etched into the sand in your mind and washes it all away. You have a blank canvas, and only you can begin to fill it in.

For most of my life I relied on the idea that by the age of twenty-five, I'd be a well-rounded, shiny grown-up with a life I was sure of and a routine that was comfortable and everything all figured out.

I cannot go back and change my own mind, but relying on that through all the uncertainty of adolescence certainly made the reality of turning twenty-five years old and having no idea what I want, what the right decision is, or who I am a lot more isolating. It would've been one thing to experience this quarter-life crisis with preparation, but to deal with it when I had romanticized the assuredness that I expected to accompany adulthood . . . was something else entirely.

It wasn't like this quarter-life crisis hit me like a ton of bricks. I did not wake up one day, look at myself in the mirror, and say, "My quarter-life crisis has begun." It was gradual, silent, and slow moving. I went through my days and I felt like I lived them too. I was twenty-two, and thanks to Taylor Swift I was comfortable being *happy, free, confused, and lonely at the same time.* I was a postgrad kid, and it was socially acceptable when I threw up from going too hard at bottomless brunch. Then I was twenty-three and twenty-four, and I was figuring it out. I was building my own business, I was going on dates with my boyfriend, I was spending time with my friends and living in an apartment in the East Village that I adored. And then, over time, I started to feel my mind want to open up and bloom—and with that I slowly began to feel a sense of lingering unease. It felt like I woke up in a strange place with no sense of direction and a crowd of strangers standing over me saying, "There's our favorite adult! Go be an adult!" There was this sudden and ever-looming idea of identity and of purpose. This encroaching concept of a five-year plan.

This idea of growing up. I tried to avoid unpacking it all because it seemed like too much, and anyway . . . I was happy, right? I was on the right path, wasn't I? But as the unease washed over the shores of my mind and kept me awake through the night, I watched people around me start to do what looked to me like moving on. And I wondered if I was actually happy and if I was on the path to the places I was meant to go.

•

In the spring of 2022, on the precipice of turning twenty-four, I was waiting to cross the street to the rental car I had illegally parked outside of a SoulCycle on Sunset Boulevard in West Hollywood (a likely place for me to be). As I started toward the crosswalk, this chatty girl named Isabela, whom I sort of knew in college, called me. I almost didn't answer her call, because we didn't really know each other and I chronically avoid phone calls. My friends knew her friends, we both wrote for the school newspaper, and she was an opera major (which is one degree of separation from the theater majors). Once, she had borrowed a dress from me to wear to a fraternity formal because we wore the same size. I had a small crush on her boyfriend before they'd started dating. She knew my ex-boyfriend Luke through extracurriculars at school. She knew a lot of people, actually, and she's the type of girl people just trust. For some reason, I stopped walking and answered the call.

"Have you heard the news?" she said, in the same dramatic tone of a prerehearsed reality TV confessional.

"Um . . . no . . . I haven't . . ." I said, somewhat eager for the gossip.

The *news* was that Luke had deleted every single photo on his entire Instagram account and posted a photo proposing to his girlfriend in a church parking lot.

It was a lot to process, despite the fact that he and I had broken up in 2019 and I hadn't thought of him in over a year. I didn't follow him on social media, so I had no clue he was now religious or that he had a girlfriend. As Isabela filled my ear with the excited chatter of someone sharing great gossip, I watched a cop walk up to my rental car, place a ticket on the windshield, get back in his car, and drive away.

Great. The only ex I'd ever truly pictured myself marrying was an engaged, born-again Christian, and I was getting parking tickets in LA. Back on the phone, Isabela asked if I wanted to hang out in New York sometime, and I surprised myself by saying that I did. We said goodbye, and I got in the car and stared at the steering wheel while I tried to make sense of it all. Someone whom I was once so tethered to, not that long ago, was getting married. I was in a new relationship (as of a week prior), and I was visiting California for the first time in my life for work. I was in an exciting period of change, and I was on the edge of feeling happy, but it was the first time I remember asking myself if I was making some kind of wrong choice. It was the first time I remember wondering if I was behind other people my age.

My relationship with Luke and all the plans we made for a future flashed before my eyes. I was the one who ended it with Luke. It had to be done, and I've never regretted it. But I had not been in a relationship as serious since then, and there was a strange nostalgia to the idea that we had both flung ourselves in opposite directions and taken up different roles and made unbelievably different decisions. It was too much to even try to process it.

I started to drive and decided I wasn't upset by this news—because I wasn't. I was confused. Part of me wasn't ready to find out someone I'd been so seriously involved with was now engaged. Not because I wanted to be the one he was engaged to, but because it caused me to reflect on what each of us had become in the three years since we were together, and on how much just two years since graduation could alter a life.

Both his and mine.

•

Luke lit a match, and soon the forest fire around me raged—let the quarter-life crisis begin. Everyone I knew was pulling in opposite directions, making different choices. One of my friends decided to move to California with her boyfriend. We had a going-away party for her, and the morning before she left, we went on a walk in Washington Square Park and she admitted she was scared. A year later she called me—they broke up. My friend Caroline got married to her high school sweetheart, and it was an adjustment to go from calling him her fiancé to her husband. My brother moved to Seattle, and my other brother moved home. Lizzie decided she wanted to go back to school and eventually committed to Northwestern. I thought we'd always live a subway ride away. People I used to know went to and then graduated from law school and medical school. Jen got a promotion at work and started to love her job. I had friends who worked as baristas as they tried to make it as actors. Daphne moved back to the East Coast after graduating from university in London, and then called me and told me she was going to move back to London. A guy I dated once was an extra in a movie. I had friends who left the corporate world for freelance and friends who left freelance for the corporate world. Sadie and her boyfriend moved in together. People moved to and from homes that they'd called homes before. I followed people on Instagram who bought their own houses and apartments. I followed other people who got laid off and were looking for new work. People got plastic surgery, were canceled for old Tweets, and went out to dinner. Others went on trips around the world, cheated on their partners, or were cheated on themselves. My friends became aunts and uncles and maids of honor and best men. There were family tragedies and health crises, mental health breakthroughs and really bad moments.

My roommates and I threw a party on Valentine's Day in 2023. We were all friends, but we also had separate friend groups outside the walls of our apartment, so we invited our people—coworkers and high school friends, college friends and postgrad friends. And every person who walked through the door, all ages twenty-four to thirty, was in a different chapter of life. Engaged, married, living with significant others or alone, starting over or getting through, starting new jobs or getting promotions, moving away or moving home. Everyone was doing something different, their own expression of their own life, their own choices playing out in front of them. Anything goes, anything is acceptable, any path is an option—there is an unfettered and uncomfortable freedom to making any choice you want, and it was the first time in our lives that this was truly the case. I looked around the room at my peers and saw these disparate ways of living, and it made my head spin.

Many of us graduate high school and then decide whether further education is the right decision for us. If it is, we keep studying, and then we graduate and get turned out into the "real world." There will be a grace period, a few years of transition as we go from college student to working graduate. And certainly we were all individuals in high school, college, and postgrad—surely we carried our own baggage and processed our unique situations differently. We had responsibilities and choices to make.

But at its core we were in a shared chapter back then—a time period in our lives that still had us fenced in, aware of boundaries, cognizant of next steps. But turning twenty-five and looking around at my peers, I realized that we were officially individual adults with the option to do absolutely anything. We were the "real people" we'd been growing toward and now had the full agency to make individual choices for our lives . . . and people were doing just that.

I was overwhelmed as the world continued to turn and expand. I no longer wanted to be a grown-up with no rules. I no longer wanted to be a dog with no leash. I no longer wanted the ability to do whatever I pleased. All of that sounded nice at thirteen, but what I failed to understand then is that sometimes it's much easier to have a rubric or a reference point; that way, when you're taking the test, you feel like you're aiming in the "right direction."

In the beginning of my own quarter-life crisis, I just wanted direction. I wanted someone to tell me I was doing the right thing. I wanted guidance. I felt behind others and then felt guilty for feeling behind. I had questions and no clue whom to turn to for answers. How to know if you're on the right path? How to make the right decisions for yourself and your life? How to balance living in the moment and also carving the foundation for your future? Will I ever feel settled? Will I ever feel sure? If there are no right ways, then how are you supposed to choose which way to go?

I wanted there to be a right way because I am someone who strays from uncertainty and appreciates assuredness. I wanted there to be a right way because I missed how it felt to be going through it with my friends. I strangely missed the moments of waiting for college decisions to come out senior year of high school on the same day as everyone else. Those communities and those shared emotions were gifted to us back then—and we took them for granted.

At twenty-five years old, anything goes, so nothing goes. Anything is the right way, so there is no right way. I was raised to always do the right thing, and now I was learning there was no one right thing.

That was a tough pill to swallow.

•

I was adjusting to adulthood. I was in a very serious adult relationship. My friends were growing up and growing away. My brothers were doing the same. I was reflecting on the first five years of my twenties, which went by in a nanosecond, scrolling on Instagram, watching everyone else pretend to be fine while I also posted on Instagram pretending to be fine too.

The uncertainty ate at me like a moth tearing through a closet of pretty clothes all hung up and neatly pressed. This was THE quarter-life crisis. This was the great junction of everything that had happened up until this point—losing all of my friends from high school because I was blamed for something someone else did. The guy who cycled through me like I was just another load of dirty laundry. My mom falling ill and my family bobbing through moments of crisis. All of my twenty-five birthdays lined up in one long row. The college graduation that was canceled due to COVID-19. The guy who broke my best friend in half. The almosts and the I-just-can'ts. A quarter of a life. All of the mistakes and all of the fervor and all of the sunburns and all of the firsts. One-fourth of the way to wherever we go next.

I am so young, and I am so much older than I was at thirteen. I am so angry at the way our world works, and I am so helpless. I wish for a do-over on all the joy I've lived just so I can experience it again. I wish to make sense of all the pain just to put it easily to bed.

And the difficult truth is that there is no universal quarter-life crisis. After thinking about it, I cannot write a true guidebook on it because of that. For some, this is still the time of trial and error. For others, they dove headfirst off the cliff long ago and enjoyed the fall, and they'll swim in the waters they landed in for now. For some, what they've always wanted is what they still want. And for others, what they wanted for years couldn't be more foreign to them today.

The thing we can all share in is this: you will never really know what is meant for you, what the "right path" is. It is impossible to choose one way to live your life and feel content in that forever. People start over all the time. We must be comfortable with the reset button. We must be comfortable with our own ability to change our minds. We must give people the grace, and the room, to change and grow and mold throughout their entire life—you are not making a permanent decision at twenty-five. There is no permanence.

Nothing is permanent. Nothing is forever. There is no forever.
And people start over all the time.

•

One common side effect of the quarter-life crisis is a very glaring realization that you do not know who you are—a lack of grasp on identity or a sudden sensation of detachment from the person you thought you were. Sometimes, you even may feel you've "lost yourself." This side effect is often then associated with a rapid, chaotic journey of trying on different versions of yourself to attempt to find something that clicks or fits. For a while, I remember thinking the only thing I truly knew to be true about myself was this: I am somebody who desperately wishes to be liked, and I will do what I need to do to get there. I don't blame myself for feeling this way, and if anything, I am proud of myself for my willingness to be honest with you about it.

My identity—at least in the beginning of my own quarter-life crisis—was being a girl who wants to be liked.

We all want to be liked. We free ourselves when we realize that it is impossible and irrational to be liked by everyone. We begin to live when we stop trying to be liked by everyone and resign ourselves to the fact that there is no one person whom everyone likes. Not even Taylor Swift. MAYBE Julie Andrews, but I'm guessing even she had a high school enemy. You could be the most fresh, lush fruit to ever grow in the whole wide world, and there will still always be people who don't like fruit.

What if this is who I am? I wondered, in an awkward mood as I approached the event I had to attend for work. *What if I am an overenergized chameleon? Always adjusting my colors to fit my environment? Always easing into and out of myself to appease everyone else? What if my entire identity rests on the shoulders of being liked— what if I am wasting myself by being a caricature of a heart and a soul instead of being a real person?*

Around me it appeared as though people had an identity outside a need for other people to see them as pretty and cool and fun. Around me it appeared as though people did not hyperfixate on the things they said in the back seat of an Uber on the way home. Around me it seemed like people did not worry they had lost themselves. At the party I felt like I bent my identity ever so slightly to be palatable, and maybe I'd bend another way at a different party—but the worry remained: Was there anything else to me?

I am a woman who wants to be liked. I was once a little girl who wanted to be liked. I have been told my entire life that it is my goal to be liked. And to be liked, you have to be easy. To be liked, you have to be quiet. I used to not allow people to get too close to me because I feared whom they'd really see—if I got them to like me from an arm's length, I should keep them there. You can still see the *Mona Lisa* on the outskirts of the crowd. You don't need to see the brushstrokes. They don't need to see the real me.

The lightning rod of a girl you see on the page is not how it feels sometimes to live inside of my head—the self-assuredness and the confidence and the clear identity was not always so clear. Sometimes I look back on myself with shaky sea legs and realize I am never one simple and singular primary color but always morphing into different shades of green or pink. A shade that changes, hardens, darkens, softens, and brightens with the seasons. I must give myself the grace to change. I must give myself the grace to grow.

You must give yourself the grace to grow.

I found myself unclear on what the word *identity* means for both the purposes of our conversation and in general. I hear it all the time—lamenting that we don't know who we are, we don't know what our identity is, we feel we've lost ourselves or lost our identity. To me, an identity is the unique makeup of identifiers and characteristics, interests, passions, and experiences that make up who we are. It is our scripture, our magnum opus, our very own Constitution. It is something only we can hone for ourselves.

We cannot sit down with a spreadsheet and a calculator and build our identity. We cannot think up our identity and then put it into practice. It is invisible to us until it is inside of us, and then it is who we are in both our quiet moments of solitude and our bright moments out in the world. That is not something you can curate or choose from a wall of options like a nail polish color at the salon.

An identity is something you build, discover, and hone through doing—and in many ways it is inevitable; it is not something we can totally control. It requires trial and error. Of course, you make choices about what you want to do and where you want to go, but the things that make your heart beat really fast, the places you feel safe, the music and books and environments that bring you comfort—those happen to us. We can choose to claim and incorporate them, and we often do, because we gravitate toward feelings of safety, security, and joy.

I remember the early moments of feeling like I'd lost myself and had no identity—which are two valid feelings for two impossible realities. The idea of losing yourself insinuates you are an object that you can lose. You are tethered to yourself, and there is some comfort in that. You can misplace who you'd like to be, but you cannot lose yourself. You are not a sparkly pair of earrings or a cell phone. You are two eyes and a mind filled with ideas and so much more. The idea that you have no identity insinuates you've never experienced anything, never enjoyed anything, didn't come from anywhere. And I do not know you, but I know you came from somewhere, and I know you have likes and interests and desires, and I know you've lived through things that color who you are.

I am still a girl who wants to be liked—that much may never change—but what has changed is my reliance on needing to be liked and allowing it to define me. And I was always me, but now I am more confident *being* me. I have sunk into myself like you might fall into the chair in the living room of your childhood home.

What I am—and my identity—has always been. I am a theater artist, an older sister, a daughter, a friend. A writer, a reader, an artist. Part Italian, part Jewish, 100 percent New Jersey (of course). Astrologically I am a Cancer, and socially I am a little anxious. I love to make people laugh. I will rest under the joy of the people I love. I am so insignificant and so significant, and I am learning to hold multiple truths at once.

I know who I am and that I always have been her. I am every age I've ever turned. I am every word I've ever written. And now I can get through my quarter-life crisis, because I have the one thing I really need—and that thing is me.

•

They say the first step is acceptance, and in this current moment, as it relates to the quarter-life crisis, I believe this to be true. We must accept that life is messy and rocky and occasionally nauseating. It is also exciting, thrilling, and sparkling. That maybe it isn't a crisis to be in chaos. We must accept that there is no one perfect way to live your life—there is no way to get a perfect score. There is no score. There are no scorekeepers. There is no right direction and no right path. It is okay for this to be scary. I am scared too. We can do this scared. We don't always have to play it cool, have our shit together, act like we aren't afraid. Fear is proof that we are alive. And for that, I am lucky.

There is only you. There is your heart and your mind and your opportunity to live and what you will do with it. That is all you can ever truly guarantee. There are your gut instincts; there is your ability to seek out joy and embrace it.

So we must accept there is no right way to do things first. No right time to get married, or to have children (and no requirement to do either at all). No right job. No right city. No right person. There is no right way to live an entire life. And you cannot plan a life either. You can spend your life collecting other people's stories at a bar you own and run, pouring beers and listening. You can spend your life traversing each corner of the world, taking pictures to send back home because you want the people you love to see sensational things. You can spend your life as an artist, sharing a gift you were given with thousands of other people. You can spend your life a mother or a father. You can spend your life a lover. You can work more than you live or live more than you work. You can curate the biggest, most genuine group of friends. You can do one or all of these things too. You will not live your life as just one thing. You are not a singular; you are plural—you contain every wish you've ever made. Every moment you've looked up at the sky and thought, *Wow*.

If you spend your time planning and making timelines for yourself that you must adhere to strictly, you waste your time building something that won't actually ever support your weight. Going for it, then, is our only option.

It is uncomfortable to sit with this fact. But it is our first step—accepting it. Shaking hands with uncertainty and welcoming it in, because on some level, we will always feel uncertain. If there is no right way, in a world that has tried to tell us who to be and what to be since our first breath, there will be no confirmation either. No outside affirmation willing you along.

It is and has always been within you to confirm and affirm that your choices are the ones you'd most like to make. It is a privilege to have the ability to make choices, to have options. If you make a choice you wished you did not make, or choose a path you deem wrong—I implore you to reframe this for yourself. You cannot choose a wrong path or make a wrong decision—you make a decision, and it either confirms something you hoped to be true or teaches you a lesson that will lead you down new paths and to choices that will confirm things you hope to be true. There is no wrong, no failure, no lost—there is you and your opportunity to live or to learn, or if you're lucky, to do both.

Welcome to the hard part—it is also the best part once you accept that both can exist at the same time: the strain and the after-party. The mess to clean and the glass of champagne.

Now that we have accepted that there is no one way to be twenty-five or twenty-six or in your midtwenties at all, we can move on. Since this is the reality, and only you have the power to make it good for yourself, then you will. We have so many options, but they all really boil down to one: making it good for yourself. Of course there are circumstances out of our control—life will get in the way, and this is inevitable too. It is impossible to plan a life because it is impossible to be entirely sure what life will throw our way. And yet you are the center of your universe. You are the person you think most about. You are navigating your ship. The opinions of others do not choose what you do and where you go. Your mother or brother or friend or partner does not get to choose what you do and where you go.

Only you can truly decide. That is scary. And I am scared too. We can make choices while we're scared, though. You don't have to trust me. But just think about it—I'm here, and I've done it before.

To reject this crisis we must: (1) rediscover ourselves through doing, (2) accept that this is reality, (3) become okay with this reality, and (4) create our life to be one that we like.

•

Part of embracing adulthood and rejecting the idea that it is any type of crisis means growing comfortable with the fact that the decisions I make will not be the same decisions everyone else makes—and might not even be the decisions people in my life would make in the same circumstances. Sometimes we might disappoint someone else. Of course, we should strive for our decisions to *not* disappoint our loved ones and the people we care about—but we have to become comfortable disappointing others before we disappoint ourselves.

I lived with Jen for two years after we graduated from grad school. We spent hours with our legs folded under ourselves on the couch filling each other in on our days and various troubles, ordering DoorDash, and drinking wine from mason jars. I had met Jen around the same time I met my boyfriend, Noah, and I feel sensationally blessed to have met two of the people I cherish most in my life after graduating from college—it reminds me that you will collect fresh new love as you grow and that your time to do so never expires. Midway through our second year living together, it was time to start talking about renewing our lease. Jen wanted to stay in our apartment, and I had pretty much decided that until I moved in with Noah—if we moved in together—I'd stay. It was rent stabilized. We were perfect roommates to each other. The location was stellar, and we had made our space into a home. I told Jen of my plan, and she said there was no rush, we had time to decide, and if I was going to move out, we'd have time to find someone to take my spot too.

As Noah and I crept toward our third anniversary, we decided we were ready to move in together—and it made sense for me to move in to his apartment when my lease went up in August. I was excited. I was happy. I was ready. I didn't see this so much as some big symbolic step as much as it was a decision I was ready to make with someone I cared very deeply for. I told Jen as soon as I made the decision, because I wanted to give her time to fill my room (and help her find someone if I could). I knew she wouldn't be upset with me (she's the most rational person I know). I knew there was nothing to worry about (I am so secure in our relationship). But I *knew* simultaneously that this put her in a situation that would be more complex than if I stayed. This situation would not cause unease between us, nor would it be some insurmountable challenge to find someone to fill my room—but the choice I was making to serve my life and joy the best was, potentially, not the best-case scenario for her. But two things can be true at once, and they are—it would be better for her if I stayed in my room and she didn't have to deal with finding and adjusting to a new roommate, but she wanted me to be happy and choose the most joyful path for myself MORE than she cared about the minor inconvenience my absence would cause.

So I told her, and for some reason I was nervous, and for all the reasons in the world, she was nothing but thrilled for me—she told me we would be roommates, sisters, forever. She told me my moving out changed nothing.

And then my very chill Aquarian cousin needed a place to live, and I connected her to Jen, and she became Jen's new roommate. And it all worked out how it needed to work out. Jen could be disappointed I was leaving and happier for me to go. I could be disappointed to close the chapter of my life where I live with my friends and also thrilled to turn the page to a new chapter. We could be so many things, feel so many things about this one truth.

Jen loves me, so she will not punish me for choosing my own version of happiness, even if it is not identical to hers, even if it is not the best option for her. Jen will choose her own version of happiness, and even when it is not identical to my own, I will be happy for her because she is my person.

You have to allow yourself to disappoint everyone else before you choose to disappoint yourself. And you have to let people feel disappointed if that's how they feel. In your mind, you must be the main character—the only person to exist. Not because you are selfish and not because you are an egotistical maniac, but because everyone in the whole entire world is viewing themselves that way—making choices for themselves that way—so be okay with doing the same. Because when you choose your joy, you make your life better for you, and this subsequently makes you a better friend, sibling, child, parent, lover, and partner. Your joy makes you a better person to the people around you.

•

There will be a quarter-life crisis, and there will be what comes after that. There will be the memories you associate so deeply with the smell of the perfume you wore that one summer. There will be the long-forgotten playlists and the Snapchat memories reminding you of bolder, less responsible days. The adults do not feel like adults, and they never will. The shock of adulthood is a polar plunge; it is the way the frozen water stings you and then, inevitably, you grow used to it. You grow comfortable. The strains of adulting may not necessarily fade, you just get to a place where you enter the chilled water with ease—you get to a place where you're better equipped to get through it.

When I was on my book tour for my first book, I got accidentally trapped in a small black box theater adjacent to the larger theater where we did our show. On my way to the meet and greet, I took a wrong turn and found myself in a pretty dress and seven-inch-high pink shoes, holding a bundle of Sharpies in one manicured hand as I rattled the antique door to the lobby with the other. It was dark in there. And I was about to text someone to come rescue me, but I looked around for a moment and the familiar theatricalities of the space came alive to me. The slightly dusty scent mixed with some type of lemon cleaning spray. The frayed black curtains held back by brass knobs, the little stage tattooed with neon tape, and the stacks of mismatched chairs kept in the corner. In my mind I was always trapped someplace like that. Someplace so banal and so mistakably unremarkable that human beings can turn to magic with words and imagination and an audience. And I thought, *The little thirteen-year-old girl inside of me is breathless at the idea of my life at twenty-five years old. She doesn't care that I don't own a home. She doesn't care about my lack of husband or child or nice fancy car.*

She cannot believe that on the other side of the door, there are girls wearing pink and holding copies of our first-ever book, eager to have us sign them. Eager to tell us they read them. She is not mad at me for my failure to adhere to our timeline. She wants to hear why we don't talk to our best friend anymore, but she'll understand when I take her through it all, step by step.

And she is so proud of me. Tonight, she is just proud of me.

•

You will get through this crisis by doing, by charging forward headfirst and with ambition and bravery. Your identity is not being a woman everyone likes. It has never been that. You are not lost, you are not trapped, you are not a phony or a fake. You really could go anywhere. Do anything. Bring out any side of yourself. There was terrible turbulence once when I was on a flight to Michigan—I remembered the time I ran the marathon in Detroit as we passed over the city, and I realized how far away I felt from that version of myself, she who lives sleepily inside my bones. I went to dinner to catch up with my friends a few weeks ago, and we got drinks and shared guacamole. I thought it would be one of those dinners that never ends, but instead they told me about how depressed they felt, how stuck—and we just talked about it. And then we got up and hugged each other goodbye, and they told me they felt a little better—I felt a little better too. I went to Madrid to see a Taylor Swift concert and met up with an old friend, and she introduced me to a group of total strangers who made me feel like myself again, and they don't even know that. And they never will.

And I don't feel like I look anything like a twenty-five-year-old should. And I have no fucking clue if I am a chicken with its head cut off or the daughter my parents raised to be a good girl. I just know I am trying, I am doing, and somehow, through it all, I am living.

And I think I like how it feels to do just that.

Does Anyone Else Feel Like They Need to Stop Scrolling?

USER3489735102: u look heavy here.

I know exactly what the comment means, but it doesn't stop me from thinking about it anyway. I was wearing yoga pants in the video they commented on. A pink shirt. I had my hair and makeup done that day. And I felt pretty when I posted it. But feeling pretty is fleeting for me these days. My fingers hover over the keyboard, shaking slightly.

You look heavy here.

Heavy how? With the weight of all these phony expectations? With the fear of one internet faux pas—the way one mistake can be written in permanent ink? Heavy with exhaustion? With joy or maybe with fear?
Or do I look heavy? Just heavy.
Maybe I am.
I wonder what it would be like to walk up to a stranger in person, graze over them with my eyes, and say those exact same words to their face. I try desperately to imagine myself

in a situation where I'd even notice, even consider someone else's body—or perhaps feel entitled to comment on how it had changed. I move my finger over the block button and block the user, sending the comment into oblivion. I set my phone on the table beside me. Walk into the kitchen and get a glass of ice water and drink it slowly, steadily, reminding myself of everything that is real outside of my iPhone's poisonous world, and yet the comment lingers with me like heat on the back of my neck.

I feel pairs of invisible eyes on me as I move through my kitchen, although I am all alone. The eyes grow fists and the fists reach for shiny silverware and they feast on me and they are starving. I will have to log back on and face them. I have to log back on and serve the people who like me and the people who don't know me yet. I have to log back on and entertain. Make someone laugh on the other side of the world. I have to log back on.

USER9384710345: that's not it girl

USER9230428471: hire a stylist

USER234672143: your daddy bought you a book deal.

USER123749463: stripes make you look wide.

USER364723814: I'm begging you to fix your eyebrows they look awful

USER431263715: lmfao this is so cringe

USER125674931: you obviously have an eating disorder ... its sad lol

I am heavy. I am fat. But if I lose weight, they speculate about the drugs I used, the eating disorder I must have. My apartment is ugly. *Why decorate it like shit with allll that money?* But when I spend money on it, they accuse me of being materialistic and out of touch. I am too close to my family. But when I stop posting them to protect them, my family must hate me—my family is tired of me. My boyfriend wants to end our relationship. When we move in together, they say I've trapped him. I am forcing him to be with me. They feel bad for him. They want to "free him." My clothes are ugly, and I need a stylist. But when I spend money on something nice, I am "promoting an unattainable lifestyle of privilege." If I post about social justice, I am performative. If I don't post at all, I am sexist, racist—a bigot. If I eat a salad, I am promoting disordered eating. If I eat a bowl of pasta, I should lay off the carbs. If I try to look good, I'm trying too hard. If I don't try at all, I'm disgusting, a slob, a mess. My dad bought my book deal—but when I prove that he didn't, "they'll just give anyone book deals these days."

I am too fat, too skinny, too concerned with appearances, too ugly. I post too much and then not enough. When I post my friends, I am forcing them against their will to be involved. When I stop posting them, I have none. I am the dumbest person in the world with two degrees, one from the top public school in the country and the other from an Ivy League. But I am a terrible writer. And I am so beyond horrifying, so beyond annoying, so beyond cringe.

When I prove their lies to be lies, they move the goalposts, never admitting they were wrong. Surely if she proves her friends don't hate her, they are only friends with her because she gives them free things and takes them to events. Surely if she proves nobody paid for her book deal, it must be easy to get one.

It is a woman's biggest crime to be happy and loud online.

And they cannot stop talking about me. And they cannot stop scrolling. And they cannot stop commenting and commenting and commenting. It is a sickness, and I am the one at the doctor's office begging for the cure.

The internet is a battlefield, and I have been drafted to the war. I am given no weapons. I am given no protection. I stand in the town square, and they wear masks over their eyes and they laugh at me and they throw things at me and they watch me wilt and wither. They try to break me over and over and over again. Some days, they actually do a pretty good job. I am not the type of person who will stand here and pretend like I am incapable of feeling. Because it is all I do—feel.

They will tell you they are not jealous. They are holding me accountable.

As the world burns from the inside, the screams of children reach us through videos from tragedies across the world, our neighbors starve, our rights are slowly peeled away—I am the one, the girl from New Jersey with the TikTok account, who must be held accountable for everything. And also nothing at all.

•

I stumbled into 100,000 followers on TikTok in May of 2020. It was entirely happenstance, a by-product of pandemic days and boredom—and it changed my life overnight. It took me a year and a half to consider pursuing any sort of career in social media—and when I did, I had plans to pursue a career in writing in tandem. After over four years of being both chronically and professionally online, I see the internet as one of the heroes and also one of the villains of my life. It has felt like the most romantic dance in the world with someone you know will only break your heart. You do it anyway, because you want to reach people—you want to make them feel something. You want to feel something yourself too.

Or maybe it feels like the only way to, as they say, "see for yourself."

I do not intend to spend my time with you here complaining about my career as a social media content creator—because while those complaints may be valid, they are champagne problems in the grand scheme of the world and the complaints all of you may have about your work. I intend to utilize my unique perspective as both consumer and creator to illuminate how damaging and fascinating modern social media culture is, especially for Gen Z. I have spent the most formative years of my life thus far unabashedly and glaringly online. I have mixed emotions about exactly how this has manifested as I've matured and grown.

I am a content creator with more than one million followers across all platforms, and I am also a random twenty-six-year-old girl from suburban New Jersey. I am both not at all normal—because people stop me to take photos with me when I'm visiting a country across the world—and completely and totally regular: I am the same girl I've always been. She has been asleep inside of me all this time, just like everyone else.

No matter how authentic I have attempted to be throughout my time online—no matter how real and how raw—I have spent over four years curating content for a social media world. A world that is not our real world, not a tangible world. A world that for some does not exist, and for others exists at a much lower volume than it does for me. No matter how authentic you attempt to be online, the very act of curating content insinuates that you are selecting what to show the world and what to hide. And the moment you start monetizing this content, your personhood fades, and you instead become a brand—a pixelated version of yourself. You are no longer skin and bones—but fodder for discourse, a jumping-off point for opinions that discard the concept that you may actually read or see them, and someone who is so lucky to have what they have, they can handle the territory the castle comes with.

I want to read a recipe from a recipe book that my grandfather wrote, and I want to bake my phone inside a loaf of bread and never think about it again. The next day I want to film myself sharing my thoughts with the world and respond to all my messages on Instagram—I want to reach out and feel.

It is a troubling dichotomy, a sticky spider's web of trying to do your best and knowing that no matter what you do, it's never really enough. Being online in the year 2024 is a nightmare and a daydream, a blessing and a curse—whether you have ten or ten million followers.

•

I downloaded Instagram in 2012, when I was in eighth grade. My friends and I spent so much time already on Tumblr, and even updating our Facebook statuses—a new world where I could keep a photo diary and scroll through my friends' diaries—felt like a new opportunity to be creative. A new opportunity to live.

I loved social media back then. I loved Tumblr, loved curating pages of pins and adding music to my page with songs that coincided with the aesthetic I'd put together. I loved watching my Facebook likes trickle in when I changed my profile photo to a picture my middle school crush had taken of me in the park behind our school. In my sweet youth, these platforms served as an outlet for all of the many things I felt I had to say.

And with the onset of Instagram, I had yet another place just to myself—another place to share the thoughts dormant in my mind. Under my handle—Act4life33—I was able to post funny memes I found on Google and poems I wrote and pictures of all my friends going to the school dance. I could filter the photos to add a saturated sheen. I could craft witty captions and then I could scroll and scroll and scroll and see what my friends had to say too. As we raced away from our childhood and toward the iron doors of high school, more of my peers joined Instagram, and it became a mainstay of culture, a cornerstone of socializing in 2013. We #TBT'd and #WaybackWednesday'd and #FlashbackFriday'd. We posted on National Best Friend Day and crafted small novellas to accompany the Pic Stitch collages we'd post for our friends' birthdays. We spent hours a day scrolling and posting and commenting and liking. We followed celebrities who became famous from movies and music, and then we followed people who became famous just for existing inside the golden gates of Instagram.

Instagram became a shiny world of its own. It became a verb and a noun. A third space—a watering hole—a place we went for sustenance and entertainment, a place we went to paint ourselves as the dictionary definition of popular and cool and pretty.

As a misunderstood girl who always felt second or third in line to get the guy or make the team, I felt empowered by the bright aura of my Instagram account. I loved the burst of magic and light that would fill me as I pressed the post button. I loved that I could be the best parts of myself, just the parts I wanted them to see. Just the funniest parts. Just the prettiest parts. In real life I sometimes felt like I was a failure to launch. I was always saying things in an awkward way. Closing my bedroom door after the party, imagining I'd be better off next time not saying anything at all. I imagined the popular girls felt protected by some type of cool-girl invisible halo. They could say the most awkward things, fall into the most embarrassing blunders, stumble over their words, and everyone would find them charming and delightful and funny. But when I opened my mouth, overthinking every word that would follow my next breath, I saw on the faces glancing back at me an expression that whispered, "We don't understand you." Instagram was the cool-girl invisible halo for me. I was creative and interesting and colorful there. I wasn't afraid to be that way—because to some degree, the world we were all building there wasn't a real world. It was an alternate reality, free from the consequences and strains of our real lives—and I did not fear how they looked at me in confusion, because I could not see them.

By the time I moved to Michigan for college, Instagram had 500 million members. Instead of our phone numbers, when we met boys on our nights out and girls who lived down the hall, we held out our Instagram accounts and watched as they typed in their own aliases, their own usernames, and hit the follow button. We were accepted into their pretty online worlds, and they were accepted into ours. We knew each other on Instagram, and that became the norm.

On Instagram I hid behind the depression of my second semester of freshman year. Hunting for the best angles of my life—a random darty from last week where I was miserable, the St. Patrick's day party I took an edible at while my ex publicly made out with another girl fifty feet away, the flushed cheeks of a night where I drank myself into oblivion, the sunset on the night I first saw Sadie cry, the realization that maybe I hadn't been the best friend I could've been. On Instagram I hid the nasty breakup. On Instagram I hid the thirty-pound weight gain. On Instagram I hid the bullies, the faltering self-confidence, the strained relationships with family members. I hid myself away in tiny cubes of unrealistic joy. I stuffed myself into smiley, well-edited photos of hands around waists and lied through my teeth about being fine.

On Instagram I began to hide.

In four short years, Instagram had dissolved from a place where I felt free to be a version of myself I wanted so desperately to hold and occupy in the real world to a place where I purposefully stuffed the skeletons to the back of my closet full of dresses and cropped black tops. I was no longer using Instagram to manifest the confidence to behave as my true self in the real world, I was using it to manufacture a persona I hoped people would believe. I used to think that if I could convince my online world of followers that I was fine, and beautiful, and cool and happy—then maybe I'd start to believe it myself.

Girls need to be small. Girls need to be quiet. Girls need to be obedient and girls need to have their shit together. Girls need to survive, and survival is contingent on doing all sorts of things that almost kill you, but there's the key word . . . *almost*.

Starve yourself to fit into the jeans so you can wear the jeans and post the jeans and everyone will know you have those cool, cute jeans. Do your hair tonight so you can post a picture having fun with your friends, and he will think you don't care about him, he will think you've moved on, he will think you are desirable. He will call you. He will want you back. He will sit and stare at your shiny eyes and the I-don't-care attitude radiating off the photo, and he will regret hurting you. Post your accomplishments right as you accomplish them so everyone knows you're accomplished, you are successful. You have an internship. You are going to move to a city for the summer and wear uncomfortable shoes and go work in an office somewhere. Everyone needs to know, or it doesn't exist, right? Everyone needs to know, or what's the point of going at all . . . right? You are going to post a picture of an Aperol spritz at a namey facey rooftop bar so everyone knows you can get into rooftop bars because you're twenty-one years old and you're not lame—you're cool. You are going to post with your date at the formal because people think you're cute and they take you to formal, and besides, everyone is posting, so if you don't post, everyone will think you didn't go or, worse, you had a bad time. If you don't post, you will be irrelevant. You will fall off the face of the earth. Posting is a confirmation of your existence, a confirmation of your success, a confirmation of your joy.

And god forbid you have a bad time. God forbid you don't like something. God forbid you have a panic attack in the bathroom. God forbid you are a human being. God forbid you breathe.

I am blue in the face. I am exhausted. I am keeping up with one real life, hanging on by a thread, and one fake one. I am putting on a show for everyone in my life, and they are putting on a show for everyone in their lives, and nobody cares about anyone but themselves. Nobody was thinking of my Instagram account, and yet I was certain if I made my Instagram life perfect, my real one would follow suit.

Time went on. Instagram hit one billion users in 2018. Some of these people have become famous just from being beautiful, or having beautiful homes, or baking sourdough bread in their beautiful kitchens. Some people post every day, and some people post only when something fabulous happens—a trip to Europe, a new relationship, an engagement, a baby, a wedding, a new house, a move across the country, a promotion at a job. Prom, graduation, formal, sorority initiation, a football game.

The news feed is an endless scroll, a bottomless pit—of people sharing perfect days and perfect smiles and perfect outfits. And there's an unspoken rule somewhere that you have to keep up—you have to post your best days and pretty perfection. You have to curate something fabulous so that you will be perceived as something fabulous in the same way your next-door neighbor and the girl you went to summer camp with and your best friend are being perceived as fabulous. If you are capable of turning off the invisible pressure to be seen online, to be present online, to build a world for yourself online, maybe you should be the one writing this book.

Because we all just want to be seen. And I cannot blame us—I *will not* blame us for that. Feeling seen is the reason we risk the shipwreck of heartbreak. Feeling seen is the reason we approach strangers we hope to turn into lifelong friends. Feeling seen is the reason so much great art of the world has been made and shared. In order to survive, you cannot be the wallpaper in the living room. In order to survive, you cannot spend a lifetime flying right under the radar. In order to survive, there is a part of us that craves and requires the feeling it is—wonderful and whole—to be seen.

And social media is a gateway drug into a store-bought version of this critical feeling—this feeling we require for our survival. Social media is the easy way out—a way to be seen exactly as you'd like others to see you. Sitting behind the easel, holding the brush—we get to choose just how we'd like the painting to look. But even if you're the painter, you do not get to decide how others view your paintings. You do not get to sit in the museum all day, explaining yourself and explaining how you'd like to be seen. You cannot control it. They will see you through their own lenses. And you must be okay with this.

So even if you are trying to be something or someone on Instagram—even if you are trying to be seen in a certain light—people will see you however they see you. But if you are trying so hard to be seen in a certain way, they won't actually be seeing you, just a curated facade. So the conclusions they draw about you are not based on reality, and the energy you poured into your online persona in the hopes of feeling seen will not be lucrative.

What I am trying to say is that you cannot choose how others will see you. The perception others have is out of your own control. You can work to become the best version of yourself, you can heal and you can bleed kindness and you can live—and still, the perception others have of you is out of your own control. You can spend your whole life trying to micromanage it, and you will never accomplish anything.

It is better, then, to just be you and allow people to feel how they feel about you, the very same way you carry your perception of others with you in your pockets like little bits of spare change. I know how scary that is. It scares me too.

Being ourselves is the most fundamental life lesson we need to embrace, and yet it is simultaneously the hardest. I am begging you to start with just being yourself. You will notice that the energy and time you utilized running from yourself was so futile when you welcome yourself back into your own life—and nothing changes, it just gets a little bit easier to be you.

•

I have known, for the past six months, that in 2024 I will get engaged. I have no idea when, but my boyfriend, Noah, and I decided in January that this would be the year. We are ready, and I am helplessly and devastatingly excited to spend my life with someone who spends his just trying to make me smile.

As for most people in their midtwenties and beyond, I cannot escape the stream of engagement and wedding content that has been relentlessly living on my timelines and news feeds for at least the last year. Each family friend and college acquaintance and random stranger posing with a ring brings me genuine joy. I am someone who wants to celebrate the wins—big, little, and otherwise—of others. I am someone who feels unbelievably excited when the people around me get something they want or have worked toward—even if that thing is something I too want but do not yet have.

But I'd be lying if I said seeing constant engagement photos from strangers and acquaintances alike online every day didn't place a warm sort of anxiety in my stomach. The inevitable comparison game creeps in even for the most genuine of people. I find myself wondering what my engagement will look like, wondering what I'll post online, wondering when it will happen and what I will wear and what we will do afterward and what the ring will look like and how my nails will be painted. The inevitable envy comes next—wishing it could be my turn because I've been waiting patiently (haven't I?). The inevitable spiral then enters swiftly stage left—will people judge me? Do people think we should be engaged already? Do people think it's too soon? Should I be posting more of my relationship online? Should I be posting less?

None of it matters. And I truly believe that none of it—Instagram and TikTok and the photos we post and the captions that accompany them—matters. But I am a human being, a human woman, a twenty-five-year-old human woman, and I am not immune to feelings of envy and tripping over the hurdles of comparison as they relate to social media and falling right into the trap. I am happy for every single person who is happy on my screen. That has been true every single day of my entire life. I can be happy for those people, and I can feel envious of the lives they're showing me or fall into the trap of comparing myself to them. And then I can feel horrible for doing so. Because I do feel horrible for it—I do not want to feel envious, and I do not want to compare myself to people who are simply and innocently sharing their happy life with their online community.

When I look at Noah in the dark and see the whites of his

eyes, and he holds my hands under his chin and kisses my knuckles, I drift back to earth, or our bedroom. I am steady here with him. We could get married in secret, and it wouldn't matter if there wasn't a single photograph to document the experience. We could elope, and we could spend our lives on a deserted island, just us two, and I would feel peace in his arms. That is true. That has always been true.

This does not mean that simultaneously the world of social media does not impact us.

Inevitably, at some point, we are going to get engaged. And because it is my job and because it is a social custom and because I want to, I will post about it on Instagram and on TikTok. And because there are human beings who follow me—human women, human twenty-five-year-old women—people will compare themselves to me, and people will fall into the trap of envy, and people will feel worse about themselves because of it. And they will also be happy for me. And all of it will be genuine, and all of it will be valid. Each feeling, even as it pertains to my own joy, felt by others, will be valid.

And these feelings will not nest inside of people just because of me or my milestone or my sharing it—but because this is how social media makes us feel. A sugar rush of instant gratification on one end of the pendulum and a desert of hangovers and self-loathing on the other. I know this because I am you and you are me. We are different, but some experiences are simply universal.

We all bring our own perspectives to our timelines and news feeds—but all of us can isolate a time where social media contributed to our feelings that we are "behind" other people, or stuck. All of us can isolate a time where social media caused us to compare ourselves and our lives to someone else and their life. When the news feed serves you ten engagement photo shoots a day, ten celebrity vacations, three people who just bought their first home, two happy relationships, and six gigantic friend groups on a girls trip, it is impossible to sit in your bedroom, where you have a stack of dirty cups at the bedside because you've been too depressed to do anything that you don't absolutely have to, and simply feel thrilled for everyone and then move on.

It is not okay to take the negative feelings that someone's innocent social media posts might evoke and utilize that as a jumping-off point to send baseless hate and negativity their way via comment sections. It is not okay to take the negative feelings you have and turn them into cyberbullying. It is okay to be jealous. It is okay to be envious. It is okay if someone else's joy and success has made you feel shitty about your current reality.

You may be obsessing over some girl's engagement photos, and she could be withholding that one of her parents has fallen ill, or that she doesn't talk to her brother anymore, or that she just started therapy for her crippling anxiety. Before I was a content creator, every single time my life and mental health were the worst they had ever been, you would not have known from the pretty perfection of my Instagram feed. Nobody is sharing the ugly stuff and the tough stuff. You are being offered a sip of someone's life, and they hold the rest of the bottle. You have no idea what that bottle contains. Withhold yourself from filling in the blanks about the lives of others that you've surmised from a few Instagram pictures.

As a society we have spent a lot of energy villainizing jealousy and envy. We teach our children how awful jealousy is, how negative envy is—and how these feelings are not to be felt. We do not want to feel them, and if we do, we should be ashamed of ourselves for experiencing such a horrifying, ugly emotion. Jealousy can certainly get ugly, and so can envy, depending on how you act based on these emotions—but jealousy and envy themselves are not ugly emotions. They are not the bad guys . . . no feelings are.

I view jealousy as a signal. I fear shoving my emotions to the wayside—no matter which they are—and not confronting them properly. When you do not let your emotions in, it is impossible to let them out. If you do not let your emotions in, they will spend hours and hours banging down your door, breaking in through the windows, and making your house a mess that you have to clean up when they are through. So when I am scrolling through Instagram and I start to feel jealous, I do not say, "Ew, I hate her." I do not say, "Why HER and not me?" I do not say, "When is it going to be my turn?" I do not say, "They do not deserve that." I say, "Why not us both?" I say, "I cannot wait until it is my turn." I say, "They have something that I want. What could I change, if anything at all, so I can work toward having that thing too?"

I say, "Look at that marvelous example of what I could have; look at that marvelous example of what I hope one day I will have."

In many ways, this very simple mindset switch is far more than a healthy way to think. It is a form of manifesting—in saying, "I cannot wait until it is my turn," you are suggesting that future you has what current you wants, future you has what that person has, and current you is working toward it. The universe rewards attitudes of abundance, of confidence that the future version of you has everything that the current version of you hoped for. The universe does not reward negativity. When yet another acquaintance of mine got engaged this past weekend and posted her photos and videos and shared with us all of her joy, I did not say, "When will it be my turn?" I said, "I am so glad she found her person, and I cannot wait until I get to have my moment with mine."

Sometimes it feels good to feel bad for yourself. I get that. Sometimes it feels good to sit in the jealousy and the envy and let it take you over. And I am not denying you the space to sit in the shit if you want to. I am not denying you the space to work through these complicated emotions. I am suggesting that instead of jumping straight to the shit, consider the scenic route— consider opting into positivity, grace, and belief. Consider accepting that it is impossible to be behind anyone, because life is not a race or a competition. Consider accepting that comparing your full cup to the sip someone else has offered you via an Instagram post is a fruitless endeavor and will only steal away your joy. Consider accepting that everything you want, you have it in your power to go out and get. Consider deciding that every choice you make is the right choice because it is all leading you toward what is meant for you. Consider recognizing that agonizing over what others have that you may not have will not get you what you want. Consider that hating someone for having what you want is not going to get you what you want any faster.

I am not here to pretend that this will be easy. I want it to be my turn too. And it will be—all of our turns. Because there is room for all of it—our joy and our pain and our time in the sun.

•

As both consumers and creators of content, we have the power to contribute to, suffer from, and work to fix the problem. We can do one, two, or all three of these things as well. Sometimes we get sucked into the shiny, airbrushed worlds of Instagram and TikTok in a trance. The pull is undeniable, and it is nearly impossible to fight the riptide. Down the rabbit hole we go, losing touch with our real worlds outside of our cell phones, getting lost in the haze of near mandatory performance online.

We consider our big life milestones in the context of our faux social media worlds and not the real one. We approach our weddings and our birthdays and holidays and travel plans within the guise of "Instagrammability" and "content." We don't even feel ourselves doing so—but we fall so far from our own zip codes and so deep into our cyber worlds that we cannot stop it.

I need you to begin to live as though there will be no phones at the function and no photographers. I need you to plan your wedding and ask yourself what you would do if not a single person, including you, had an Instagram account. I need you to plan your birthday party and ask yourself what you would do if there was no pressure to put it anywhere online. I need you to go on your bachelorette trip and ask yourself what would bring you the most joy, what you would want to do if every single person left their phone at home. I need you to get dressed in the morning like there is no OOTD or fit check to be had. I need you to go out to dinner as though you could not put up a story of the person at the other end of the table. I need you to go on a first date as though you would never post proof of your encounter anywhere.

Because it is not real.

I need you to download an app that blocks social media from your phone for a few hours, every day, at whatever time you choose. I need you to mute, block, and unfollow any account, run by any person, that does not make you feel good. I need you to go outside and meet a stranger and turn them into a lifelong friend. I need you to lie in the grass and feel the way the sun lightens your hair and tans your skin. I need you to turn on do not disturb and meet an old friend for dinner, and I need you to take turns saying "remember when." I need you to listen to every good song, watch all the good movies, go to the bookstore and buy five books and commit to reading all of them. I need you to make really bad art so you can make really good art. I need you to go look at someone else's art, and I need you to pick your head up on your commute and look at the children playing I Spy with their mother next to you on the subway. I need you to notice the expressions on the faces of the people around you. I need you to hold your mom's hand. I need you to take a really deep breath of fresh air. I need you to go out dancing and have no concern for the way your mascara looks or how close you are to random people dancing next to you. I need you to feel your lips against someone else's lips, and I need you to live in that moment—in the breath they pull from you—without stopping to wonder how it is you will announce to the world of Instagram that this is your new boyfriend. I need you to swim in lakes and run on dirt paths and wear and eat whatever and go wherever you want. Because you want to live. Because you want to see the world. Because you want to experience life instead of just posting about experiencing it.

When you cook a meal for someone you love, and you are drinking glasses full of red wine and listening to a song you both love, when you are holding their hand while the plane takes off—while you are in the shower and they are hovering over the sink shaving—I want you to feel all of those things.

When your best friend calls you with good news, when you pick up a new hobby and it becomes a part of your routine, when you sit on a park bench that has been marked with someone's memory—I want you to feel all of those things. When you have a breakthrough in therapy, when you paint a picture and hang it up in your living room, when you get home after a really hard day and your heart is there waiting for you in the bedroom, when you get something you weren't expecting in the mail, when you feel really beautiful at the dinner party—I want you to feel all of those things.

And then I want you to tell me how an Instagram post could ever re-create the feeling of the first time you slept side by side. I want you to tell me how an Instagram like could ever manufacture the joy it is to watch your siblings become the people they've always wanted to be. I want you to try to explain to me how an Instagram comment could ever replicate the peace it is to look around a table and see all of the people who love you eating bowls of pasta.

The thing is—and this is coming from someone whose every bill is paid by Instagram and TikTok and who is undeniably indebted to both—an Instagram post will never be real. Your Instagram profile will never be you. The affirmation and validation you can glean from these havens of manufactured joy is akin to Monopoly money—you can't actually buy anything with it, no matter how much of it you manage to earn.

•

When we think about the issue of comparison as it relates to the internet, we think about both mutuals (people we know both in real life and online) and the content creators, influencers, and celebrities we follow online.

The modern-day influencer, as a by-product of TikTok, has become the new reality star. Without the manufacturing of a production company and a streaming service and the time required to shoot and film a reality TV show, TikTok stars give us a real-time, self-shot glimpse into their daily lives. Each account, each profile, serves as its very own little reality television show—complete with Get Ready with Me Story Time videos, recaps of evenings out, the sharing of personal relationships and information, vlogs, and more. We have never had access to public figures in the way that the TikTok influencers of today give us access—with very little barrier to entry.

In order to stay relevant, the great TikTokers and macro influencers have to do one of two things:

The first is to have a niche or aesthetic that is inextricable from their brand—this way the audience knows what to expect and feels comforted by the familiarity of the platform. These creators may focus on cooking, dance, home decoration, or fashion. They have an individual niche and are the best creators on the platform at what they do. There may be ten thousand cooking creators on the app—but the ones maintaining relevance, gaining opportunities, and growing are the most professional and/or unique within the niche.

The second way to stay relevant is to be as transparent, unfettered, public, and accessible as possible. Always give new information, always tell new stories, always share personal information. Give your audience access to you.

People think being a content creator and influencer is easy—and in the grand scheme of jobs, it is easy. It is more flexible than a nine-to-five job or a service job for a million reasons—many of which are obvious. Being a content creator is both a massive privilege and a massive responsibility . . . and these are two aspects of the job I won't ever deny. The real challenge comes in what you are willing to do and what you are willing to sacrifice to stay relevant. And a lot of times that sacrifice comes by way of your privacy and personal life.

The more you give, the bigger you grow, the better the opportunities . . . and the more your audience wants. You sacrifice your privacy for the unbelievable and undeniable perks of maintaining relevancy as a social media content creator, and yet it still comes at a cost to everyone. The more you give, the larger risk you run of your audience inevitably comparing themselves and their lives to yours. Because while you're showing them your life, nobody wants to watch someone's content if there isn't some element of aspiration or inspiration. And as the creator, no matter how authentic and raw you may be, you're still showing an audience your life vis-à-vis your crafted and curated brand. Your brand is the you that you are online, the things you share online, which will inevitably be a slightly different, more manufactured version of the you that you are to your most intimate and close friends and family. It is not possible for you and your brand to be identical. It is impossible to truly, deeply know someone via the ninety-second videos they share on a daily basis online.

The more lucrative TikTok, influencers, and social media become for brands and subsequently capitalism and the economy, the more addicting the engineers behind the apps will make the algorithm. These apps *want* you to compare yourself to the shiny, symmetrical faces crowding the most popular pages on their platform. They *want* your self-esteem to wither away and your anxiety to heighten, because they *want* you to purchase things you will be told (on said social media apps) that you need to make these feelings go away. At the end of the day, even the creator you have the most genuine relationship with is still trying to sell you something. In some ways, we all are.

According to the anthropologist Robin Dunbar, the average person can maintain ten to twenty close social relationships in the real world—but online, the average number of social relationships skyrockets to anywhere between one hundred and one thousand people. It is no wonder social comparison is far more common in our online world—we have more opportunities to compare ourselves, and are simultaneously being fed content apt for comparison.

The levels of hate and negativity faced by content creators

(specifically creators who are native to TikTok) are the direct consequence of social comparison online. The more someone who does not perceive themselves to be thriving consumes content from someone who is purposefully showcasing a life where they are, the more they will subconsciously compare themselves and harbor resentment and sometimes even hate for a creator they may have formerly liked. As you supply personal information and access to your life to your audience, the consumer's parasocial attachment to you grows and deepens—psychologically, your audience is now tethered to you. If you do, say, or post something that does not fit the perception they have of you, they will feel betrayed, frustrated, and angry, even if you did absolutely nothing wrong. Because you are more accessible than a celebrity—and still present as a normal person, although your life is nowhere near normal—your audience feels welcome to say or comment whatever they want under your videos. You are not real to them. You are successful and you are rich and you are well-liked, and because of that you can handle anonymous vitriol, nastiness, stalking, hatred, and baseless lies.

We've all heard someone say, "I used to love her when she just started making content, but now I think she's just too much." We want to encourage women to grow, to maintain success, and to follow their dreams, but when they attain the success and the dreams, that's when we decide they no longer deserve it. The most frightening part of this creator/consumer relationship is that the majority of creators identify as women, and the majority of people sending these women hate also identify as women.

I cannot fully place the blame on the "haters" and the "trolls" (as we so fondly refer to them in the industry). They are watching people go from college students or working professionals to millionaires—with millions of followers, loads of attention, incredible opportunities, free products, and free trips—simply from being themselves and sharing that with the world, or simply from sharing their passion or art with the world. Regardless of who you are, watching someone who was in your shoes yesterday skyrocket to internet fame will evoke feelings of discontent. Especially in the current state of the world, when wealth inequality is at an all-time high and there is a very real, very terrifying cost-of-living crisis unfolding before our eyes. Especially when the algorithm has been created and manufactured to promote social comparison between consumer and creator on a daily basis.

We have such a hard time balancing several truths at one time—but in this case, we need to. Influencers are not good or bad. The culture of content creation and internet fame is not good or bad. There are out-of-touch content creators, and there are out-of-touch people who work in sales, business, marketing, and law too. When we muster up anger, negativity, envy, and disgust for large institutions working to harm us, corporations ruining the environment or exploiting people, and the government's inability to listen to its people and serve us, and then we project all of that anger onto internet content creators (the majority of whom are female and also not at all to blame), we are not accomplishing anything. We are not accomplishing anything for feminism, we are not accomplishing anything for social justice, we are not holding anyone accountable, we are not making any real change.

If you think that your Reddit thread, your nasty comment, or your call for "accountability" on whichever creator you've chosen as the subject of your hate is accomplishing anything, I implore you to think long and hard about what that accomplishment is.

Did your legislators change their way of lawmaking? Did they pass legislation to protect you? Has the cost-of-living crisis been remedied? Has the wealth gap closed? If you are trying to teach that influencer something, did your methods work? Have they changed? Have they been held accountable?

And if they did do something wrong and did apologize or change their ways, why is it that instead of accepting that and moving on, or choosing to revoke your fandom altogether, your gut instinct is to say, "This is so pathetic, she only changed because we put pressure on her to change."

What is the world without the opportunity to grow—to learn—to change?

If the people behind these anonymous accounts really wanted to hold someone responsible, they would be pleased, content, and excited if their intervention amounted to real change. If these people truly and deeply cared about accountability and social justice and making our world a better place, they would not be utilizing woke intellectualism and moral superiority as a mask for their true desire—to cancel people. To end their careers. To watch them suffer because they seem to have too much, their lives are too good, they are too lucky—and they don't deserve all that.

Ultimately, there are bad content creators like there are bad people in every single job in the world whose lives are not visible and accessible via a social media platform. Content creators can absolutely contribute to some of the very real problems plaguing our nation, but they are not lawmakers in office. There have certainly been creators who have needed accountability, call-ins, or potentially to lose their platform altogether. I do not tolerate bigotry, sexism, racism, homophobia, elitism, classism, or hatred of any kind—both in my internet world and in my real world. But I am not speaking of the creators who have needed to be removed from their positions of fame online. I am speaking more broadly of the cancel culture that permeates every pore of life online, and the ever-present fear that the failure to overexplain yourself, qualify every statement you make, and be flawless at all times could cause you to face intense repercussions.

•

It is so complicated to be a woman in the world. It should not be surprising to you that it is also unbelievably complicated to be a woman online. The expectation to adhere to beauty standards is ever-present, written in invisible ink. When you reject, push back against, or simply do not meet the Western standard of beauty online, the hate and vitriol you receive will be worse. In my time being professionally online, I have fluctuated thirty pounds. I have noticed a startling difference in the way I am treated in comment sections and by brands and opportunities I receive based on my size. These comments and this treatment were never explicitly directed at my weight—but it is clear to me that it affected the algorithm, brands, consumers, and opportunities.

In college, I always thought I was really pretty. I cherish the memories of believing I was pretty. Sometimes I wonder how much work and inner peace it would take to awaken her from her sleep inside of me. I miss feeling that way—so pleased with how I looked and so unconcerned about it too. In the last four years, I have heard every single criticism of my face and body you can imagine. I always sound like I have a cold. My nose is ALWAYS red. My eyebrows look horrible when I don't do them and horrible when I do them. My hair is "the worst hair" people have ever seen. My arms are fat. My body shape is weird and wide. I force myself to have a thigh gap. My smile is atrocious—too gummy, too crooked. The list goes on, and on, and on. Things I never noticed about myself before have become permanent insecurities. People will say I don't have the right attitude, the right mindset to handle this job—but I promise you if you spent four years having your appearance torn apart, you too would stop feeling pretty. You too would wonder what the fuck is wrong with you.

You too might fall victim to cosmetic procedures or purchase loads of skincare products all promising the same result and underdelivering. You too may spend the time and energy you used to spend enjoying your life trying to figure out how to become prettier. Maybe you wouldn't—but imagine how you feel simply *scrolling* Instagram and TikTok, and now imagine multiplying those feelings of inferiority and insecurity by a thousand.

It is a vicious cycle. I go get Botox and lip filler so I can tolerate my smile again after they've ruined it. So the comments will stop and I can look at myself in the mirror again and like what I see. But my decision to get a cosmetic procedure impacts other women who are watching my content—and as they compare themselves to me and then other women tear me down, I feel backed into the corner of altering myself so I can fit the most unattainable standard in the world. We all contribute to a vicious cycle. The more insecure we are, as women, the more profitable we are to the beauty industry, the wellness industry, the diet industry, and other industries that rely on our insecurities to make a profit. The more insecure with our looks we are, as women, the more we can be micromanaged to fit the arbitrary and uncontrollable beauty standard. The more we are pitted against one another, the less we can come together to fight our actual shared enemy—patriarchy and internalized misogyny. I will never judge a woman for a choice she is making in regard to her own body as it relates to cosmetic procedures and surgeries. That said, I also won't pretend like these are feminist choices. Not every choice made by a woman needs to be a feminist choice—but we should not be pretending it is inherently feminist to get cosmetic surgery. It is directly abiding by the patriarchal Western beauty standard in order to survive in a world plagued by misogyny and social media rabbit holes. But it is not the woman's fault for feeling like she must alter herself to survive. It never has been.

It is complicated—as both creator and consumer—to sit here and reckon with how being online in a public way and in a private way has impacted me, my self-esteem, and my confidence both for the better and for the worse.

•

I would be remiss if I did not mention all of the incredible benefits of social media that I have recognized as both consumer and creator. The ability to connect, to keep in touch with loved ones and friends around the world, to educate, to share information, to fight for what we believe in, to share and consume art are all made possible by TikTok, Facebook, Instagram, Twitter, and more.

Not to harken back to pandemic times, but social media made it possible for us to share, grieve, laugh, entertain, and fill our days with light and joy and passion. During the pandemic, in many ways, I think we *needed* TikTok. Not to mention, just four years ago the landscape of TikTok was quite different than it is today. It was freckled with positivity and something that felt like hope. It anchored many of us, saved many of us, and helped us to find hobbies, recipes, and other ways to fill our days and find purpose. It is no wonder to me that as the world crumbled slightly in post-pandemic years and influencer culture skyrocketed, such a dichotomy would lead to the inherent toxicity and negativity of TikTok comment sections today.

(But in tandem with the heightened negativity of comment

sections, I would be remiss not to recognize that influencing may be the first industry where women consistently, conventionally, and GREATLY outearn men. Female influencers earn far more than male influencers, despite the fact that they face the negativity on TikTok far more than men do.)

So what can we do? Where do we go from here?

We can start by taking an inventory of how we, as individuals, use social media—how we feel when using it, how often we use it. What works for you in relation to your online presence? What doesn't work? If you find that following or consuming the content of an acquaintance or a content creator or a celebrity makes you feel bad—you need to give yourself the option to mute, unfollow, block, and unsubscribe from that content. Content that is consistently making you feel bad about yourself is not content you should be watching, consuming, or allowing into your life.

I use the mute button liberally. When someone I know gets into the habit of posting or sharing content that doesn't serve me, I do not feel bad when I mute them. This is a boundary that does not harm anyone and instead serves as a way to protect my peace. It is not normal to know what everyone is doing, eating, and wearing all of the time.

If you find that you cannot focus because of social media or feel the ways it slowly corrodes your ability to think or live freely—set up a system with an app that blocks your social media apps for a few hours a day. I have my social media apps blocked from 9:30 p.m. to 9:30 a.m. on all weekdays. This way I start and end all of my days without the noise, distraction, or comparison that social media so often tempts me with.

The next thing we can do is just be kind. I am not a perfect person, and I have made many, many mistakes before. If you have found yourself in comment sections anonymously negging, harassing, or bullying a creator—if you have found yourself in

Reddit threads or Discord chats ruthlessly tearing apart the life of a creator whom you do not know—I implore you to put down your phone, walk away from the computer. Take a deep breath. Remember what is real. Perhaps it is a futile effort to reason with those whom I believe to be unreasonable. That being said, I don't think you are bad people—or a bad person. I think you are misunderstood. I think you are looking to feel seen. I think you could be lonely, could be jealous, could be bored—and while I don't know you for sure, I do know there is something more out there for you.

There is joy. There is positivity. There is success. There is goodness. I think you just need to choose to stop pouring negativity into the world—choose to stop pouring salt into the wounds of innocent girls just trying to share their story with the world—choose to just stop. Commit yourself to something else, because many of you are nothing if not passionate and relentless.

I am not saying that you're not allowed to dislike someone for no reason, have a personality conflict with them, find their content annoying, find them out of touch. I am asking you to choose the block button, the mute button, or to talk about them in the privacy of your home with your friends. I am asking you to not make your baseless dislike of someone else their problem. I am asking you to look inward and wonder if maybe the reason you dislike them . . . is because they have something you want. I am asking you to choose to ask yourself to go after the thing you want instead of hating someone else for having it.

I am asking all of us to understand not everything is about us and not everything concerns us, not everything is a direct threat to us. It is okay if someone has a different opinion than you. It is okay if someone has a different preference than you. It is okay if someone doesn't like your favorite movie, book, or musician. I am asking all of us to understand that someone sharing their joy, their success, and their glow with the world is not automatically bragging—is not automatically making a statement on those who do not currently have the same level of joy or success. I am asking all of us to feel joy for those people, to hope we can get there one day too.

The third thing we can do is push back against the systems attempting to pigeonhole us, stifle us, and squash us—especially those of us who are women. You do not need to be "coastal grandmother aesthetic" or "strawberry core" or "deer pretty." You do not need to be "cottagecore" or have "copper cowboy hair" or "almond milk latte nails" or "blueberry muffins makeup." You do NOT totally need this brand-new blush that is going to literally change your life. You do NOT need this new pair of leggings that snatches your waist to the gods. You do NOT need this new perfume that will cause people to fall in love with you.

You need to be yourself. You need to be yourself. You need to be yourself. It is essential to your survival in this world to be yourself. You cannot exist in the real world as a figment of your social media presence. You cannot manufacture who you are. You are not an aesthetic. You are not a niche. You are not a "core" of any kind. You are a person. With a heart and a mind and a purpose. And that purpose has really nothing to do with your social media presence. It has to do with what you will dedicate your life to—whether that is love or work or a passion or a hobby or a family or friends or just having a good time.

And when you log in online—you need to be brave enough to be yourself too.

This world critiques and berates women for the way that individuals choose to be themselves. We hate women for their interpretation of the performance of individuality that we require from them. What do I mean by this? We require that women are deeply individual—have a unique set of traits and interests that make them who they are—and then we attack them for doing their best at this phony dance of individuality. We hate women who are basic and enjoy things that other women like too. We hate women who are different and enjoy things that are unique and undiscovered. It is so troubling, so impossible, so exhausting.

You just need to be yourself. And you need to celebrate and allow others to have the space to just be themselves too.

Last of all, I do believe there is a way we can appropriately and intentionally use social media in a way that protects us all. We should be able to reap the benefits of social media without experiencing the detriments at the same volume. These detriments will always exist, but I believe it is possible for us to be held accountable for our small sliver of space on the internet. This will protect our spirit—this will protect our peace. We cannot control what other people post and how other people handle themselves as it relates to social media. We cannot fix a system that I believe is a symptom of much larger societal problems. But we can control our boundaries, our social media persona, and how we view, post, scroll, and show up online.

•

I get stopped on the street several times a week by young women (and sometimes men too) who follow me on TikTok. I am familiar with the expression that graces their bright faces when they notice me walking toward them, and I always stop so we can have a moment of tangible, real interaction. Interaction between two women with shared interests or some tiny detail that makes us similar in some way. Two women with souls full of hopes, goals, and dreams. With dating lives and family lives and trauma and trouble and joy.

I cherish each of these special interactions. They put it into perspective and make it all worth it. They remind me that each of you is a person—a person just like me. They remind me that there is a reason I show up every day in my real world to post in my internet world—it is for community, for love

Recently a girl stopped me on the streets of New York City. We pulled away from the hustle of the sidewalk and tucked ourselves under a shopfront, and she had someone else with her—a boyfriend, a partner, a friend—and they stood awkwardly beside us as she and I chattered on and on and on. It felt like we were two old friends catching up. It felt like we'd known each other forever. In some ways, I guess we have.

"She is so funny," she said, turning to the person next to her, face painted with an expression of sheer joy.

"Like, you have no idea how funny. She's just SO funny." And she turned back to me and looked at me and said, "Please don't stop."

And then the two of them were off—to conquer their day and live their lives, sucked into the pedestrian traffic and exhaust and concrete of the city.

My life did not start so quickly after they skipped away. Instead I was transported back to the dimly lit bedroom of the first person whom I ever loved. He would tell me all the time, "You're not funny. Like, not at all." And I often thought being funny was sort of my kryptonite, my superpower, the thing I could always lean on when I had nothing else—my humor, my ability to entertain and bring other people joy. Of all the things I could be to someone else, to be funny was my favorite of all.

Naturally his inclination to put me down was born of his own need to feel better about himself. But it never stopped me from feeling like the butt of the joke. So to be stopped on the street by a girl with golden eyes and a bright smile and her own trials and tribulations, and to hear her say "she's so funny" over and over like she just needed someone to hear her, that was more than just a compliment in passing for me. That was a lifeline, that was a reminder that if I just show up as I am both online and off, I can truly be seen.

User023840932 was never interested in making me feel seen. And that is their right, in many ways, I suppose. But as they make a space that I am so intent on making safe for so many people feel unsafe for only me, I do my best to let it roll off my back—to understand that the gift I have been given, the platform, the privilege, the responsibility, would never come without its own set of challenges.

Some days I am exhausted by the world online, and other days I am invigorated. I allow myself to be both. Because yes, I am heavy—with thrill, with opportunity, with the need to do good with the role I've been given. I am heavy with passion, with the experience of being an artist in the twenty-first century, with the ability to reach out and wipe the metaphorical tears from your face. I am heavy with wonder, with excitement, and with the simple fact that I was meant to be here . . . right here. I was meant to reach you both online and on the page and maybe one day in other places too—like on the sidewalk in New York City on a day where we both wish to be in some air-conditioned store but we've instead decided to stand on the hot concrete and know each other for real. I will do my best for you when I open up Instagram and post on TikTok. I only hope we can all choose to do our best for each other too.

Does Anyone Else Avoid the OB-GYN?

Content Warning: This chapter contains discussions of eating disorders. If you or somebody you know is struggling and looking for help:

National Alliance for Eating Disorders Helpline: (866) 662-1235

Crisis Lifeline: 988 or text HOME to 741-741

I worry so much about other people I often neglect to worry about myself.

I care so much for other people I often forget to care for myself.

I worry so much about other people worrying about me that I choose not to share the ways I'm hurting—both physically and emotionally. I'd always rather suffer in silence. Nothing sounds worse to me than someone else worrying about me. I can't bear the thought of someone I love staring at their own reflection in their coffee mug, lost in thoughts of *Is Eli okay?*

I pretended to be fine through every heartbreak. I pretended to be fine for semesters, and sometimes even years.

I am used to being the girl that is fine, and I excel at it too.

I do not know why this is. And it was never really to my own detriment . . . until. It is always until. You are always fine until something happens and wrecks the ship or sinks the life raft. You are always fine until you are not. And then you are a person who is not fine, but also incapable of asking for help, incapable of breaking down—because you are more afraid of other people worrying about you than you are of how it feels to keep all your pain deep inside. So you keep going—heartache after heartache, trauma after trauma, stuffing it all away. It can't be good for you, but I know no other way.

I have always been fine. Sometimes I think it's because I had to be; sometimes I think it's because of birth order, or astrology, or just the way I am.

I never want the people I love to worry about me, and I've done a stellar job at making sure they don't. Ask my parents, for one, and they would tell you I am the child they worry about least. Not because there is nothing to worry about, but because I store all the darkness somewhere only I can see it. And for the longest time, this was just a secret I had with myself—I am a superhero. I am perfect at pretending to be fine. I am amazing at pretending to be okay. I am amazing at hiding every bit of pain, every semblance of feeling—just so the people I love don't have to add me to the list of the people and feelings and heartbreaks they are losing sleep over.

So it is no wonder that the following story went exactly the way it did. It is a cautionary tale, in some ways, about what can happen to you when the plane is going down and you put on someone else's oxygen mask before your own. It is the story of what happens to the girl who fails to take care of herself because she is always her own last priority.

I love you. I love her. I love us. And I am so sorry.

•

I am fifteen years old and a hostess at a restaurant, and my favorite person to work with is twenty-one, self-tan-obsessed, and wildly entertaining. She is shiny and adultlike and intentional. I am much like Cher Horowitz in *Clueless*, a virgin who can't drive. One interminably long shift during a lull in service, she tells me that when the time does come for me to lose my virginity, I have to PASTAUTI—or pee after sex to avoid UTI.

I never forgot the tip, never forgot her, and in a strange way, am reminded of that interaction every time I pee after sex. I stuck to the rule and went UTI-free for most of my teenage years and young twenties.

I am twenty-four years old, and I get five UTIs in the span of only a few months—and each doubles in intensity and pain. I call my friends who get UTIs all the time because they don't PASTAUTI. I'm confused because I have the same sexual partner and the same habits I've always had. They recommend I use an online prescription platform to chat with a doctor and get a UTI prescription with ease. That's what they do when they forget to pee after sex and wind up with a burning sensation when they pee a day later. I do it four times, and it works temporarily each time.

But when the fifth UTI rolls around, I make an appointment, figuring that something else may be going on—or that maybe the strain of UTI I had may require an additional or better antibiotic. It is the end of winter 2023, and I am in so much pain as I hobble to the appointment that I can hardly walk. The heaviness, the burning, the pain in my abdomen (which feels eerily similar but far more intense than a UTI at the same time) is excruciating. The doctors test my pee and, sure enough, find the type of bacteria that isn't treated by the standard UTI antibiotics; I need something stronger, something more effective. They tell me to clean my vibrators well. They tell me to always remember to pee after sex. They wish me luck and send me on my way. And the antibiotic works, and I go back to taking care of everyone and everything I need to take care of. And then three weeks later, the pain returns.

I am on a plane back from my alma mater—the University of Michigan—and the pain has magnified, but it is now accompanied by nausea and a level of bloating I've never encountered before. I read *Tomorrow, and Tomorrow, and Tomorrow* on the flight, trying to distract myself from the intensity of the symptoms, which again, make it nearly impossible for me to walk.

The next day, I go to urgent care, and the doctor is male. I point at my right ovary and tell him I think that is where the majority of my pain is coming from. I tell him my appetite is gone. That I've been in bed for twenty hours with a heating pad. He sends me for an ultrasound and says he thinks I may have PCOS (polycystic ovary syndrome), considering my OB-GYN had found cysts on my ovaries in the past. I keep myself on a regime of Advil and Midol, make appointments to meet with a new endocrinologist and a new OB-GYN the next day, and continue to suffer. Two days later—after receiving a PCOS diagnosis *and* hearing that my new OB-GYN thought I could also have endometriosis—my pain hasn't subsided and my appetite has not returned. My mom drives me home from my endocrinology appointment, and my entire body is shaking and I am freezing cold, but I smile and laugh with her and tell her I am okay. I just need to rest. An hour later I spike a fever, and the pain becomes so unbearable that I ask my boyfriend to take me to the emergency room.

I had never been to the hospital before for anything other than an anxiety attack I mistook for an inability to breathe. I used to knock on wood when I told people that—out of fear that I might change my fate if I didn't. I'd never been there for surgery, a broken bone, or an ailment of any kind. I was lucky enough that I'd only ever been to hospitals to visit loved ones. I avoid *Grey's Anatomy* like the plague. Turn the other way at the sight of blood. I have been emetophobic (afraid of vomit) since I was a child. So it has been a blessing that I have not had to frequent hospitals throughout my life. Though maybe if I had, I wouldn't have feared them so much.

At the hospital, a nurse suggests that before seeing the doctor I get an MRI to test for appendicitis. She says she highly doubts I have it, considering I've been in pain for days and am not experiencing the typical symptoms of someone with appendicitis, but still, worth checking, considering I identified the majority of the pain to be exactly where the appendix is located. Her eyes are a glass color, and she has a comforting face—like she was born to be a caretaker or a healer—and for the few moments when she pushes me in a wheelchair toward the testing room, I feel unbelievably grateful that she is the nurse on rotation that night.

When I was a kid, appendicitis was my biggest fear. Well, throwing up or seeing someone else throw up was my biggest fear, and my second biggest fear was surgery, and my third biggest fear was the hospital. I also feared other people worrying about me too. Put all of my fears together, and you have my personal fear of all fears: appendicitis. At that moment, though, rolling toward the testing room, I feel strangely calm. *She said there isn't a big chance I have appendicitis, didn't she? This is probably a cyst that burst or an infection, isn't it? I haven't had enough time to prepare for emergency surgery anyway, and I have been a good person, and I haven't done anything to warrant bad karma, have I?*

Maybe you've had appendicitis, and maybe you think I'm being dramatic right now. Or maybe you've had something way worse, so you cannot possibly comprehend feeling so torn up over a potential appendectomy—one of the most routine, common, simple surgeries done by surgeons daily, worldwide. I validate your feelings and ask you to do your best to open your heart to mine too. They say don't reason with the unreasonable, and sometimes that is how I feel about my own mind. I understand that my phobias may seem unreasonable, and for that reason, I often beg them to leave me alone. At the time, in April of 2023, wearing a pink sweat suit in the hospital waiting room, I didn't yet know that the phobias and anxieties I was experiencing were actually OCD-related obsessions, which had gone misdiagnosed as anxieties for two decades. I can look at myself in the mirror and tell myself not to be afraid, or that my phobias are invalid, or that I have it so much better than so many other people—but I cannot control the way these fears take over and force me into submission. I cannot explain in so many words how it feels to be controlled, like a player in a video game, by the things that scare me. I only know that it feels like my fears are sharp-toothed cheetahs racing after me—and they are beautiful and shiny, and no matter how far I run, no matter how fast, no matter how well I hide, they will come for me. They can smell me. They could find me if they were blind. I wish some days to be beat up with fists and not thoughts. I wish to be hurt with weapons and not ideas.

You can call me dramatic. Or call me out of touch. You can tell me people have it worse. You can tell me I am being irrational or insane.

All I would say in return is that I want nothing more than to be freed from the psychological prison that I feel trapped in. It makes me feel weak, the way my own brain—one full of so many ideas and creative stimuli—will succeed almost instantly when it tries to take me down. I want to be strong. I want to be fine. I need to be fine. I have no choice but to be fine. And behind the closed door, after the party is over, I am curled in a ball trying to will myself into normalcy again.

Two hours later, when a doctor comes into the waiting room where I am scrolling on my phone, lying on a cot, and tells me that I have chronic appendicitis and will need to be admitted to the hospital for the next seventy-two hours at the least—I do not freak out like someone who is terrified. I don't even really react. He explains that sometimes the appendix bursts or perforates and the body builds up tissue around it in order to protect itself, and he assumes it has been doing this for the last six to eight months. If this happens, the appendix cannot be removed immediately, and will instead need to be treated with IV antibiotics, a few weeks of oral antibiotics, and time prior to surgery. It is both uncommon and unideal, because if the patient's condition does not improve after a few days of IV antibiotics, the surgery will have to be done regardless of the potential hazard to other organs nearby. He marvels at the countless times I was misdiagnosed when my condition was so obvious (pain in the right side of the abdomen).

When one of your worst fears happens to you—even if it is something as seemingly minor as a hospital overnight stay or appendicitis—at least in my experience, you don't immediately feel fear. There is no metaphorical cheetah tearing apart your brain. No immediate spike in stress, or heat on your neck, or feeling of discomfort. You don't necessarily even immediately react. You become someone different in that moment. You walk into the room as a person with a gigantic fear, and you walk out having experienced it. It is so strange, it just leaves you sort of numb. There was no time and also no real desire to process any of the implications or the situation as a whole. So I was admitted to the hospital, and I stayed there for three days. And the entire time I was there, I did not feel fear. I did not feel anxious. I did not feel much of anything at all. My boyfriend and I watched the *Hunger Games* series on my laptop when he came to visit, and we took walks around the quiet floor where I was staying, him pushing my IV alongside us. I messaged my endocrinologist and OB-GYN on their patient portal and filled them in on the newest development—and they both said we would wait to discuss treatment options for the PCOS and potential endometriosis. Once I got the appendix situation sorted out, we could make a game plan and go from there.

I was discharged three days later; my white blood cell count had improved, but I felt the same if not slightly worse. I would be on a two-week dose of strong oral antibiotics and could not exercise, drink alcohol, or do much of anything other than rest. The doctors said that each day would be marginally better, marginally easier. We scheduled surgery for early June, because by that time, I would be in a much safer state to be operated on sans complications.

It did not hit me until we were pulling away from the hospital in my dad's car, driving to my parents' house, where I'd spend the next week recovering and resting, how emotionally exhausted and confused I felt. My appendix had been slowly perforating over the course of a six-month period, and I'd been misdiagnosed with UTIs and then diagnosed with PCOS and endometriosis despite the fact that the bulk of the pain was not actually the fault of either of those two diseases. People around me, when I complained of what I'd been experiencing, said they were sure I was fine. I dulled the severity of the situation in line with their thoughts. I always trusted doctors. Always trusted medical professionals. That was a way I quelled my fears—I always relied on them for the reassurance that I was or would be fine.

It felt like I'd been failed by a system, and also like I'd been failed by myself. *How could doctors at urgent care, who see appendicitis cases daily, misdiagnose me when I was pointing at my lower right abdomen? How could people around me think I was fine as they watched me hobble to and from appointments, spend days in bed, and lose my appetite? How could I—someone so in touch with the way she feels—ignore how horrible, how unwell I felt?*

Was all of this the result of the desire to be fine, so much that you are willing to compromise your own health and safety? So that everyone around you will think you are fine even when you are, very clearly, not fine at all?

What lengths will I go to, just to be fine? How much time will I dedicate to taking care of others, leading me to fail to take care of myself?

It is unbelievably difficult for me to relive these experiences through the practice of writing about them. I am trying my best, and that is always what I can promise you. I want so deeply to be able to look back on that few-month stint as a distant memory—something I am grateful ended up being okay. But instead, I cannot get a headache or develop a cough without the very real fear that it is something far, far worse ... and any doctor I see could misdiagnose me or miss it altogether. I cannot develop any sort of illness or ailment without fearing that my tolerance for pain and understanding of when something is bad enough to warrant emergency medical intervention is off or wrong. And most of all, I cannot forgive myself for how difficult it is for me to struggle—because of how deeply I fear that it may impact the people I love most.

I have not, in over a year, thought very much about everything that happened because the stain of that series of events lasts on me like a permanent tattoo. I relive it in the villainous cycle of obsessions and compulsions I experience throughout the day. I relive it in the anxieties creeping up behind me, lurking beyond each corner of my home and each next door I reach to open. And I struggle so deeply with the traumatic aspects of this time in my life because I can acknowledge that receiving a PCOS and endometriosis diagnosis, even as a by-product of chronic appendicitis, provided clarity and answers for questions I've been asking medical professionals and myself for years.

And beyond the realizations this experience brought me, as it relates to my own mental and personal health, is the objective throughline that is so startling to me—women's healthcare is neither taken seriously nor adequately researched, and thus, we fail women when it comes to their bodies and their health.

Not only do I feel I failed myself, I feel a system failed me too.

•

Historically, women's bodies are both underresearched and underrepresented in medical studies in general. Prior to the 1990s, doctors considered male bodies the norm and women's bodies the other. In light of this perception, women were rarely, if ever, included in clinical trials. Scientists have gone so far as to avoid conducting any studies on mice that are female, as it can both be more expensive and require more work than just using male mice—so even the *mice* used in medical trials are male. And this is a massive, extremely problematic oversight, because as you can imagine, biological sex does have a very legitimate impact on the way certain diseases present, along with medication side effects, symptoms, doses, and even medications themselves.

To put it in perspective for you—the medical field only recognized that women with heart disease experience different symptoms from men with heart disease in 1999. Heart disease is the leading cause of death in the United States for both men and women. Things haven't improved very much in the twenty-five years since, either. As of 2022, women are still vastly underrepresented in clinical trials for leading diseases—despite the fact that in 1993 Congress passed a law requiring women be included in clinical trials. If you were curious what explanations the medical field has for such gross oversights . . . It was historically believed that the fluctuating hormone levels women experience throughout the month make them more complicated to study and thus more expensive. Throughout history, there have even been bans on pregnant women, single women, women using contraception, and more from partaking in clinical trials because it was believed that many of these factors could impact the trials in some way. And because, historically, fewer women are medical professionals than men, there weren't any women in testing rooms and boardrooms to advocate on behalf of their own.

It is so impossible to read all of this and feel anything other than enraged and scared.

Women have been overlooked as it relates to our health for decades and decades and decades. So it should not surprise you either that diseases that predominately or only impact women are beyond underfunded, while the diseases that predominantly impact men are beyond overfunded.

When I was eight years old, I was diagnosed with hypothyroidism—a disease of the thyroid that is far more likely to impact women than men. Throughout the second decade of my life, in tandem with puberty and getting my first period, I experienced the difficulties of having a disease that is underresearched and undervalued (because it predominantly impacts women). It is not so much that doctors do not care, or do not want to help you.

It's that they do not have enough of a fundamental understanding of the disease OVERALL to provide you with the attention and care you deserve. Hypothyroidism means that the thyroid does not make enough thyroid hormone to keep the body operating normally. Symptoms include (to name a few) weight gain, weight fluctuation, extreme fatigue and brain fog, the inability to tolerate cold temperatures, and the inability to lose weight. When I got my first period and went through puberty, I began to struggle with maintaining the weight I'd been for years prior. I'd gain ten, twenty pounds in a month, and it would take a year to lose it (if I tried, but it was seemingly impossible). I went to an endocrinologist and asked for help and was dismissed. I switched doctors five times after, each time begging for help, begging for answers.

Once, sitting in the bright light of an endocrinologist's office in my teens, the doctor looked at me and said, "Most of my hypothyroid patients are far, far more overweight than you are. Most of them are struggling with fifty-pound weight gains, not fifteen pounds. Just eat healthy and change your exercise routine."

I continued to struggle with monthly ten-pound-minimum weight fluctuations. I ate healthy. I exercised every day. I went to doctor after doctor and begged for help. I was exhausted, I couldn't maintain my weight no matter what I did, my hands and feet were always freezing cold. And nobody helped me, mostly because they had no way to. It is no wonder this yo-yo caused me to develop a hyper-obsessive relationship to food and exercise. I was in high school, tracking my calories for the day in an app on my phone called Lose It! I was exercising daily and would hardly allow myself a day off to breathe and rest. My tumultuous relationship with food and exercise was packed in my suitcases with me when I left for college. There, the issues compounded, and I developed a binge-and-restrict eating disorder, which often flies under the radar—because it can feel really embarrassing to speak about, which I can relate to all too well.

I can only speak for my personal experience. Weight is a very personal topic. Health is a very personal topic. And I blame the lack of research and funding into diseases that predominantly impact women as the reason why I was sucked into a vortex of obsessive tendencies with food and exercise for seven years of my life. I blame the lack of research and funding into diseases that predominantly impact women for some of the most difficult moments of my life. I blame my inability to ask for help as well, which is something I associate with the perfectionist tendency to always be okay.

My freshman year of college, I tried, for the first time, to make myself throw up, and failed. I made the decision to make myself throw up with the ease of someone deciding what they'd like to order from a menu at a restaurant or what plans to make on their day off. My emetophobia became an afterthought once the idea of being smaller had been introduced, when a solution crossed my desk. The idea flashed into my mind one evening in February 2017, and it felt like a problem solver to me then—not some kind of an illness. Not something that could raise alarm bells. I figured that if I could succeed at purging—if I could succeed at that one thing—I'd be proud of myself. It felt like a way out of the binge cycle I was in, a way out of my obsessions with food and exercise and my body. A lot, it seemed, had gone wrong at that point. But maybe I could make one thing right. If I couldn't succeed at anything else, bulimia was the least I could do for myself. And it didn't seem like it was going to be too hard to accomplish.

Earlier that day—Valentine's Day—my dad had sent me a lemon Lulu cake from Mother Myrick's Confectionery. Myrick's is a Vermont-based bakery, one I have fond memories of from childhood. Opening the gift reminded me of the spirit my dad and I share, the sugary energy I inherited from him that pulses through my veins. They ship their famous cakes nationwide, and it was carefully shrink-wrapped and placed in a neat white box, tied up with a red-and-white ribbon. The cake was a sunny yellow sponge, the color of lemonade, with a sweet and tangy fragrant scent, even through the wrapping. The powdered sugar had hardened on the outside like a translucent frosting, giving it a crisp shell. I didn't bother opening the box; I put it on the windowsill alongside my other snacks.

I wouldn't let myself have the cake, I decided, grabbing my coat from the hook on my door. I didn't deserve a cake. I hadn't done anything to warrant a celebration. I was struggling in school and in my personal life, struggling in my body and my mind, and the last thing I needed was a cake to celebrate all that failure. I sent updates home, and I made sure everything looked perfect, I made sure everything looked fine. But in Ann Arbor, in my dorm room all alone, where I could be honest with myself about how horrible things had gotten, the cake mocked me. It whispered in my ear—*Do something good, and then, maybe, you can have me.* Truth be told, I didn't feel like I deserved much of anything back then. I'd never dreaded school before. Never dreaded socializing. Never dreaded being surrounded by other people. I was afraid that if I was around that many unfamiliar faces, sober, I'd just burst into tears. I didn't want anyone to see me like this unless I'd done enough preparation to hide it. I wanted to hide under the covers. I wanted to go out already drunk enough that I wouldn't focus on what I thought I lacked, or what people might think of me—my misshapen self, a person I didn't know anymore.

The switch in my demeanor came as winter did, and each new scenario compounded on top of another, making life seem more desolate. A gut-wrenching breakup followed by weight gain followed by unkind social circles followed by the fear that I'd amount to nothing. And somehow, the lower I sank, the better I got at hiding it.

On my walk to class, a friend in my sorority shared messages from a group chat she had with some of my other sorority sisters. They were talking about me. Saying I was fatter in person, that my Instagram wasn't an accurate reflection of how bad I really looked. I wish my friend hadn't sent me the screenshot. I know she was just trying to protect me. Maybe she was trying to tell me subliminally to stop editing my photos, but I felt like I had some unspoken pressure to make myself look happy online. I had no other choice. I had to signal to everyone I was fine.

I had to be fine.

At least then nobody would ask if I was okay.

But this was the straw that broke the camel's back. I wasn't fine. I was broken. And I couldn't bear to let anyone in close enough to see the cracks. Nobody seemed to think I was pretty or cool except Sadie, whom I feigned happiness in front of. I didn't want to drag the only sun in my life down with me.

That Valentine's Day I went to my afternoon classes and came home and caught a glimpse of myself in the mirror. I sucked in my cheeks and thought about how my face used to look and decided to go for a run. I couldn't accept this new body, though no less beautiful than my former one. And both bodies struggled with a disease that made my metabolism hardly function—and nobody ever seemed to want to help me with that. I'd struggled with food and exercise before, but this was the beginning of a slippery slope—a lengthy battle with binge-eating disorder that began with overeating dining hall food, past the point of fullness—just because I needed something to fill me, to make me feel whole. When I was overstuffed, to the point of feeling sick, to the point where the skin across my stomach was taut and firm, I wouldn't have the energy to feel sad. The hurt would be redirected to a pain in my stomach, instead of a pain in my chest and heart and head. My body reflected a cycle of abuse, and I didn't want to face my own eyes.

My roommate went out to a party that night, and I opted to stay in. I skipped dinner and let the hunger eat away at me. I felt like a success. I watched Instagram stories, answered text messages, and switched my pillow to the cool side when the heat of my cheek had warmed it. And then I felt so empty, I got up, swung my legs over my lofted twin bed, and took the lemon cake down from the windowsill, where it sat, shrink-wrapped, in its beautiful box. It looked too pretty to eat. Too pretty for someone like me to have. I opened it slowly and decided I'd allow myself a few bites. Sitting on the floor with a plastic fork, a few bites turned into a slice. It was buttery and sweet and tangy and perfectly sour. With each bite, I felt further removed from reality, from the world outside, where people were enjoying themselves and holding hands and shouting the words to overplayed songs. Each crumb, each morsel carried me further and further from myself—and that was all I wanted anyway. I wanted to become a separate entity from who I was. I itched to be free of my own skin.

When I finally looked up, half the cake was gone, my lips were speckled with powdered sugar, and the insides of my gums were raw and stung by citrus.

Another failure. I threw the cake away, hoping that would prevent me from having any more. The feeling of freedom, of bliss, was quickly replaced by a feeling of self-loathing so overpowering, I tried to promise myself I'd never eat that much ever again.

And then the thought entered my mind—with such ease,

such simplicity—I should just go throw up. I could just become bulimic, and then at least I could fix one thing: the food. I couldn't stop eating altogether, because food was a source of comfort and control, and most of my meals, after all, were shared with friends and classmates and clubmates. Despite how lonely I was, I wasn't very often alone.

I slipped out the door like I was heading to the shower. The halls were empty and dimly lit, and the bathroom was unoccupied. I checked for feet under the stalls to be safe. I kneeled and couldn't remember the last time I'd gotten down on my knees. Maybe to pray, in church, years ago during communion. Maybe to give a blow job, though I don't remember ever doing so on my knees.

The tiled floor looked clean enough. I stared at the toilet for a while, letting my reality settle around me. I pushed a finger down my throat, and then another. I coughed, my mouth filled with spit, and I spit into the bowl. I tried again, pushing deeper, more aggressively. The same: just a cough and a spit. My eyes welled with tears.

I tried one more time, with all the force I had. Nothing. I leaned against the side of the stall, pulled my knees into my chest, and sobbed. My fingers were wet. There was a tiny scratch in the back of my throat. I do not know if I've ever felt so at war with myself as at that moment. I wish to reach out across the years, across the states between here and Michigan, and hold that girl in my arms and tell her I am so sorry. And tell her it is not her fault.

I went back into my dorm room, took the rest of the cake out of the trash, and finished it. Then I turned off all the lights and pretended to sleep when my roommate arrived home from a party and shuffled around for her water bottle and makeup wipes.

I've never spoken of this outside of the padded walls of my therapist's office.

Because I have been more terrified of people worrying about me than I was of ruining myself.

•

In May 2023, my life paused while I recovered before my appendectomy. I do not remember a time, in the past decade, where I've had the chance to pause like this. It was comfortable and incredibly uncomfortable simultaneously. I don't think we really have many opportunities to pause and reflect for an extended period of time, and looking back, it was some of the most valuable healing I've done, physically and emotionally, in my life.

In May 2023, my mother begged me to start taking care of myself. She told me I worry so much about other people I forget to worry about myself.

In June 2023, I had my appendix out, and ten days before the surgery, my debut book's cover was revealed in *Cosmopolitan*. I wore a pink dress, and we had a party.

In June 2023, I was so scared, both of not being fine and of continuing on the path I was on. In many ways I was failed by a system, in many ways I had abandoned myself, in many ways I failed to understand what self-care really was—and how vital it is to our survival. I realized how lucky I am to have gotten away with the avoidance of my health and well-being or failure to prioritize myself for so long. For twenty-four years, I got away with it. Now I won't take those same chances.

What happened to me is a failure of our medical system, but also a failure on my own part. I do not fault myself with this failure, as I believe it illuminated a really important lesson. I feared not being okay so much that I allowed myself to get to a really scary place before seeking out the proper help. I failed to take care of myself because I was expending all of my time and energy taking care of other people, and eventually, inevitably, I paid the price.

And then the world begged me to slow down, and I had no choice. I slowed down, and I saw myself as a shell of who I thought I was. Crooked, halfhearted smile where fullness used to live. Pale cheeks and a body struggling to stay upright because the swelling in my abdomen was so severe, I had to stand at an angle. I didn't like this version of me—not because she was not beautiful or motivated or passionate—because she had failed to keep her eye on the one person that mattered to her most . . . herself.

You have to take care of yourself. First, because you cannot take care of anyone else if you are dangling by a thread. Second, because you are truly, deeply, and painfully all that you really have. You have to water yourself, you have to feed yourself, you have to listen to yourself. You have to take care of yourself the way your grandmother asks you to when you part. You have to take care of yourself because your ancestors did not survive for you to spend your entire life ignoring your needs. You have to take care of yourself because your best friends need you and you need them, and you cannot need one another if one of you burns out as a result of abandoning yourself. You have to take care of yourself because your younger siblings admire you. You have to take care of yourself because a woman went through the world for you to be here. You have to take care of yourself because you deserve to enjoy every sunrise you're up early enough to see. You have to take care of yourself because there are happy hours to be happy at, there are love stories waiting to write themselves into your life, there are people who have not yet seen you through their pair of eyes. You have to take care of yourself because you deserve that. The very first thing you deserve, in the long lists of things you deserve, is to be the type of person who cares for themselves.

Self-care looks like so many different things. There is no right way. You will find your peace in the boundaries you set. You will find it in the routine you build for yourself that you actually like. You will find it in the way you move your body, the realization that it is such a privilege to feed yourself, to fill yourself. You will find it in the precautions you take to avoid burnout and the prescriptions you use when you find yourself in a period of turmoil. You must become an expert not at being okay, not at pretending to be fine—but at caring for yourself in the personal, individual way you need. Because you will crumble sometimes. We all do. But then you will nurse yourself back to health.

It is not easy—both to find the time and energy to take care of yourself and to understand the way that you uniquely need to be cared for. We often feel it to be selfish or self-indulgent to spend time, energy, or even money on caring for ourselves. But if you do not care for yourself, you will not be able to care for anything else—not your loved ones, not your pets, not your work, your hobbies, your passions, your home, or your future either. We must accept that self-care is not an indulgent, selfish form of treating ourselves and is an undeniable human need that each individual requires in a different way. Self-care does not necessarily require spending money either. It can be the boundaries you set in order to spend a weekend or evening recharging at home. The elongated shower you take to reframe your mindset after a long day. It can be carving out the time for a long walk outside, a phone call home, making yourself a comforting meal. You can spend money on yourself too (obviously retail therapy is very important to me). You can put that money toward therapy. A monthly massage. A new product you've really been wanting or, in a very Carrie Bradshaw way, a pair of shoes.

Do not treat yourself like you are the boarding gate at the airport—just a place people pass through while they're waiting to get to their final destination. Life is too short. And you are too worth it for that.

What I need you to understand is that for so long I didn't think I deserved to take care of myself. I didn't think I deserved help when I was on my knees in the bathroom of East Quad looking for a quick solution. I didn't think I deserved help when I was hobbling around New York with a burst appendix, pretending like I could just handle it myself. I didn't think I deserved to take care of myself or to ask for help because I didn't like myself. And it's hard to take care of someone or something you do not like.

I pushed and pushed and pushed myself to my own limits. I neglected myself. I put myself in the path of pain because it was better than feeling nothing at all. And at my breaking point, I decided I couldn't live like this anymore—not that I had much of a choice; I couldn't *survive* if I kept up with old habits and old ways. I wish it hadn't taken a life-altering, traumatic health scare to get me here, but the silver lining is that I am okay, and it paved the way for so much growth.

I got medicated to treat my PCOS. Found doctors who truly heard me when I described how intense and painful my periods are and how difficult it is to exist with the cocktail of hormonal imbalance and thyroid issues I'm dealing with. I read books about how to best take care of yourself when you struggle with these things. I rebuilt my habits around what I learned. I invested in my health from the inside out and also the outside in. I stopped saying yes to things I didn't want to do, reintegrated therapy into my life in a new way, and was finally diagnosed with OCD.

I spent so much time working on myself—in all the various ways I needed to. When I took a break (because the work is never really over) and put down all my tools, I looked around and to my surprise, found I had not neglected my friendships, my partner, or my loved ones. I managed to care for them in deeper, better ways when I focused first on caring for myself. I managed to care for my home, my work, and my passions better too. When my energy was focused on being the best version of myself and on living a life I truly enjoyed, and not on how little I felt I deserved, how hard I had to work to pretend I was fine, the way I cared for everyone, including me, was better.

•

I used to play things painfully safe. Mostly because I didn't have the time for spontaneity or fun or truly living my life. I was busy carrying everyone else's loads when they hadn't even asked me to. And besides, I figured the safer you play things, the less risk you have of worrying anyone. The fewer risks you take, the fewer opportunities to get sick or hurt or burned out. I needed to conserve all the energy I did have. Being spontaneous has always scared me. I like plans. I like to be in control. I like to know where I'm going and how I'll get there and exactly what it'll look like when I get there.

But that isn't life, and I know that now. Playing it safe isn't a bad thing, necessarily, but when everything you do is safe and calculated, you miss out on so much of life's greatest tiny joys and surprises and serendipity. When all you do is play it safe, you sacrifice so much of your one and only opportunity to live.

It took a full year from spring of 2023 to do the inner work and self-care and dedicate the attention to myself that I needed to truly heal. And after that year, I felt a little flower open up inside of my chest, and I—for the first time ever—had the desire to be spontaneous. To throw aside my rules (maybe not all of them, maybe not always) from time to time and just let the wind take me. To let go of control and see what life is like when you don't decide you're the type of person who takes no chances.

That's how I ended up on the rooftop of an Airbnb in Madrid, all alone, listening to the sounds of an unfamiliar city below—a year to the day that I was admitted to the hospital in 2023. I had gone to Madrid for the Eras Tour (I am not above chasing Taylor Swift around the world, thank you very much), and I returned with a bit more of myself in tow. The day after the concert, I met up with an old friend, and we caught up at a bar for a few hours. Her friends (whom I'd never met) met us there and then she left to go on a date, and I stayed with her friends. After a formative year and twenty-three years before that of skating by—after four years of being perceived through the lens of an iPhone app and after ignoring the sensible part of me discouraging me from taking a spontaneous trip to Madrid—in the presence of these strangers, I felt like myself again. It is strange how this can happen. How you can feel so lost, so far gone from yourself, so broken and perceived for so long, and then some random Thursday in a foreign country with a bunch of people you've just met, you realize you've found yourself again. The work has worked, in few words. The life is back in my face. The wind is back in my sails. The care I have for myself is not an unknown concept to me. It is as familiar as the lines in my palm and the crinkle in my nose when I'm sad.

They saw Eli, and I felt them see me.

Not Eli the writer. Or Eli the TikToker. Me. Just me. I was nobody and I was everybody. In the eyes of kind strangers, I crawled back into the home inside of myself I'd once lost the key for, and all of my belongings were just the way I'd left them the last time I was there. The bed was unmade because my exit was so hasty last time, and I collapsed into its warmth and promised to never leave myself again. Because I wasn't passing through this time. I wasn't a visitor in my own home or my own body.

I was home. I am home.

Does Anyone Else Feel Like All Their Friends Hate Them?

I miss how easy it was to be eighteen years old. I thought it was so hard back then. Nearly a decade later, everything's changed, and I cling to myself for dear life. I cling to the idea I had of myself then too. I already let her go; I can't let myself go too.

There will be best friends. And there have been best friends. Past tense, the us—no more. Not for lack of trying, though. I squeezed her hand tight in mine and tried hard to hold us together, but her fingers slipped from mine like the end of a story we all wished to be interminable. I knew all along the writer would have to find a place to end. *But how are there no more pages? How is our story over?*

Everything I knew about myself at eighteen years old is part of a long-forgotten archive now. In my naivete, I thought hanging on to past friendships would help me to hang on to the girl that I was when I made them. In my desperation, I cut my hands on the shards of that friendship—what we had left—thinking we could glue the pieces into something prettier now that we had to start from scratch. A childhood spent in matching outfits and a teenagehood spent on shared secrets and never-have-I-evers— where does all of that go when the friendship is nowhere to be found? Her memorized home phone number, for a home she no longer lives in, is as inherent to me as my own last name. I wonder if her lucky number is still thirteen. And I wonder if she still thinks back on it all like I do.

To lose a friend is to lose a thousand reflections of your own eyes, a road map back home even when you think home doesn't exist. To lose a friend is to lose a person, one of very few, who is only in your life because they truly like your company—not for sex or for blood or for work—but because they see you, because they have decided their world is brighter with you in it. Because you see them back. To have a friend is to have the only real no-strings-attached relationship the world has to offer.

The friendship I knew so well is in the rearview mirror now. Every day I take a heavy step forward, away from us. Tomorrow hurts like hell when you've left an entire lifetime in yesterday. Sometimes I like to look back on the days that have breezed through the windows of my life, when any whisper of an end to our alliance would've made us laugh. She was, in many ways, the love of my life. And now she is the love of so many others. And I am too. And I hope it is everything she needs.

•

We've just left our high school graduation, and the weather is New Jersey's best. June, bright, hopeful, long. Our high-heeled shoes are tossed at my parents' front door, and we sit on the porch with our legs tucked under us, a plate of cupcakes on the table. We sip on half-full glasses of champagne. Juliet and Anna have been two of my best friends since kindergarten, and we've made it through every school dance, case of mono, pep rally, and Spanish class together. Tonight, our graduation gowns are slumped over armchairs in my parents' living room, and we speak idly of our plans for the evening.

Juliet is my other half. At eighteen, she is my favorite person in the world. Her hair is the color of honey, and she has freckles and blue eyes. She is creative and weirdly flexible and a vegetarian. We are the same in all the ways that matter.

Anna has lots of close friends both in and outside the confines of our friend group—likely because she's extremely likable and the most reliable, responsible eighteen-year-old I've ever met. Anna always knows what to say. I think she deserves the world and is the prettiest person I've ever seen, and I think a lot about when she'll discover that herself.

Our small trio is a part of a larger friend group of almost twenty girls, marked with a group chat the rest of our high school class knows as the Group Chat—which is synonymous with constant drama and chaos. It is a revolving door of familiar characters, girls leaving the chat and being re-added when the dust settles after whatever boy drama or exclusion has created the latest argument. Within a group of twenty friends, there will always be subgroups of three or four—the friends we call "best"—and Juliet and Anna are that for me. Parallel to our group chat is a group of about twenty guys with whom we spend our weekends—most of us have been involved with one (or a few . . .) of them, which is the occasional cause of our group chat's meltdowns.

But tonight, it's graduation, and everyone is in a good mood, and no matter what has happened over the last four years in the confines of our group chat, I've always had Juliet and I've always had Anna. In fact, the three of us have a side group chat with three other girls who also try to steer far from the drama. Graduation day was chaos—with many of our friends off to dinners and celebrations with family. Juliet, Anna, and I gathered our parents and headed for my house, where we sit now, trying to figure out what the rest of the group is doing. It is in our small six-person side chat where we find out that one of our friends, Carsyn, is throwing a party, and Juliet, Anna, and I are the only three people who have not been informed. The other girls tell us we should just text Carsyn and ask to come. They are sorry we weren't invited, but they are still going to go. And as much as we'd like to be surrounded by people who want us around, we are eighteen years old, and we want to fit in. So I text Carsyn and ask her if she has room for three more, and she tells us that her mom said she can only have forty people. So Juliet, Anna, and I sit and watch as well over forty people from our graduating class, and then kids from surrounding schools, post from Carsyn's backyard on Instagram. Carsyn was insecure and cruel then, and even though we knew we were better off, she still hurt us. I haven't spoken to her since and honestly haven't thought much of this interaction until now. I'd be the first person to tell you if Juliet, Anna, and I didn't deserve the invite. If we were annoying or mean or had done anything to deserve being so blatantly excluded. But the three of us avoided drama, hardly drank (and often took the role of designated driver). We were far from liabilities, and the real reason for our lack of invite never came. So the three of us ended our high school career together, on my parents' porch, drinking Corona and champagne and laughing about how pathetic it was to be us.

Looking back, I don't feel sad thinking of myself sitting at home on graduation night. What I remember was the way it felt to have two people in my corner, Juliet and her clear blue eyes and Anna and her remarkable sensibility. I remember the way it felt to know I had Juliet and Anna—to realize that I didn't need to be around forty people who hardly cared about me, because I had two who really did.

•

I want to be able to tell you that Juliet is still my other half—that I lounge on her couch in her Manhattan apartment and talk about things that matter because graduation nights and group chats faded but we never fell apart. I want to tell you I was at her engagement party. I want to tell you the last decade went differently than it did.

But I can't tell you that. It would've been unthinkable to the two of us, at twelve or sixteen or eighteen, that we'd no longer be best friends at twenty-six. We exchange happy birthdays; sometimes we stumble upon something fleetingly nostalgic—an old photo, a diary entry from the second grade—and we'll send a text. The exchange is always a few lines, always pleasant. They also always leave me with an open and hollow ache.

We made it through college on each other's side. It only took half a semester for our disorderly group chat of twenty-plus girls to fall apart while our smaller subchats remained. I know a few people who managed to maintain friendships with everyone they knew in high school, but more often than not, I think you hang on to a select few while the rest fade to acquaintances. It is only normal that at twenty-six you are not the person you were at eighteen, so it strikes me as rare if you've managed to change in tandem with everyone you knew at eighteen, without any whisper of growing apart. I spoke to Juliet, Anna, and three others in the smaller side group chat daily. Juliet's house was my first stop every Thanksgiving break and summer. We cried the day her parents moved out of their childhood home and into a house a mile down the street. We kept each other up-to-date on my crazed dating life and her adorable college friend group. We visited each other at our respective schools, and it didn't really concern us that our larger friend group had dissolved. We had what we always had, and what we always had was each other.

I will not waste space breaking down what went wrong between us. What I failed to do, what she failed to do, how we hurt each other, or the mistakes that were made. It isn't just my story to tell, and there is really nothing Juliet could ever do to cause any emotion to overpower the love I still have for her. Even if we are no longer best friends, I will love her forever, and that will remain unchanged. So while the details will be spared, it pains me to know that you are sitting here now applying these very words to your own Juliet. It is okay if the part of you that is still the eighteen-year-old girl who called her your best friend still wishes things were different. The version of me that is twenty-six might not call Juliet my best friend, but the versions of me that are ten years old and seventeen and twenty-one still do.

Our dissolution didn't happen overnight. It wasn't like we were arm in arm one day and the next things were over. There was no big blowout fight, no major confrontation, no petty drama that you can point to when you identify what exactly went wrong. I can admit to mistakes I made, and I have. We just began unraveling like a spool of thread, and when we were a tangled mess on the floor, Juliet cut herself free. Eventually I realized I had to cut myself free too. Sometimes I wish she had stayed there with me, because I think we could've gotten ourselves out of the first mess we ever found ourselves in. But what I wish more is that she will continue doing what is best for her. Losing us was best for her, and I have made peace with it in the years since. I have seen her since we grew apart, and because knowing someone as intimately as we knew each other does not fade, I could tell, instinctively, that she doesn't hold any resentment or negativity toward me.

It was our first year postgrad when we began to lose sight of each other, and in the four years I've had to process the end, I've realized that Juliet does not need me anymore. And although I don't believe friendship is always contingent on needs, it is Juliet's right to leave when something is no longer serving her, even if I cannot understand everything clearly. At many points in our friendship, I needed Juliet. Now I just want her. Want her joy, her comfort, her trust, her words. And it is hard to have come to the conclusion that this was for the best and that we weren't meant to carry each other into our midtwenties the way we always sort of figured we would. But when something is not right for one person in a relationship, it is not right for either person—so what Juliet knew first, I have come to understand now.

Still, with all this clarity and all this closure, there is no feeling as acutely painful as losing a friend. I remember being on a drive, alone with my boyfriend's mom one time, and her recounting the greatest friendship breakup of her life. She is thirty years older than I am, and I was misty-eyed realizing how universal these feelings are, across generations, spanning cities and states. Especially when there is not one specific moment that was the catalyst for the breakup—truthfully, we grew apart, and it is more common than I wish it was. When I grew apart from Juliet, I also grew apart from the other few girls too, including Anna. I fear sounding dramatic—because it is not like we all dislike one another, it is not like I can't text them and ask them to grab a drink and catch up. This was not so much a friendship breakup as a separation or a dissolution. We distanced ourselves from one another. Things happened. People were wronged. But nobody really prepared me for how it would feel to grow apart from the people you were taught you'd always just have.

•

Friendship is taught to us through nursery rhymes and storybooks and cliché quotes. *Good friends are like stars; you don't always see them, but you know they're always there. Make new friends but keep the old; one is silver and the other gold. True friends will be there no matter what.* Girl Scouts sold me the idea that my friends at eight years old would be my friends for life. Claire's sold best friend bracelets and earrings and necklaces that we bought and wore religiously. The acronyms BFF and BFFL were thrown around regularly in my childhood. In *Hannah Montana* and *Wizards of Waverly Place* and even *SpongeBob*, friendship was portrayed as pure and eternal. Even if Miley and her best friend, Lilly, spent an episode fighting, they always wound up back together by the end, because they were best friends *forever*. SpongeBob and Patrick disagreed and argued, but ultimately, it was a *forever* thing for them. It is comforting to have something like that to believe in. It is life-affirming to rely on the idea that one aspect of life—our friends—will be forever, unchanging, endless. Our crush might not like us back, we might do poorly on the pop quiz, our parents could get divorced, but friendship, we are taught, is forever and ever.

But this is unfortunately not realistic. And when you go through your first friendship breakup or when you grow apart from a "forever" friend for the first time in college or postgrad, the pain is so unique because it is so unexpected—it's something you were never taught would inevitably happen to you. Would inevitably happen to all of us. Friendship breakups and dissolutions are not normalized in pop culture and media for children, and in our teen years, the friendship breakups we do see portrayed in the media are dramatic, messy, and the culmination of some blowout fight. The idea that we could naturally grow apart from our friends, outgrow them, or lose them is not something we are taught to prepare for and, thus, not something we are well equipped to handle.

We're taught that romantic relationships can end at any time. It is the expectation and the universally understood fact that you and your romantic partner will either be *together forever* or break up. We see people who grow apart from their families, or opt out of a relationship with them for safety or circumstances out of their control. This is normalized for us in pop culture, television, film, and books from a very early age. But the idea that friends could be anything other than forever is not as common a conversation. The norm, for whatever reason, is that friendship is a constant. While there are thousands upon thousands of dating experts online and off, guides to dating, and universally understood norms of dating culture, there are not thousands of friendship experts, friendship manuals, or universally understood norms of being and having a friend. So while we are taught, at some point, that having a romantic partner requires work, love, care, energy, time, respect, trust, honesty, communication skills, effort, and more, we're never taught those same lessons about finding, having, and maintaining friendship. We are simply taught they will always be there . . . *forever*, no matter what.

We've neglected to teach children about the reality and the necessity of friendship, how difficult friendship can be and what it requires. And I think it is the very specific American and Western obsession with individualism at fault. I'd go further to say it is the very specific Western belief that community is unimportant that is at fault. I'd go even further to say that friendships are not relationships that directly contribute to capitalism in the way a Western society requires. Romantic partnership may turn to marriage, which benefits capitalistic society and will contribute to the continuation of the perfect American nuclear family. Work relationships and professional relationships benefit capitalist society for obvious reasons. Community and friendship are not taught as a necessity for survival in Western cultures, but I believe they are. You've likely heard someone say *it takes a village*—which is an old proverb that is taken both literally and metaphorically in cultures around the world. The saying reflects the belief that it takes a community, a literal village of people, to raise a child and properly care for this child's needs. It is custom, in many countries around the world, to do favors for your neighbors, to rely on your community for your needs and even wants, to ask your people (and people you may not even know) for help. Perhaps it is hard to wrap your head around if you were raised in a country that rejects community and embraces individuality, but in many places, community is far more important than individualism, nuclear families, or even success. In America specifically, we've become uncomfortable knocking on a neighbor's door to ask to borrow an egg, reaching out and asking a friend to give us a ride to the airport, or asking someone to take our dog for a walk when we have to stay at work late. In practice, community legitimately threatens capitalistic Western ideals, because capitalism relies on individuality. Capitalism relies on the idea that each and every person is in control of their own life. Without saying so, capitalist societies discourage community building, asking other people for help, taking and giving favors, and the village approach. We view favors to members of our community as asking too much, when realistically, these types of favors foster friendship and build deep bonds.

So we hardly teach our children about the importance of friendship, and when we do, it is sugarcoated and dumbed down, despite the fact that all of these children will inevitably find themselves one day as adults, heartbroken in the aftermath of a friend breakup or after growing apart from someone they platonically loved. If you are always taught that friendship is forever, that friendship is unending, that friendship doesn't require the same tools that romantic partnership requires, you are not prepared for the inevitable dissolution of your friendships as you move through life—you are not prepared for how it feels to lose or outgrow a friend, or how to handle it. We are taught to expect romantic breakups, and we are surrounded by resources for how to handle those. We treat romantic breakups like they are inevitable—because most people will, obviously, go through a romantic breakup in their life.

But I'd venture to say that even more people will inevitably experience a friendship breakup—and yet these are not normalized, not spoken about, and not given their own spotlight. How can you rebuild yourself when you've never been introduced to the tools to do so? How can you process something that you're not allotted the space to process?

•

While friendship breakups can happen at any time and any phase of life, college and postgrad are both periods when you are especially apt to lose, grow apart from, or break up with friends. It is unrealistic to expect you will be the same person at twenty-one as you were when you began college at eighteen, and as both you and your friends change, you may change in separate directions. Those high school friend groups and childhood best friends may no longer serve you, and you may realize the child you were friends with in elementary school is not someone you'd seek friendship from in their adult form.

I am not at all suggesting it is impossible to maintain relationships from high school well into and beyond college, because I have several friends whom I have known since elementary school who are still in my life today—I am suggesting that it is unrealistic to believe that our friendships will persist through all of life's chapters.

College, specifically, is set up perfectly to enable socialization and friendship. From dorm layouts and roommate assignments to group projects, clubs and teams, Greek life, community activities, jobs, and parties—college is in many ways an extrovert's dream. Of course it is valid to have difficulty making and maintaining friendships in general (and I will get there), but I'm more so suggesting that generally, college is a place where everyone is looking to make friends—and there are tons of opportunities and systems in place to help facilitate those social interactions.

I met Sadie in October during our first semester of college. We had recently joined the same sorority, and some of the girls had facilitated a meetup over dinner in the dining hall of the dorm where I lived. Sadie was in a class nearby and decided to come. I remember exchanging awkward small talk with her near the frozen yogurt machine and fearing she was too cool to become friends with me—the lone theater major in our sorority. But something about her felt so comforting to me. I had made a small group of friends in my first month at school, and I felt content with my social life—but I hadn't found that person who gave me the excited spark of new friendship yet. And then along came Sadie. And I instantly felt like I'd known her for my entire life. We were like two magnets that had spent the first eighteen years of our lives on opposite coasts of the country and now we were standing at the frozen yogurt machine in the East Quad dining hall, buzzing with the thrill of finally finding each other. She was notoriously on time and occasionally sarcastic, always painting her nails a deep shade of blue and wearing her naturally curly long strawberry blond hair straight and down. She was cool in every sense of the word—like a breeze on a stifling hot day, a cold drink when you are dying of thirst, an icy torrent of honesty and sincerity when you need it the most. I was involved with a guy from my drama class named Ezra at the time, and I immediately pitched Sadie the idea that she should go to our upcoming sorority formal with his roommate. We still argue whether that was the best idea, but we come to the conclusion that our friendship blossomed in the mess that ensued between my first college boyfriend, his roommate, and Sadie, who I was certain was my best friend, though I had only just met her.

This was nearly nine years ago, and though our relationship has changed in some ways, we still use the title "best friend" with pride when referencing each other. We moved through our four years of college relatively inseparable, despite our opposite majors (psychology for Sadie; theater for me), our opposite extracurricular activities (the rowing team for her; the school paper for me), and our opposite friend circles (her freshman year hallmates; friends from my major). We are friends not because we have the same hobbies or interests, not because we took the same major or played the same sport, but because we were drawn to each other, and we built on that initial attraction, and we built an irreplaceable foundation of trust and honesty, communication and joy that we rest our friendship on now. We were never gaining anything from each other—help in class, a ride to practice, someone to know in club meetings—because we didn't occupy those spaces together. The only reason we showed up in each other's lives was because we wanted to show up in each other's lives.

There is something so pure about loving another person

simply because they are them. Not for sex or companionship or a hand to hold at the function. Not because you are related or you work together or you run in the same circles. Just because they are them and you are you and you cannot imagine your life without them on the other end of a phone call. It is simply their presence you love them for. And that idea—that friendship is the only relationship that is truly a just-because—is one of the most sensational things in the world.

Because society did not explicitly teach the value of friendship—especially for and between women—it took meeting Sadie in college for me to truly understand the necessity and importance, but also the challenge it is to be and have a friend. It is not that the friends I made prior were not as good or did not teach me anything—it is that I was lucky enough that my first major hardships (from heartbreak to mental health) were experienced in college, with Sadie by my side. And when it was two o'clock in the morning and I couldn't sleep, or felt worthless and undeserving, or had a call from home that my mom wasn't doing well, or just needed to crawl out of my own skin and be far away for a while—I was never alone. Because there was this implicit knowing that Sadie was there. She was just there.

•

For most of my life, I had been taught—whether explicitly or implicitly—that the most important type of relationship was romantic. Though nobody ever told me outright, the world pointed me in that direction. Each book I read, song I listened to, movie I watched, television show I became enamored with centered on romantic love. Falling into it, falling out of it, finding it and keeping it. Not only does the media sell a pretty constant stream of romantic love to viewers and audiences, almost everyone I've ever met has wanted romantic love in some way. Romantic love is viewed as this impossible-to-ignore current, pulling you out toward the seas. It is a gold medal, an A-plus, a perfect score, a round of applause. Friendship and friend love is not depicted in the same way, in media or societally. So it is no wonder that I lived under the false perception that the most important relationship I could ever have was a romantic one and it was my job to find and maintain a romantic relationship. Especially as a young woman, I felt as though society was telling me that romantic love was my golden ticket . . . and friends were something I'd find along the way. I don't know how, and why, it isn't the other way around. Romantic love is something you find on the path to holding your friends so close.

I think many of us fall victim to this one-track-minded worldview. In our midtwenties we are celebrated for our engagements and marriages, first home purchases and pregnancies, and not necessarily much else. After college graduation, the celebrations we gather for (outside of birthdays of course) consist mostly of events that center some type of romantic union or romantic love. It is no wonder that we truly believe that this type of love is the kind we should pursue, the kind that we feel we need to survive.

I'd like to turn that on its head for just a moment. Of course I do feel incredibly grateful for my romantic partner. I feel incredibly blessed that I've found someone to waste away the days with, who is committed to us, who makes me feel like I always have something to look forward to. I need a lot of things without which I couldn't survive—food, water, oxygen, shelter. Without Noah, though, I would survive. It would suck and I would hate it and I do not wish to ever lose him—but if we were pulled in opposite directions, my world wouldn't end. And *the* world would keep turning, and I'd be able to breathe regardless of whether we were together or not. I do not say this to diminish what we have. We are each other's light bulb—providing a sheen of warm, glowy light to the other. We are each other's first call, last view every night, and first every morning. I do not wish to lose him, but I also know I don't need romantic love for survival.

I don't believe any of us really do. It is something we want, and something we are entitled to want. I want it too. I have it, and I never want to let it go. But we would be fine if we didn't have it—and that is because we need love to survive, but that love doesn't necessarily need to be romantic love. A steady flow of love to and from yourself is necessary for your survival, yes. But it can come in many forms. And you can wish to have it in many forms as well. Romantic love, friend love, familial love, love for a child or a passion or a hobby or a pet or even just yourself.

Men spend a good deal of time reducing female friendship to silly and meaningless, citing women to be "so dramatic" and "so catty" and "so bitchy." They use the example of friendship breakups or dissolutions, pointing out that for the most part, men have maintained the same friend circle since college or high school or even before. It is my belief that friendship for non–cis men is cavernous and bottomless and just . . . deeper. Reason being, for non-men, friendship is a necessity for our survival in a patriarchal world. It is no wonder we have made, and subsequently lost, more friends than they have—we have reached a level so intimate, so vulnerable, and so profound that we are bound to fall apart at a higher volume than friendships predicated on shared interests and hobbies. Our bonds to one another serve as a way to share and gain information, to build and foster community, and to provide support as we survive the inevitable turbulence of being a woman or a gay person or a nonbinary person in this heteronormative society.

I am not saying that cis men cannot form deep relationships.

I am saying that the depth, closeness, and intimacy many female friendships reach is due to a society that requires us to come together in order to get through.

There was a long period of time in which I believed, truly, that the most important relationship I would ever have would be a romantic relationship, with a man. In my singlehood, I made myself crazy hunting down my perfect match—my soulmate—my other half. I was hell-bent on the fact that my life would improve drastically once I simply found my guy. I believe many of us feel that way, and it is a natural feeling. I don't want to make it seem like I was ever a truly bad friend or that I ever neglected my friends—but up until my early twenties, I feel as though I didn't understand the importance, necessity, and brilliance of my female friends. I took them for granted in the way society taught me to. I was searching so fervently for the guy with the sparkly eyes and winning personality, I failed to stop and recognize that all the love I could have ever asked for was right in front of me the entire time.

When Jen came home from a work trip and walked through the door to me, as I sat on our couch, an open bottle of wine resting on the coffee table, and crumbled into my arms in exhaustion and frustration, I held her and we mended her wounds together. I felt rage for those who wronged her and a surge of love between us so pure and crystal clear. When I flopped on the couch beside Daphne in her Notting Hill flat five minutes before my twenty-fifth birthday and she kept her eye on the clock so she could blast Stevie Wonder's "Happy Birthday" when the clock struck twelve . . . I felt this unbreakable bond, this unbridled joy between us. When Isabela flew across the country with me to support me on my book tour, just because she loves me, I pinched myself out of the fear that the women I'd managed to surround myself with simply were too good to be true.

And it was not for nothing that, when I practiced such pure gratitude for the love already in my life in the form of female friendship, I found the romantic love I had spent so long chasing. Now I am rich enough to say I get to have both.

•

Though my friends make it easy for me to be their friend, in my belief there is no relationship that is necessarily easy or simple. Relationships are hard. Not like grief or getting fired or losing something that meant a lot to you—hard like a challenge you welcome. Relationships are hard like the *New York Times* crossword puzzle on a Sunday, or a marathon you complete after training for months. They are hard because they require work and dedication; they are hard because in principle they are hard. It is when you agree, without saying so, to put in the time, energy, and effort required to sustain them that they become easy. But they'll never be truly easy—because people require things from us, and we require things from people too.

And as we ease into chapters of our lives that are more challenging than others—like our twenties and postgrad, for example—friendships may grow more challenging. If we follow the traditional route of pursuing higher education after high school, postgrad and our young twenties are the first time we are surrounded by our peers but aren't necessarily in the same boat as they are.

Even though college feels like a step up in independence from childhood, there are still structures around us in the form of clubs, organizations, classes, community-building activities, dorm rooms, and more that facilitate socialization and friendship. We are no longer having playdates or bonding with our rec soccer teams, but in a way, we are—just the scenarios have changed and our faces are more mature. And there's beer.

Then you graduate, and all those structures that you never even really acknowledged, never even thought of as a constant or as a necessity, fall away. There is no activity fair urging you to join this or that social circle to find friends and community in the vein of shared interest. There are no group projects with lectures of three-hundred-plus project partners to choose from. There are no sororities and fraternities, dorm rooms with planned activities to bring people together. If you want to find friends, it is for the first time simply and solely up to you. If you'd like to seek out a community, there is nobody presenting you with a flyer or a pamphlet and begging you to join theirs.

Though no two college experiences are identical, you are in a similar boat—if not the same boat—as your peers from a broad point of view. You are in, likely, a four-year degree program with structures set up around you that give you just enough leeway . . . just enough freedom . . . but still push you in the direction of community and socialization and composition at every turn. And then all of that fades, and you have friends in every city in the country (and sometimes the world). You have friends who move home and friends who move in with their partners and friends who are bartending and friends who are working nine-to-fives and friends who are unemployed. You have friends chasing their dreams, friends dating, friends getting married, and friends staying single. You have friends making every choice for themselves under the sun, and you are expected to do the same. And all of a sudden your shared ship is now a solo rowboat, and you're hoping to meet your friends somewhere on their own journey in their own boat.

Suddenly, in the "real world" we cannot be consumed with

superfluous, silly things like *community* or *friendship* or *having a good time*. We have to get real. We have to get serious. We have to focus on our careers. We have to hustle while we're young. We have to make something of ourselves. We have to adult. We have to find someone and get engaged and marry them and have a kid. Society no longer sells us the idea that we need friends or that friendship is important—so when we inherently *do* need friends, we almost feel embarrassed to be admitting it. We almost feel like our time for making friends is over. We almost feel like it is silly or a waste of time to pour everything into our friendships.

And then naturally we begin to pull apart from certain friends, or we lose others, and the aftermath of that type of earthquake is so shockingly grim, and we have nowhere to turn to cry or bitch or fall apart. It isn't supposed to mean so much. . . . It isn't supposed to matter so much. Right?

But it hurts so much because it is inside of us, it is in our bodies, it is in our very own nuclear codes—we need friends to survive. And sometimes it takes losing a friend to realize just how important our friends really are to our survival and our existence on this sad and occasionally cold earth.

•

When I watched Juliet slip out of the front door of my life and take all of our memories, the exact way she remembers them, with her, I was gutted. I still am. Juliet matters to me and she always will. Even if we aren't right for each other in this chapter. Even if it is not written in the stars that we will be forever friends. It has taken me over four years to process our ending because nobody presented me with the tool kit for or the handbook on just how to lose a friend, or how to manage without someone you always thought would just be. For a really long time, every day felt like waking up the day after you threw a party and having to clean your sticky floors and pick up any signs of celebration and glee and tuck them away.

And I wish I could offer you more of a tool kit or a cheat code for how to get through this unique conclusion like I can a romantic breakup. But one thing that really helps me is relying on psychology to explain the phenomena of our social relationships.

Dunbar's number is a theory (one we've already touched on) that posits that we can only really maintain about one hundred fifty social connections at one time. Only five of these will be our closest relationships, then fifteen good friends, about fifty friends, and one hundred fifty meaningful relationships overall.

Juliet and Anna could not have existed in the same moment as Jen, Caroline, and Isabela. And I don't mean to suggest I had to let some friends go in order to make new ones. And I don't mean to suggest there isn't a world where I could've been friends with all of them. But based on the above, if I can only truly maintain fifteen good friendships, it would be impossible to fall into the perfect love stories with Jen and Caroline and Isabela if I hadn't made my peace with the dissolutions of certain friendships or just growing apart from other friends. It brings me to a strange, watery, sentimental peace to know that this number isn't fixed. That the glow of the love I feel from the birthday card Jen wrote me this year is only possible because I don't have the same from Juliet right now. The way Caroline can quell all my anxieties and existentialism is only possible because I don't talk to Anna every day anymore. And maybe one day I won't have Caroline and Jen anymore in the way I do now. And maybe I will. I can't know. I have to hold them so fucking unbelievably close when I have them today. I have to pray they are mine forever while realizing that there's a chance that they are not. I will live in the precious moment of each dinner or cocktail we share. Of each secret they pass me. Each moment I feel so lucky to just know them. Each restaurant we make our place.

What a beautiful thing. How fleeting it all is. To know and accept that it won't always be the same and still choose to believe regardless. To hold them around the waist and shout the lyrics to a song we both know at each other at the bar. To board the flight with them so we can tie a memory to a new place together. To stamp the passport of our lives with one another's lipstick marks and perfume. To one day get to look back on it and pray my daughter will have the same level of sentimentality when she thinks of the women she loved so deeply, so truly, but that maybe she doesn't love in the same way anymore.

Certain people will be in your life forever. Certain people will course in and out. Others will be a blip or a moment or a month. You will truly not know until you're at the end of it all, staring back at all that has been. All I can hope for you is that you gave each of the people who graced your life the love you believe they deserved. All I can hope for is that you valued your friends like the precious gems they are. All I can hope for is the pain that certain friendships caused you will be eased by the restorative qualities of others.

Juliet got engaged recently, to her high school sweetheart. I found out on Instagram, which is how I find out most things about her these days. This is how it is, and that is okay. As I looked at the pictures of her earnest smile, a strange memory stirred inside of me—a remembering of picking out our engagement rings at the age of ten, planning to marry the ones that got away and boys whom we don't even know anymore. Maybe I'm wrong, but I felt like she liked the same emerald-cut shape sixteen years ago that she wears on her left ring finger now. There is a strangeness in the fact that I am not at the engagement party, not on the invite list or at the other end of the FaceTime, sparkly diamond and shrieks of glee flashing on the other end. It is tender like a wound that is slowly healing, to live in a time that we don't share in each other's joy the way we thought we would.

But it is how it is meant to be. And from afar I am sorry—to her and myself—for what went wrong and for believing, in my naivete, our union would be forever.

So much has changed. And I cling to the version of me that I was when we shared everything with each other. I am also sentimental for this version of me who will sit around a table tonight with women who love me for me, whom I met a few years ago, who have already left an indelible mark. I will cling to me, I will cling to us, I will cling to her too.

To be a friend, to have a friend. It is, in so many ways, the best thing I have ever been. The best thing I am. The best thing I will be.

Does Anyone Else Hate Socializing?

"Get ready with me for a night out," sings a bright voice that lives inside my TikTok app. Said voice is matched perfectly to well-kept blond hair, the most symmetrical face you've ever seen, and full bow lips. The stranger on my screen has racked up 250,000 likes for her makeup application and explanation of her plans for the night. Cool-girl pop music plays behind her, and her pretty friends breeze into and out of the frame with questions about outfits, plans, and borrowed pairs of high-heeled shoes. I am transfixed by their girlish glee, their young-twenties energy, and their hypnotic, carefree personas. I hate them, I love them, I want to be them. I want to wear their expressions and exist in their skin. I am a gross, misshapen thing beside all their femininity and thrill.

I am also on the couch with delivery food on the way, a reality TV show about people with equally outgoing personalities and fulfilled social lives playing in the background. It's a Saturday night, and I have no plans, though after "getting ready" with girl after girl on TikTok, I briefly begin to wonder if I should. I thought I felt okay forfeiting socialization for my own company, but that feels called into question with each flick of my finger on the For You page.

Is there a right way to experience your twenties? I wonder, as I tell the delivery guy to please leave my food at the door (avoiding one of very few social interactions I could have that evening). *Am I wasting away my glory days?* I think, catching a glimpse of my frizzy hair and dry skin in the mirror as I retreat back to the couch. *Is the key to happiness going out on Saturday nights, making unforgettable memories (or perhaps forgettable ones)? Is this the one time in my life left that I'll have to be carefree? To be free at all?*

I wouldn't call the phenomenon FOMO, because it isn't like I fear missing out on something in particular, or there's even somewhere I could go. But as I catch a glimpse of New York's effervescent, sleepless skyline twinkling on the Hudson River, I wonder if I am lame. If I am wasting my life away watching *Love Island*, ordering takeout, and wearing sweatpants. As always, like a tradition I wish to forever forget, I push the thoughts and feelings down. I'll address them next Saturday night, when they creep up behind me again, tapping me on the shoulder in the sneaky, flirtatious way they do. Loser. Loser. Loser. Ugly loser. Bland loser. Boring loser. Friendless loser.

I open TikTok and I feel like a loser. I sit alone and I feel like a loser. I want to be these beautiful girls with wonderful social lives, and I also cannot imagine being anyone but me.

How did I go from Big Ten school party girl to some kind of social pariah? What is so scary about a party or a crowded bar? Do I even want to go to the hot social gathering of the evening? Am I wasting my life if I don't?

In the years since I've graduated from college, I have become some kind of slow-motion hermit crab, slowly retreating back to her comfortable shell—hidden, safe. Society calls me an introvert, and I call myself a loser and a weirdo, and I wonder if this is something we can help, if we can choose how we socialize and how we like to put ourselves out there. How do you socialize in your twenties? Is there a right way? And is my way wrong?

•

One of the perks of my job is that I am invited to tons of parties and events a week. On any given night there is an invitation waiting in my inbox, an RSVP list I could be added to, and sometimes even a free Uber code dropped into the app—further encouraging my attendance. And I hesitate to sound ungrateful or as though I don't deserve these invites because I both appreciate them AND sometimes accept and attend. But the majority of the time, I don't, and I wish I was one of those people who viewed an invitation with excitement devoid of anxiety, and not both dread AND anxiety. I can't help it. I wake up the morning of a big social gathering where anyone could be there, and I feel an elephant sitting comfortably on my chest. I am not excited. And in fact, I've hated myself for years because of the worry a party invitation brings me. For me, a party means getting dressed. And getting dressed is difficult for me because I don't know how to have a sense of personal style, and I feel like everyone on TikTok is always urging us to "just wear what you want!" And "prioritize personal style!" But it sounds like a buzzword to me, and I don't even know how to go about finding my personal style, so I haven't tried to. A party also means unknown—an unknown guest list, an unknown vibe, and an unknown set of events that will take place. Parties feel irresponsible or impractical. Then I will pack a small bag of Zofran and Advil, anticipating nausea and a headache before I even walk out the door. I will get in the car or ride the subway, and I will worry my makeup looks patchy or my hair is stringy or my deodorant has magically stopped working. I will envision the other guests and how out of place I will seem among them. I will remind myself not to talk too much, but I know I will anyway. I will say something weird. It will be awkward. It'll feel like a balloon popping in slow motion, and before I know it, I've had two much-too-strong cocktails, made an excuse, and left early, replaying every interaction in 2x speed in my mind on the way home. But everyone online has to think I'm good at this. I upload an Instagram to look like I had fun. I close my eyes and dread tomorrow.

Every time, for the most part, I will have wished I just stayed home. And it becomes a cycle—where I fear attending, and when I do attend, my fears get the best of me and I perceive the entire night to be a wash, further contributing to my desire never to attend another event again. But then I open up TikTok, and it is an exclusive island for only sexy extroverts, and I am a sad, bloated woman acting like a child in the back of a Toyota Camry, wondering why setting powder doesn't look as good on my skin. Wondering why I can't just get over myself and go somewhere and have a good time. Wondering if I'll ever find a place where I feel seamless and light. Where I feel like I belong.

I've always felt like I never fit in anywhere. Too sorority for the arts kids and too artsy for the sorority girls. Too weird for the cool kids and too cool for the weird kids. Too normal for the artists and too artistic for the normies. This feeling came with me from high school to Ann Arbor, Michigan, where I attended college. The first two semesters nearly confirmed what I always knew to be true: I didn't fit in anywhere. At the *Michigan Daily* newsroom, everyone talked to one another, and nobody talked to me. When I tried to talk to people, for the most part, it felt like they didn't want to engage with me. So I often just stood there quietly during our weekly meetings, wishing someone could see how desperately I wanted to belong. It wasn't like anyone disliked me; it was more like they looked at me and decided I already had friends and already belonged and didn't need to belong there. Most students who worked on the paper frequented the newsroom several times a week—to study or work or socialize. I didn't gain the confidence to do that until I was an upperclassman. At the sorority house, if Sadie wasn't home, I ate alone. Nobody talked to me in the crowded dining room. This was supposed to be a sisterhood—I was supposed to fit in here. And again, if I spoke to them, it was like I could tell they really didn't want to talk to me. Nobody was outright mean. I just felt forgotten. Constantly, it was as though everyone figured I belonged somewhere else. And nobody knew that truthfully, I felt that I belonged nowhere at all.

For a while I figured I was the problem—too quirky, too artsy, too loud, too much. I wished to be one of those universally adored people with great hair and an inherent sense of style. Someone all the girls wanted to be, and all the boys wanted to be with. But I was never that. I was the eternal bridesmaid, everyone else's biggest cheerleader, the last pick to join the team. At least it felt that way to me, as I tried to show up in rooms I wound up just feeling awkward to be in.

It is for precisely that reason, among others, that since high school, I've never had much of a friend group. If friend groups work for you, I am genuinely happy for you, and I am not trying to villainize your experience or suggest that you are wrong for it. But I think for a lot of us, either they haven't worked or we don't have one and fail to realize that in order to have a fulfilling social life, we (1) do not need one and (2) actually would benefit from not having one.

Because I never felt like I fit in with one type of person or one group of people, I resorted to collecting individual friends instead. It was, at first, a method of survival, and eventually became a lesson that shifted into a choice. As I look at all the memories my friends have kissed onto my physical self—a friendship bracelet from Sadie, the hair care tip I took from Gabriela, the daily ritual phone call to Daphne, the vernacular I adopted from Jen—my heart surges.

It was individual women, and individual moments, that made me realize that belonging was something you had to seek out yourself. That we all deserve it. That if you are unwanted somewhere, it is better to leave than to stay and try to convince people to desire you. It was Lizzie who left the party with me because the guy I had a crush on was publicly making out with his untouchably gorgeous ex-girlfriend against a wall a week after we'd had sex. It was Lizzie who saw me first, giving me the confidence to befriend nearly everyone else in our theater program. It was Sadie who whispered in my ear at the crowded basement bar during one of our first outings with our sorority that we should live together the following year. It was Sadie who saw me and made me feel as though I was worth being seen. I continued to collect sparkling individuals, and they became my lifelines—a girl I met in class, and another who finally broke the ice in the newsroom. A girl whom I joined a club with, the neighbor down the hall, the one I always sat with in the big lecture hall, my now ex-boyfriend's friend's ex-girlfriend.

Eventually, as I moved from my underclassman days and toward junior and senior year, I was grateful to not just belong to one group, to not just subscribe to one place, but to have a colorful, genuine, irreplaceable group of friends I called mine. Not a friend group, but a group of individual friends. And it was because of that that my social life in college began to soar. There was always something to do, always somewhere to feel a tug on my heart—the idea I could belong, because I had so many friends in so many places. There wasn't just one friend group plan, one friend group party, one friend group weekend event—but an array of people, places, and things to explore. My lack of subscription to one friend group, to one ideology, to one place, allowed me to grow as a person, to develop deeper friendships with each person I was lucky enough to call a friend, and to explore more of the world than I would've had I joined a group with a pack mentality.

Socializing in college is difficult. Having a social life takes work—the work to make and commit to plans, work to align schedules and ensure you're prioritizing time for community. And it is difficult whether or not you are in a friend group. It is difficult to show up in front of a person, or a group of people, and say—*I think you should love me for me, and I'll love you for you, and we can hang out forever and do nothing together*. It takes vulnerability, which takes bravery.

It is inherently easier to have a single friend group with one cohesive social schedule—it requires less effort on your part to make plans, and it's easier to maintain friendships when you're always seeing the same people in similar settings. That said, I think the work required of maintaining many individual friends throughout your life makes those friendships deeper. You have to work harder to see these people, you have to be more intentional about reaching out and planning, and you have to *want* to work toward making sure that happens as well. It is not a bad thing to not be a part of a friend group. In fact, I think the effort you put into maintaining your individual relationships makes you a more well-rounded friend overall.

Simultaneously, I think this distinction better prepares one for the transition out of college life and into postgrad life as it relates to socialization and our friendships. There were points throughout college where I wondered if I was weird, or lame, or undesirable because I didn't have a friend group—but now, at twenty-six, I thank my lucky stars that I didn't. When you graduate from college you will likely move to different cities than some of your friends. Perhaps you will be lucky, and you'll all move to the same city—but still, it will be different. With new adult responsibilities, full-time jobs, roommates, and opportunities, maintaining friendships (even within a friend group) is different outside of college than it was when you were in college. For me, having the experience of maintaining deep individual relationships in college prepared me for the shift to long-distance friendship and adult friendship in general. As we cycle through iterations of ourselves, ease into and out of chapters of our lives, circumstances change, environments change, and *we* adapt. Having, maintaining, and making friends will change too. Though it grows more difficult to maintain our friendships as we ease into our twenties, I also believe having and loving our friends gets even better. Because we weather stronger storms together, because we hold on tighter to one another, because we fight harder to make it work—our bonds grow more ironclad.

And yet the beast named Insecurity weaseled her way into the bags I packed after saying goodbye to my college town and moving to New York. Though I had silenced her with my resilience and ability to maintain friendships throughout my upperclassman years in college, the growing pains of a transition to a new chapter dragged her from the depths of my soul and gave her a seat at my table once more.

•

In college, the farthest Sadie and I lived from each other was a five-minute walk our freshman year. The remaining three years, we shared a roof and, as a result, 99.99 percent of our waking moments as well. We walked to class in our big puffy coats, often silently, just enjoying the cadence of our steps falling in line. We got ready on the floor in my room, passing makeup products and bottles of perfume back and forth with ease. We shared clothes, meals, and secrets. Fell asleep in my bed watching the latest Netflix documentary, kept each other up-to-date on the various dramas of the classes we didn't take together. I didn't give much thought, during those long days we shared, to what would happen in the spring of 2020, after we threw our graduation caps in the air and our friendship scattered around our feet as they fell. She was moving to Chicago, I was going to New York, and it felt like she took a melon baller to my heart and brought a piece of it with her to her new apartment with a roommate who was not me. Plenty of my friends moved to New York—from all the many chapters of my life—and I never failed to consider how very different my relationships to all these people whom I had carried from chapter to chapter would be now.

In college, it was customary to study, grab dinner, hang out, or party after classes on any given weekday, but our new adult schedules didn't allow for so much social flexibility. Many of my friends worked or took classes till six p.m., had a laundry list (literally) of pesky to-dos and adult tasks to accomplish afterward, and ultimately wanted nothing more than a doomscroll session in bed to end the day before the alarm went off not ten hours later to do it all again. Now social prime time is Friday night, Saturday day, and Saturday night (potentially Sunday). But that's all pending birthdays, extra work or tasks to accomplish, connecting to long-distance friends and family, family time and events, dating, self-care and solo time, recharge time, and more. And even if we have Friday night open, our friends may not—because our socialization time has gone from pretty widely available to hardly available at all. The friends you might've seen every day you may now see once every other week—if you're lucky—and just like all these other major life transitions, nobody really reminds you to prepare for socialization in adulthood (which often looks like sending out a monthly Google Cal invite for a dinner). As a consequence, the all-too-common feeling that everyone hates you or you have no friends is amplified in adulthood. Because you're seeing your friends less than you are used to seeing your friends and don't receive the in-person validation that everything is status quo with your friendship. You have to rely on the fact that as your responsibilities grow, your priorities multiply, and you simply won't have as much time for your friends. This hurts. And it is hard.

I often like to think that as humans we're composed of metaphorical gas tanks—we have a tank for family, one for romance, one for work, one for play, one for self-care, one for friendship, one for socialization, and one for our hobbies and passions. It is not the job of your romantic partner to fill any tank other than their own—the same way it is not the job of your friends to fill any tank other than their own. But I do feel at certain times in our lives we rely on one tank of gas to keep us going more than we do the others—and in college, we're pretty reliant on socialization and camaraderie with friends to keep us afloat. College is like an island of friendship and good times—you're almost constantly socializing, even if you aren't trying to. Suddenly you're cut free in the real world, and you're almost never socializing, even if you are trying to. You don't even get a chance to wean off the high of having constant social stimulation, constant camaraderie, and community. It is like one day the dealer packs up shop and you can no longer get a fix—and you're expected to adjust, act like an adult, and proceed as normal.

But this transition from postgrad to adulthood is not normal. Being twenty-three years old does not feel normal. Your reaction to an abnormal situation—your heightened anxiety, loneliness, and the itchy feeling that something just isn't right—however, is normal.

If you are here with me, struggling to have and maintain a social life in the third decade of your life—know that you are not by yourself in feeling out of control, in shutting your bedroom door and deciding to stay in, and feeling worse for it. We will do it together. As we always have. As we can to survive.

•

I wouldn't have considered myself a party girl in college, but I went to a very social school and went out two to three times a week throughout my four years. Though I enjoyed that time in my life, one perk I found to postgrad life was less of a consistent pressure to socialize in the form of partying, drinking, and hitting the bars. It felt normalized, in a way college didn't really boast, to have a night in with friends—and I realized quickly that I'm much more comfortable socializing in ways that don't include crowded bars or clubs. And though there are hordes of young people who agree with me, there are an equal number of young people who live for their next night out (as they should, as is their right), who love clubs and bars and parties. They populate my TikTok feed and often also my own life, being that I am friends with tons of people who prefer a night out to a night in. I felt myself confront my youth as each weekend came around the bend, wondering if I was wasting it on couch cushions and bottles of wine shared in a cozy apartment. I am not getting younger. I am growing up with each passing moment—and should I just go out? Should I hit the bars? Is my idea of fun a waste of health and energy and being a twentysomething?

Not only did I feel less motivated to go out, I also felt a heightened anxiety and overwhelm when I did. These negative emotions were compounded by the people my age who seemed to enjoy and look forward to going out, especially when those people were my friends. I didn't feel a fear of missing out, I felt a fear of wasting my life. A fear that I was washing my potential to enjoy every day down the drain with every canceled plan or evening spent at home.

Some nights, I'd succumb to the pressure—fear of ruining my glory days and regret driving me out of the house, into an uncomfortable pair of shoes and an Uber, a slight discomfort settling within me, right under my breastbone. At the pregame with friends of my friends, I'd find myself going into the bathroom trying to catch my breath a few times, wondering why I came, what to do with my hands, whom to talk to when the conversation with one quasi stranger ran dry.

I can tell myself over and over and over again that nobody is thinking of me, and even if they are, it is out of my control, but all I can think about is the way it feels to have a pair of eyes on me, processing my face and nodding. For a while, I did this. I went to pregames and parties and bars and clubs that mimicked my college experience—places that people my age populated, places the majority of people in my circles enjoyed frequenting. And when I wasn't having a good time, I failed to consider there was very likely somewhere else I could go—somewhere I was wanted, somewhere I felt comfortable—and just because one environment wasn't bringing me joy, hiding away at home wasn't the only other option. There were other places. Other environments. Other ways to socialize in my twenties. I just had to do some digging, but nobody had offered me the shovel.

It was like I wanted to hate my life so I continuously placed myself in scenarios where I knew I would. In bed before going to sleep, after the function where I hated myself for going more than I'd hate myself for missing out, I scrolled for an hour. Each girl explaining her plans for the night ahead on my TikTok app is prettier than the last. Each outfit is more stylish. Each video is a reminder that I am a freak with abnormal tendencies who is flushing her twenties down the toilet. Girls with their arms interlocked laughing carelessly on their way to the club. A group of friends in matching bikinis on a boat at a bachelorette party. A huge friend group doing a Secret Santa. A girl leaving the club at three a.m. with her eyes twinkling.

I wonder what is wrong with me and then I wonder why it would be their fault for enjoying their youth, enjoying their lives, if something was wrong with me. Perhaps if it is hell when I do go and a slightly better hell when I don't, there's some other middle ground, someplace that might feel like an even slightly better hell or, if I'm lucky, some kind of heaven.

Maybe I'm not meant to have a cool, flawless party-girl life and that's okay—even if it feels like everyone on TikTok is meant for that, even if it feels like I'm the only one who isn't. Because here's the truth—someone else's joy is not a threat to my own. Someone else's idea of fun is not a threat to my own idea of fun. Someone else's preference of how they spend their time is not a knock at me for how I prefer to spend my own.

I am not sure why I was internalizing it as though it was, but I was. I was spending all my free time forcing myself to do things I hated or beating myself up for not forcing myself to do something I hated. I was comparing my life to others' lives online and determining that it wasn't as fulfilling or exciting, further discouraging me from going out and claiming a version of my own life that was fulfilling. I wanted to make new friends but was preventing myself from making them. I wanted to enjoy going out into the world, socializing, and I was stopping myself from opening the front door. I wanted to discover what my idea of fun was, in my young twenties and my midtwenties and eventually my late twenties, and I was letting someone else's TikTok discourage me from doing so.

Social media certainly exacerbated these growing pains—but it wasn't anyone's job but my own to recognize that. I am the only person accountable for the content I consume and how I consume it—who I block and mute, how much time I spend consuming content, and what type of content I linger on or scroll away from. We cannot allow ourselves to feel threatened because our idea of fun is not the same as the majority of people's our age. We cannot allow ourselves to feel threatened because we don't like something that a lot of other people like. We cannot intentionally cause ourselves harm and isolation because we don't want to do the work needed to find an environment that makes us feel seen, makes us feel heard, makes us feel wanted.

For several years, I continued on like this. An endless loop of feeling sorry for myself for staying home, or forcing myself up and out and regretting it. I lived under the false pretense that there was one way to have a social life in your twenties, one idea of how to have fun, and because I didn't like it, I resorted to thinking I'd never have a healthy social life, never have fun again. Once in a while, I'd have a night that felt like a gift from God herself—no anxiety, no wishes to be elsewhere, no tears of gratitude falling down my cheeks on my ride home. I cherished them as though they were rarities, as though I didn't deserve to have a normal social life that was a version of normal I enjoyed.

But those few nights were a spark, a little kindling—a fire-starting log that reminded me that there was goodness to go claim out in the world, out in the night, a place where my uncomfortable shoes and setting powder and I belonged.

•

My little brother Jack's favorite movie (for a while) was *Field of Dreams*. The plot is not necessary to the following story—and I don't really remember it anyway. What I do remember is the quote one of the characters hears while he is walking through a cornfield at night.

The quote is "If you build it, he will come."

You've probably heard it before, and you probably didn't know it came from a random movie about baseball. The idea of the quote is what stands out to me so much—if you build something of quality, with care and passion, the audience you're trying to attract will come.

I'd take it a step further: if you build the life you want, the life you like, the life you actually enjoy, your comfort, your belonging, your peace will come too.

The key here is the act of building—the key here is that to find your comfort and your peace, you need to do the work to carve out a life where your comfort and peace feel welcome. I was wasting the time I could have been using to build myself a life I liked trying to re-create the lives of others, and feeling depressed and angry when the mimicked lives of others didn't feel right to me.

The girls I watched on my Saturday nights alone seemed to have built the life they wanted. And perhaps it was easy for them because their idea of fun and joy is the norm for girls in their young twenties. Perhaps they were also pretending, putting on a mask as though they were having the time of their lives and clicking the upload button just like I did every now and then. Perhaps we're all pretending. All masquerading as totally cool, flawless, and fine. Maybe someone was spending tearful nights comparing themselves to my video on their For You page. Nothing happens in a vacuum. But it is up to each of us to individually identify the things that make us feel good—the social events, the environments, the Friday night plans—and commit to doing them consistently, putting in effort to elicit joy, so long as that is still our idea of joy and fun.

My idea of fun was different from most twenty-two-year-olds I knew. My idea of a healthy social life was different. My idea of my own joy was different. That doesn't make them wrong or make me wrong. There is no single textbook definition of individual joy, fun, or peace. Unfortunately we don't wake up one morning feeling at ease, feeling content with our lives and the people we surround ourselves with. We have to go out and find those people, find those places, find that peace.

•

Our childhoods and teen years are freckled with so many reminders of friendship and camaraderie—we are constantly around our friends, constantly reminded of their importance, and constantly placed in scenarios wherein making new friends and socializing is far easier than it is in adulthood. What is done for you is now something you have to do for yourself, and nobody tells you this is coming—they just rip the safety net out from under you and let you fall to the floor. The invisible framework for how to live a life prioritizes friendship early on, and as you age throughout your twenties, any prioritization of friendship is discarded for new priorities—romantic love, a career, monetary success. Notice how I said *invisible*, though, because to me, this is not a real framework—not one we need to rely on.

You are allowed to prioritize socialization and friendship in your twenties. You are allowed to prioritize making new friends and building a social life that you like. It is not silly—not pointless—to spend a good deal of your time hanging out with friends, making plans with friends. To me, these people and these experiences will save your life in the ways a romantic relationship or a job will never be able to. It is actually, in my book, admirable, when the largest chunk of your free time is spent around your friends. I think you deserve a gold medal. Seriously.

I needed that reminder so badly at twenty-two. I needed that reminder so badly at twenty-three. I needed that reminder until I realized that it didn't make me unfocused on my career or directionless to prioritize my social life and my friends like the universe was telling me (in a silent way) that it was. My social life will keep me fed, keep me alive, keep me afloat, so that I have the energy and the desire to focus on my career and my passions and everything else too. I need gas in the tank for the car to drive. I can't keep stalling in the middle of the road.

I was waiting for someone to ask me, "Eli, what do you WANT to do?"

"Where do you FEEL like you belong?"

"Where have you been lately that has brought you joy?"

"Who makes you feel safe and secure?"

Nobody was going to ask me those things; I had to ask them to myself. But I am asking you now. Pause, take a moment, and answer these questions for me.

What is your dream Saturday night? Have you been going where you feel wanted? What do you want to do with your time? Are you content with your friendships? With your social life? What is the ideal social life and experience for you? What would you have to change from your current reality to get there?

My dream Saturday night begins with an early three-drink dinner (a dinner where we each have three cocktails and spend a hefty amount of time talking and laughing) at one of my home base restaurants, with a small group of my girlfriends, or maybe just one friend. Sometimes we'll go to the piano bar (Marie's Crisis, anyone?) or go see a Broadway show or some live music, or stop by a cool art event. Sometimes we'll take a gummy and go home to watch YouTube videos. Sometimes we'll stay in, and I'll cook while my friends drink wine and sit in assorted chairs, or just on the floor, and recount bad first dates they've been on.

I feel wanted when I'm in settings around other theater people and writers—and the greatest friends I've made from the app that lives inside of my phone come from some kind of arts background. My ideal social life and experience is one where I have ample time to recharge, and am spending time with the people whom I love because they are just themselves, outside of bars or clubs or crowded parties. And that is okay. That is normal. And I can absolutely make a video on TikTok doing my makeup and rattling off my plans for the evening even if they aren't glamorous or exciting or don't include bottle service.

My ideal social life is accompanied by social anxiety that I have dealt with since I was young. I am not a failure for the panic that arises within me when faced with social settings. I am a girl trying her best. I am a girl who is proud of herself for going anyway.

How badly did I need to know that if I built it, my joy, my peace, and my comfort within my own body and my own life would come? Sure, it requires effort and energy and time. Yes, it requires getting real with yourself and your wants. But the payoff—comfort and security in the way you choose to exert yourself socially—is so beyond worth it.

And maybe one day will come where I want to be a party girl again, and go out until four in the morning. Maybe one day will come when this version of my own joy changes. That will be okay too. It is so beyond normal to change your mind. I am not sure when we began to villainize ourselves for the human act of changing.

•

As Gen Z and Millennial women continue the trend of marrying later in life than prior generations, as we put off childbirth until later years, and as unprecedented numbers of us choose not to marry at all, our need for community in the form of friendship grows. Our need for healthy social lives grows. As we gain more mobility in the world, more opportunities to earn money, more opportunities to work and succeed—we fly the nest and branch out far more than women in other generations. We move to cities our ancestors never laid eyes on. We turn thirty years old and decide to pick up and spend a few months in a different state or even a different country. For women, this ease of movement is unprecedented. And to me, fundamentally, these shifts require us to be making new friends at older ages than prior generations.

My mother, for example, moved home after college, and so did the vast majority of her friends from high school and childhood. She married at twenty-four years old and had me at twenty-six, and her friends had similar trajectories. She is still close friends with the majority of her childhood friend group. Simultaneously, the adult friends she made were women she met in circles with other mothers. Her open-ended need to make new friends was not as obvious as it is for me, legally single at twenty-six, living in a city without many of my friends from high school and college, with no plans to have children or get married in the foreseeable future.

However, because it is not as normalized to have a need to

make new friends in our adult lives, we feel childish, embarrassed, and awkward to either admit we'd like to have or make new friends, and we are simultaneously unsure about how to go about it.

Having a desire to make new friends, having a desire to have new friends, has never been and is never going to be silly or embarrassing. You may feel embarrassed by your desire to make new friends at the age of twenty-six, but I promise you, many of us who are freed from the invisible framework for how to live a life need new friends too. It is okay to want to start fresh with your social life at the age of twenty-five. It is okay to want to make new friends at twenty-six. It is okay to want to make new friends at thirty or forty or fifty years old too.

It is time we got serious about how important friendship and friends are for our survival. I need my friends like I need oxygen. I need them to get through my worst days. I need them to be on the other end of the phone on my best days. I need their hands to hold, their eyes to pass me messages we can't say out loud at this crowded bar. I am so lucky to have people who need me like I need them.

Putting yourself out there will always be terrifying because it is always accompanied by the very real potential that you may wind up alone, you may get rejected, and you will be perceived. But the worst-case scenario is you introduce yourself to someone, or you join Bumble BFF or a Facebook group or put yourself out there in a book club or community group, and you don't meet a new friend (which is doubtful). The best-case scenario is you meet the person who will make every day make sense. The best-case scenario is you meet the girl who will become the home to your secrets, your safe space, your flashlight, always guiding you home. The best-case scenario is you meet someone to get ready with before a Saturday night out, or do nothing at all with.

The risk is real, yes. But the reward is too.

•

I am too much for some people. There are also those who cannot get enough of me, though. And those are the people who I choose to center. I have the best fucking friends in my world. I hope I have them forever. I also hope I have the chance to make new friends in every phase of life, in every chapter yet to write itself.

I stay in on Saturday nights with my boyfriend, and we watch a documentary like I used to with Sadie in college. I send her a photo of our takeout dinner, and she sends me one back of what she and her boyfriend have ordered. We recommend new shows to watch. We book flights to visit each other. We tell each other "I love you," and we mean it.

I call Daphne in the Uber on the way to the event I'm going to on a Thursday. Her voice is like aloe to my soul. She is the greatest antidote to every bad day and even the good ones. She tells me about her day, and we trade stories about the nothingness that happened to us that we will forget in a week or two. As we say goodbye, I know that it doesn't matter if someone doesn't like me at my destination or if I am too much for someone, because I am not too much for the witty blonde on the other end of the phone. I will talk to her tomorrow and then the next day and then every day into the future as long as we still talk. Knowing that much is enough to keep me afloat.

Isabela is waiting for me on the sidewalk out in front of the party. She has the best hair, and she is always smiling. I knew what she'd be wearing before I left the house because she sent me a mirror selfie. We had to make sure we weren't matching, because we always buy the same clothes as each other. Because we wear the same size, we share everything except for our names. She grabs my hand, and standing next to someone so shiny and bright is like a coat of armor. I hope I make her feel the same way. We became friends at twenty-three, right before twenty-four. How lucky I am to know I will continue to meet women so shiny and so bright, to share pairs of shoes with into the future.

This is my idea of fun. This is my idea of peace. This is my joy. I go where I am wanted and I want to make each person who walks through my own front door feel wanted too. And when it isn't my idea of fun anymore, when it doesn't bring me joy anymore, I have stored my shovel and my tools for safe keeping. I can rebuild it whenever I'd like, and they will still come.

Does Anyone Else Fear Moving Away and Growing Apart?

I am nineteen years old and waiting for Sadie on a cool bench outside of a school building on campus. We have an unspoken tradition of meeting between classes on Tuesdays and Thursdays, when our schedules line up. I have a huge crush on a guy who doesn't know I exist. I have an English paper due. I have a flight to New Jersey to catch in a week for Thanksgiving. I have all these problems that seem like dust bunnies, pesky and irrelevant, looking back now. And I have this redheaded best friend who is always punctual, perpetually loyal to our time together, even if it's just fifteen minutes in between class. The tradition always goes the same way. I sit on the bench in the midst of the busiest part of campus as hundreds of students pour out of hulking buildings and stumble their way to wherever they're going next. I scan the crowd—students hand-holding and doomscrolling, stopping to make small talk and hustling to Espresso Royale to try to get a table to study. And then there she is, catching my eye, laughing hysterically like we are long-lost twins reunited for the first time in decades, flipping her long hair behind her. It is random and funny and fate that we found each other—to have left for college expecting camaraderie and friends but never anticipating each other. Every day we tell each other we can't believe we spent eighteen years wandering around our hometowns with no knowledge of the other's existence. It is so good to be so young. It is so good to feel unstoppable and to know we never have to live another day without having each other's phone numbers.

Sadie is from Phoenix. She is West Coast perfection—stylish in a carefree way, sunny and on trend and, in many ways, what California would look like if she was a girl and not a state. She often reminds me she was born in Brooklyn, but her family moved to Arizona before she was old enough to have any memory of New York bagels or Prospect Park jaunts. So she is a West Coast girl to me.

College was like a snow globe. Four years contained under a rigid, shiny dome, and everything that mattered was protected underneath its translucent exterior. The first three years we were so high off each other's company, so drunk on adolescent glee and vodka lemonades and acting adultlike that we didn't discuss what would happen after graduation. We hardly considered the day we'd wake up in different homes, in different lives, in different cities, or different states. Maybe we thought it would never happen. Maybe we were avoiding the possibility that we'd move in different directions after graduating. I can't say for sure. Nobody ever told me what would happen to my relationships when the snow globe shattered and spilled me out into the real world. They just reminded me over and over and over again that this was the best four years of my life.

In the fall of our senior year, she accepted a job in California. I had never been to California, having spent my entire life on the East Coast. California felt like another dimension—another world—and even its name felt too big, too clunky in my mouth. The outer edges of each syllable were sharp and biting and foreign. After she fell asleep the night she accepted the job, I decorated her bedroom door with streamers and a silver banner that read CONGRATS! I even put a little gift at her door. It was midnight, and I was moving silently, considering what it'd be like to maintain our relationship over miles and time zones and everything else. I didn't yet know where I'd end up after graduation, but California wasn't even an option. I didn't know anyone who lived in California before college.

Our other roommates were making plans in tandem. One would move to Chicago for a job at a fancy bank. The other would stay in Michigan for med school. Two would move to New York City. One would teach at a school in Brooklyn, and the other would work for a different fancy bank. Six girls under the same roof, booking flights to cities on opposite ends of the country so they could begin their lives. Packing bags in our dilapidated college house that we'd unpack in a new apartment, somewhere else. I didn't want to stay in college forever, and felt like I'd be ready to move on when the time came—but the moving on, the spreading out, the expanding of our wings seemed so daunting, so heavy, so heartbreaking. It was an inevitable that felt like a wound that needed a little more time to heal.

•

On March 11, 2020, I decided I'd be moving to New York City to attend Columbia University's journalism masters program. When I told Sadie I'd been accepted, she screamed, folded me into her arms, and then we jumped up and down in excitement until we were both sobbing into each other's hair—the gravity of what New York meant for me settling around us. Over 2,500 miles would stretch between the two of us, when we'd spent nearly half a decade with no more than one mile of space between us at any given time. It was sobering. It was cunning. It was easier to just avoid the thought of it.

It was a Friday night, and celebrations were in order—as was our second semester senior year routine of weekend partying. Sadie sat on the floor of my attic bedroom to do her makeup, like she did every weekend night, but neither of us had any idea this was the last time we'd ever do that for the rest of our lives. It was always the same routine: I'd straighten my hair, standing at the full-length mirror next to my bed while she sat with her feet tucked under her, on the ground, doing her makeup with a combination of her makeup and my makeup. We'd listen to a playlist exclusively of Chelsea Cutler, Taylor Swift, and Halsey. Then I'd make us vodka lemonades and we'd swap—Sadie would straighten her hair at the full-length mirror, and I'd sit on the ground and do my makeup. Once we were done with hair and makeup, I'd make us another vodka lemonade, then we'd sort through each other's closet, pick our outfits, and meet the other four girls we lived with in the living room for the pregame.

This is not only one of my favorite depictions of girlhood—getting ready side by side, lip products and hair tools crowding the already-too-small sink or vanity or desk. It was religious, it was sacred, it was so seemingly mundane and so inherently meaningful simultaneously. And I am much more careful with the memory of it now than I was in the moment. I took it for granted.

That particular day, March 11, we were midway through our getting-ready ritual when we received an email from the university canceling our graduation and all of our remaining in-person classes due to a foreign virus that is now all too familiar: COVID-19. Our plans for the remainder of the semester came undone as the six of us pivoted from end-of-college celebrations to packing our bedrooms up three months prematurely and going home. For the twelve-hour drive between Ann Arbor and New Jersey, I pondered the idea of home and how we could all be booted so swiftly from a place sold, advertised, and presented to us as home before it was time to go. May would've arrived eventually. Graduation would've happened someday. We just never thought we'd pass the day in our childhood bedrooms and not doing our makeup on my attic bedroom floor.

In many ways, the class of 2020 experienced a transition from college to the real world that mimicked ripping off a Band-Aid—no pomp and circumstance, graduation traditions, or senior week to stamp the end of one chapter and ease us gently into the next. The high dive was the only option. There were no metaphorical hands to hold. No time spent processing the goodbyes that would inevitably come. It just happened.

The growing up, growing apart, moving away part of our lives, a part of life that comes for everyone, happened prematurely—like a snowfall in the middle of September or a beach day in early May. Sadie and I said goodbye two days after the announcement came that we'd have to leave campus if we were able. She fled to Arizona, and I drove to New Jersey. We wouldn't see each other without the help of a FaceTime call for eight months.

•

Though the class of 2020 had a sudden, precipitous nosedive into the adult world, every young person transitioning from the educational system they've been familiar with for the prior twelve to sixteen years to the adult world will feel a series of shifts and growing pains. Many of these pains we've discussed so far. Some of these will come in the form of our relationships, be it our friendships, familial relationships, or romantic relationships.

Some of these will be in the form of our hometowns, childhood bedrooms, college towns, and more. The idea of growing away from our loved ones, physically or emotionally, simply because we've made the decisions best suited for our own lives is harrowing and intense in a really emotional, human way. Obviously, people move away from their families and friends in order to move toward themselves, but I never really considered what it would feel like if that ever happened to me. I didn't know to expect this shift. I didn't prepare myself for the slightly stale guilt and acrid sadness that would accompany growing away from my loved ones. Not apart from them, but away from them. They were still mine, I just didn't have my eyes on them anymore like I once had. In many ways, I don't have anyone to really blame for my lack of preparation for such an emotional part of adulthood either. The idea of moving back to or near one's hometown, or spending the majority of one's life there, is becoming less and less common.

For women, not only do we have increased opportunity in terms of our careers, we have increased mobility and increased methods of family planning (including scientific breakthroughs like egg freezing). It wasn't until the late aughts that laws like the Lilly Ledbetter Fair Pay Act were introduced, further enforcing and strengthening antidiscrimination laws for gender-based discrimination and penalties for violators. According to the US Census Bureau, there's been a 25.6 percent increase in women working full-time since 2000. It is important to note that this figure may partially reflect the need for women to commit to full-time work as the cost of living has increased, but simultaneously we cannot deny that increased opportunity for women has also led to said increase. With this in mind, there has been a larger influx of women moving to cities they've never lived in or been to for job or education opportunities. At the same time, this means our friend circles are bound to be spread out around the country (and oftentimes even the world) as our friends set roots down in cities far, far away from the cities we land in, or where they are originally from.

Sadie made the decision in October 2020 to abandon her California plans and move to Chicago full-time. Selfishly, I was overjoyed, considering Chicago is far more centrally located than California. She moved into a giant penthouse apartment with one of our friends from college, Alyssa. I seized with envy when she FaceTimed me to walk me through her new digs, showing off their bar cart and pretty wall art and other girlie decorations in their new, spacious home, which was half the cost of the walk-up I was living in (a windowless bedroom, with three roommates, one bathroom, and a guinea pig, no less). I had yet to visit Chicago due to pandemic restrictions, and we were keeping up our relationship on FaceTime calls and text messages alone—a far cry from being nearly attached at the hip a year prior.

One night, after getting ready for a date on her own bedroom floor, Sadie called me from the back seat of an Uber. I was doomscrolling on Twitter in bed on the Upper West Side, considering whether or not it was worth it to get up and go grab a drink with a guy from Hinge who very likely wouldn't become the next love of my life. I sparkled at her name on my phone and quickly answered.

"I'm on my way to a first date right now," she said, her voice pitching up with nerves.

"What the FUCK, why didn't you TELL ME?" I gawked, a bit of separation anxiety settling into my chest. What else did I not know about her cool new life in Chicago? Were we slipping through each other's fingers? Was there any way we could truly keep up what we had over miles and time differences and totally severed lives?

"Dude, I don't even know if I should go. I'm, like, second-guessing it," she said, ignoring my concerns and getting to the point.

"What? Why? You're already on the way there," I said, wishing I were there to get ready with her. Wishing I could have planned a date on the same night, in the same city. Wishing we were somehow bound at the hip again.

"I don't know, I don't know if I, like, want a boyfriend. I just don't know," she replied, being quintessentially Sagittarius and overwhelmingly independent (as she always is).

"Don't waste your time on anything you don't feel like doing," I said.

"Okay but, like, I'm already on the way there. Can I even cancel right now?" she asked.

I considered. "Just go. You're already on the way there, just have a free dinner, and if it sucks, it sucks. Who knows," I suggested, imagining her midpanic in the back of a Honda Odyssey, pulling her hair back and fanning her face with a blue-manicured hand.

"Okay, okay. I'm about to be there. And you're the only person I told. Like, I didn't even tell Alyssa—I just left. So I'll call you after," she said, and she began advising the Uber driver on where to pull over.

You're the only person I told. Her secret is safe with me. It always has been. Always will be. She lives with that guy now. He pokes fun at me for almost advising her not to go on the date. We're both really glad she did.

Sitting on my bedspread, staring at the ceiling, I considered how out of order and strange it felt—to be hearing when she was already on the way there about a first date she'd planned, and not because we had spent an hour rummaging through her closet together, picking out exactly what she would wear. Having to assess his Hinge profile via screenshots, and not because she passed me her phone and let me scroll myself. There was space between us now. I was a grad student in New York City describing my new friends to her over the phone. I was trading stories of nights spent with Lizzie for her nights with Alyssa. We weren't replacing each other. We weren't angry. We were straining against the reality that we no longer lived in the same city. When it was two p.m. for me, it was one p.m. for her. We no longer traded dull details of the day when we convened in the living room each night. We heard an abridged version of a week over the phone when we had time to spare. I felt like I didn't have time to spare anymore. It had been so much easier when we could knock on each other's door. When we weren't a missed call or an "i miss you" text, but a "How was your day?"—face-to-face.

Daphne was in London. And she'd been in London for a few years, so I was used to the ocean between us. But I missed being seventeen years old with her. Jen lived in a Hell's Kitchen studio apartment. I had met her two weeks prior. Isabela lived down the street, but we didn't know it at the time. Lizzie was trying to figure out what was next for her. Anna moved back home. We all make our beds in foreign cities, plane rides away from one another. We spread out and try our best. We comment on one another's Instagram posts and pretend everything feels normal. We go to our yoga classes and awkwardly grab coffee with a person we're hoping we can make a friend. And I feel alone in New York. I don't know whom I can trust. I don't know how many times a day it is appropriate to text your long-distance best friend. We're all choosing what's best for our future, and no two futures are identical, so we have slowly melted away from one another. It is a physical distance first, but naturally there is an emotional distance as well. Living hundreds of miles from your best friend is different from living down the hall from her. Even if you talk every day. Even if you're hell-bent on nothing changing. Nobody allows us the time and the space to process growing up and growing apart. Our to-do lists are crowded with more tasks as the days turn to weeks, which fade into year over year. We are so busy, so booked, so impossible to track down, that there is no time, really, to let ourselves sit in the reality of growing apart. I hope these pages can serve as our time, albeit brief, to do so together.

Because things will change. Friendships will end up a memory because the tides of life take a girl you used to know everything about east, and you west. You will keep up with her via Instagram. You will see her for a happy hour drink when she is in town. You will talk to the people who matter most to you every day because you will commit to making it work. You cannot stay where you are. You cannot drill your feet to the floor. Things will change because they have to.

But that doesn't have to mean they will be worse.

•

Daphne moved to London when I was nineteen years old. I had to use my imagination and fill in the blanks about her life for four years, because I wasn't able to visit her until I was twenty-three. I didn't think she was serious about moving to London until she boarded the plane. I never had a friend move that far away before. I never resented her for moving. Our bond was so seamless, so natural, so without forks in the road—it just felt like we'd be fine either way. Whether she lived in New Jersey or Connecticut or London. Surely with a time difference of that size and two lives happening so far from each other—a classic American college experience and a classic teenage expat experience—we missed each other every now and then. I don't know what stopped me from being scared I'd lose her. I think it's that she is just so unbelievably sure of everything, at all times—and I trusted she'd be sure of this too. We'd be fine. And we were.

No matter how fine you are, though, the reality is that your best friend is creating a life far away from you, without you involved, in person, on a daily basis. And at some point, your homeostasis was knowing everything about their day-to-day.

It is factually accurate that it is easier to maintain a friendship when you get to see the person a few times a week or even every day than when you don't see them at all. Inherently, often, the person you are the closest to at any given time will be the one you get to see all the time. So although I never doubted that Daphne and I could handle a five-hour time difference and a seven-hour flight between us, I still felt a twinge of heat and emotion whenever I got new details of the life she was building a world away. New friends, new phrases she used (like *flat*, instead of *apartment*), new favorite restaurants and coffee orders. My best friend going out to claim, discover, and hone the best version of her life was at once the biggest heart surge and heartbreak of my life. She hadn't left me behind, because in many ways, I was going after the same things—just doing them for myself.

There is a myth, one that intensifies in young adulthood, that you cannot be friends with people who are not in the same boat as you, who are not sleeping under the same stars or going through identical motions. As high school students and higher education students, we were navigating, for the most part, similar experiences to our friends. It is uncomfortable to be released from that communal, uniform, and parallel experience to an open-ended, unrestricted field of options and paths for one's life. We sell people the idea that if they are pregnant, it is mandatory that all their friends also be pregnant people or mothers. Or if we are in a relationship, we must have friends who are also in relationships, and if we are single, our friends should be single.

Certainly it is comforting, comfortable, and necessary to have friends who can share in your misery and joy—who can understand exactly what you are going through because they too are going through a similar thing. Mothers should have friends who are mothers. Single people should have friends who are single. But you do not need to be in the same boat as all of your friends to cultivate, maintain, and enjoy meaningful, long-term relationships. It is natural to gravitate toward people who can relate to a transition you're experiencing, or a common life milestone—but you do not need to be experiencing the same emotions or living a similar life to someone to be their friend or to have a deep connection. It is a beautiful thing to split a bottle of wine across the table from someone, have them unpack their week in front of you before allowing you the space to unpack yours, and realize that while nothing you brought out into the conversation looks the same, something still is—you want to listen, and you are there for her. She is there for you too.

I am all too familiar with the idea that women, specifically, will ditch their friends when they find themselves in a new romantic relationship. And while I do believe that there are certainly circumstances wherein our friends will get into romantic relationships and entirely abandon their friends and leave any sense of platonic community behind, I do think we need to be realistic about these types of situations—especially when we experience them in our adult lives. If your friend completely abandons you when she gets into a new relationship—I want you to give her one honest attempt to fix it, by telling her you miss her and are so happy for her, and also want to see her more. If she does not take this gentle reminder as an action item—and things don't get better—then you need to make a decision for yourself as to whether or not you'd like to continue to hone this friendship in your adult life. However, we also need to understand that naturally, if you were to get into a romantic relationship today, you're going to have less time for your friends than you did before—or less time in general for other areas of your life, because you've introduced an entirely new relationship dynamic that you will want to water and give your energy to. There is a way to prioritize your romantic relationship while also maintaining your friendships. Of course your friendships may shift a bit, as your friends introduce romantic partners into the mix and start building joint lives with said partners, but that doesn't mean it has to get worse. When I first met and started dating Noah, I made sure to consistently make my friends feel special, show up to the majority of the plans they instigated, and continuously instigate plans myself. I made sure to be mindful about checking in, about making them feel just as special as I sought to make Noah feel—because they matter. Because I can prioritize more than one person and more than one area in my life. Now that I am really making plans for the future with Noah—ones that will hopefully involve getting married and starting a family—I know how important it is for him to be a priority. I completely understand if I may see my friends a little less once they introduce a romantic partner into their life—as long as we are able to continue to give one another the time and energy we need (even if it isn't as much as we had before). These are nuanced topics and challenging life shifts—but I do believe there is a way to prioritize both your friends and your romantic partner. I do believe we need to be understanding and gentle with our friends when they inevitably have less time to spend together. And I do think we need to be okay with the fact that our friendships will change. And change can be uncomfortable. And change can cause friendships to end too.

Sometimes we change in the same direction as our friends; sometimes we change in entirely different directions. Sometimes we change in opposite directions and find our way back to one another. The way we show up for one another, the way we spend time together, and our relationships in general will, inevitably, change as we do. That is okay. It is all we can do to cherish each and every moment we have in the here and now, in this chapter with our friends, because one day the page will turn. Things will be different. We will grow nostalgic for the memories we put the time and the love in to create and to hold.

After moving out from the apartment I'd lived in with Lizzie, we drifted from each other a little bit.

It was a natural drift, a current inevitably pulling us in different directions. We had different schedules. Different groups of friends here or there. Our weekly text check-ins slowly faded to biweekly, and then monthly. Then we were surprised to hear from each other much at all. It went on like this for over a year. I still loved Lizzie. My love for her never went anywhere. In fact, in the absence of seeing her often, of hearing from her every day, I feel it amplified. She crossed my mind regularly, and I felt that on the other end of the rope that was our friendship, she was still holding on, that we'd find our way back together.

Lizzie is gentle. She is also fierce. She is a spectrum of sentimentality and artistic prowess and emotions she wears upfront, like a bold sweater or a graphic T-shirt. In our college years, Lizzie and I moved our own emotional mountains with help from each other, navigated showing up for ourselves and each other, spent hours crafting texts to crushes and planning evenings out. She was someone I needed so desperately, whom

I didn't even realize I needed until she was already mine. I didn't even realize how desperately I needed her until we slipped from each other's lives, before getting back up and walking back home.

In May of 2023, I had an extra ticket to the Broadway show *Life of Pi* and I decided to ask Lizzie to come with me. Time had passed, we had both grown and changed as individuals, and I missed her. We made plans and we didn't discuss, over text, the distance and space that had amassed between us since the last time we saw each other or spoke. We hugged and got drinks and talked about how much we missed each other and attempted to catch up on a year of our individual lore before the house lights dimmed. After the show, in our respective taxis, she called me. She said her Uber driver had been blabbering on and on and on about the meaning of friendship and the importance of finding and maintaining true friends. She relayed the story, telling me she was thinking of me.

"Being with you tonight made me feel like myself again," Lizzie said, and I could feel the emotion behind each syllable, because I felt exactly the same. Being with Lizzie felt like being the best version of myself.

We had grown apart. We had grown as individuals. We hardly saw each other for a year. But like two magnets vibrating across opposite ends of twinkly Manhattan, we found our way back together. At a time where I needed her. At a time where she needed me. I talk to Lizzie every day now. Missing her was enough to realize how permanent I want her place in my life to be. Friendship is complicated like that sometimes. Sometimes you do slip from someone's grip just to reach back out for it again.

I often spent so much time worrying about how people in my life would react to me choosing my own version of happiness, or claiming my own best life, and I would make decisions that I believed they would want me to make over the decisions I wanted to make for myself. At the end of the day, you are the only main character in your story, and you're not the main character of anyone else's. The people who deserve you—the people whom you deserve, the people you are lucky enough to have in your life who are lucky enough to have you in theirs—will CELEBRATE you for going out to claim your own version of happiness. Even if it isn't the same decision they would have made. Even if it isn't their own version of happiness.

It is through the example of a friend like Lizzie that I now understand that it is possible to grow up, grow apart, and even grow away from our friends, to make decisions for ourselves that mimic the best version of our lives while simultaneously preserving those friendships. It is through the example of a friend like Lizzie that I now realize that the friends you want in your life will celebrate you for claiming your own best life, even if it isn't like theirs.

Maybe you know this. Maybe you're struggling through this now—asking yourself if it is possible to maintain friendship with someone who is living their life in a way that is drastically different from the way you are. Maybe your best friend moved to Spain to find themselves, and you wished they could find themselves in Miami, down the hall from you. To love someone is to allow them the space, the grace, and the encouragement to grow.

Here's the truth—everything is temporary and no two lives will ever be lived the same way. So if you were to discard every friend who isn't living their life like you are in favor of those who relate to you all the time, eventually you'll have to discard those friends in pursuit of different people who relate to you all the time. Because we change. Because everything is temporary. Because you will not relate to someone consistently, every single day, for the rest of your entire life.

Your friendship to someone should not be contingent on whether or not you relate to each other directly right now in this current moment. In order to preserve your friendships, in order to have long-term friendships, you must be willing to understand that you will have to meet one another where you are—even if it is the other side of the world—even if you aren't always on the exact same page. Of course it is a case-by-case basis, and this time in your life will see you float toward some people and grow apart from others, perhaps because you no longer can relate to one another or perhaps just because.

But what I'm trying to explain is that there are no stages to life. There is nobody tracking your progress against an arbitrary list of milestones you must reach. There is you and there is me. There is your life and how you'd like to live it. My most meaningful platonic relationships are with people who differ greatly from me and perhaps live their lives in different ways or in different spaces, but who most importantly align on the things that matter. One of these being our mutual willingness to work to keep the spark of our friendship alive.

•

I am twenty-four years old, and I am on a flight to visit Daphne in London. This trip marks the third time I have visited her since she moved. I have my own coffee order at her favorite coffee shop, Gail's. I have my own favorite SoulCycle instructor at the studio where she spins. I have my own inside jokes with her two dozen friends (because she is nothing if not the most amiable Leo alive). I have my own favorite restaurants in her neighborhood. My own favorite traditions to re-create whenever I set foot into the place she has spent so much time making her home. I think she will be there forever, and I am okay with this. I would do anything to be seventeen years old for just a day, so I could roll by her house in my car and shout out the window for her to come outside. So we could just drive to nowhere, as we did so many times, meandering and talking and singing along to a playlist we made together.

But what's so much better than being seventeen years old and living down the street from my Daphne is knowing that she is the happiest she could ever be in her flat in Notting Hill. It became clear to me the very first time I visited her, the first time I'd been to London. She was so excited to hold my hand and parade me around to all of her favorites, to introduce me proudly to every friend who already knew so much about me because she never shuts up about me just like I never shut up about her. Nobody could ever take my place when it came to her. Nobody could take her place when it came to me. We were so secure in this, so deeply rooted in it. So infatuated by what it meant to be each other's best friend—there was no competition, no pettiness, no resentment of moving far away or building a life somewhere else. There was just the pride and the thrill of bringing each other into this somewhere else. Of course she made new best friends too. Girls from all over the world, in fact. But because we are so intentional about what we mean to each other, it is not threatening when one of us introduces a new person into our lives—instead, it is a beautiful thing. How lucky is that person to get to love Daphne? How lucky is that person to get to have a piece of her pie, to bask in her shimmery light? I know how it feels to be loved by her—why would I want anything other than for other people to get to experience the same thing? If you find it to feel threatening when one of your friends makes a new friend, I implore you to ask yourself if this friend is truly acting in a way that is threatening to your friendship *or* if you feel insecure in the relationship.

Of course sometimes it is the former, in which case I would say this person isn't a friend worth having. But oftentimes it is the latter. It is a beautiful thing to meet wonderful people whom you feel a connection to and want to spend time with just because they are them. We should encourage our friends when they find people who make them feel alive, to water those seeds. We should want our friends to live the fullest, most connected lives they can. We should hope they want the same for us. To be a good friend, we must encourage our friends to make their lives as colorful and shimmery as possible, while holding space for them in our own. It is the best-case scenario when a friend does the same for you.

Isabela—the sweet, quirky girl who called me three years ago to tell me my ex-boyfriend was engaged—is the fastest friend I have ever called "best." From the minute we first met up, we just both sort of realized we were going to be in each other's lives for a very long time. I don't remember having a gut instinct like this in my adult life before. She fit so naturally by my side, and I by hers. This year, on Daphne's birthday, Isabela was seated at her birthday dinner in between Daphne and me. They made jokes to each other because they are close like that. They spoke in depth about books they recommended to each other because they have similar tastes. I was struck with such sentimentality—such gratitude—that Daphne encouraged me to prioritize Isabela in my life, and that Isabela immediately valued Daphne as a friend of her own.

I have good people. I know good people. I love good people. It wasn't always this way, and it didn't happen overnight. I have never worked more diligently and cared more passionately about anything. Like any relationship, friendship requires work, energy, and time in order to maintain. And I am not a perfect friend. Nobody is. And it hasn't always been this good, and this bright and this reassuring.

And these friendships will change. And it will be okay when they change. It might be sad. It might be for the best. I will lean on my loved ones like pillars. I will be a statue to lean on when they need me. I will accept that this is my reality—that 100 percent security is impossible—that I cannot control and manage other people; I can only control and manage my reactions to those people. And it is in my best interest to recognize that I may have two hundred friends throughout my entire life—and not all of them will be forever friends. And that is okay. What a gift to love anyway—not knowing if we will all be forever. What a gift to carve a place for someone in your heart, even if that space won't always be theirs.

•

My younger brothers are not the ten-year-old little boys they once were. They live with their partners, and they have real jobs, and they are not just building robots in my parents' garage or annoying each other like they once did. They are adults. With lives of their own. And inevitably, as they've grown, I've had the privilege of growing with them. I've had the privilege of our relationship changing. It is the biggest gift of my life to watch my siblings grow into the people they've always wanted to be—to delight at life's surprises, to find and keep and hold love. It is also bittersweet. I have always been their older sister. Always will be their older sister. And what that role means has changed as they've turned twenty and then twenty-two and then twenty-four. I linger on our goodbyes and make sure they know I am proud of them. I still see them as the kids they once were, but I marvel at the people they have become. And as we have all found our respective partners and taken next steps in our romantic relationships—I've realized that we have more change to encounter yet. The idea of "family" is ever in flux and is something to be defined by each individual person, being that sometimes, our family is not whom we are biologically related to, but is chosen. When I think of my family now, I think of my brothers and my parents. One day, when I think of my family, it will be with my future partner and the children we have together. Nobody prepared me for what it feels like to see that on the horizon, to watch as decade-long traditions have to fold in order for new ones to pop up. I want to hold on to the *we* that we are today forever, and yet I know that I will feel the same way about the traditions I create with children of my own one day.

I hold on to this: We are always changing. Always growing. I will miss these moments when I am gone and other beautiful, sparkling moments have taken their place. I will feel it all. I will feel grateful for it all.

•

This time in our lives can be lonely. Isolating. You can feel like you are in the middle of nowhere, with no maps and nowhere to turn. Nowhere to run. I have been you. At the party, surrounded by twenty shining faces, sparkling hearts and minds who I know love me, whom I love back. And deep within my soul, like a peach pit growing in my stomach, I have felt so deeply, so intimately, alone. Alone in my struggles, alone in my open-ended thoughts, alone in the way my mind has blossomed and expanded and formed into something new. Alone in a crowded room. Looking at him, looking at her, and wondering, *Is there any way they feel as shitty as I do? Is there any way they feel so alone?*

Sometimes I succumb to this story, this lie, that I am on an island of one. I am on an island never discovered. I am on an island where we never talk about what hurts. We never talk about what scares us. We never talk about what's real. Because everyone has their shit together—right? Because everyone feels seen and heard and valued, except me, right?

I do not know. I do not know whom I relate to. I do not know whom I can reach out to. I do not know whose hands I can hold and say, "Wow. You get me. You really get me." I am a worn-out girl. I am a tired girl. I have been through too much and I have been through nothing. My thoughts are hunting me. They are chasing me. I just want to be free. I just want to feel seen. I just want my friends to drill their feet to the floor. I just want to cry into her hair like I did the night we found out we'd be moving so far, far away from each other. I want this moment to never end. And I want to repeat what has been, and I want to fast-forward, and I . . . don't know what I want. I don't know what I want.

I just want us to all stay friends forever. I know we won't. I know a door closes so another can open. I know this, and I feel nonetheless. But isn't it good to feel? I think it's a good thing to feel.

•

I am getting ready to go meet a group of friends for dinner. I haven't seen them in a while. I am getting mascara on my upper eyelid as I try my best to do just the opposite. I didn't want to go. I could hardly peel myself out of bed, and I almost canceled, but I didn't. Because you always feel better when you see your friends, I remind myself. You always feel better when you see your friends.

I take the subway to the restaurant, and there's this crushing dread following me there. Right down the tracks, straight to the restaurant. That it won't always be like this. That we won't always live right down the street. That plans won't always be this impromptu, that we won't always be twenty-five.

But I know I will adjust. Just like I did when Sadie and I moved away from each other. Just like I did with Daphne. I need to hold so tightly to the now that my knuckles get white. I need to squeeze all the life out of today.

Because around the dinner table we will order a round of drinks. One of us will order an espresso martini and then everyone else will follow suit, because that's how it always works with espresso martinis. Then someone will break the thick layer of ice, our jokes and our banter, our giggles and our gossip, and they will say they're scared. They got laid off. Their partner isn't giving them the love they deserve. I have a sick parent. You have a brother who is going through it. We have no idea how we're going to do this. And the waiter brings our food, and we move on to talking about our weekends, our plans for the rest of the month, our friends who couldn't make it, pop culture, or politics. And then someone will say they've been depressed. Someone else is swimming through a swamp of grief, and they will say they are sorry when they start to cry. And I reach out across the table and hold their hand, adorned by so many pretty rings and a small tattoo, and I will love them so much I'll wish it were me hurting and not them. We will lament. We will bitch and moan and laugh and pay the bill. I will tell a secret I've never told anyone. We will linger after we've paid. We will get up and go our separate ways.

On the subway home, I will sigh relief out my nose and ears and mouth. I will exist as relief. I am relief. I am relieved. Because I am not alone. I have these beams of light shining on me. All across the city, all across the country, all across the world. I have friends who are going through it too. And it is enough to tell someone exactly how you're feeling and to hear them say, "I'm sorry" or "I know how you feel." It is quintessentially midtwenties to pour your existential crisis on the dinner table like a spilled cocktail and have everyone sop it up with their lap napkins because they care.

It is human to want to share. It is human to be scared to share. But what I've realized from having and being a friend, and having and being a mess, in my twenties—we are all going through something. The least you can do is speak about it to people who love you.

And how lucky I am that I love Daphne so much I sobbed as I wrote about her rhetorical digs and silly attitude. How blessed I am to hold memories of Sadie with her carefree persona and blue eyes right near my heart. How insanely fortunate I am to have all these people I can call when I need to have dinner with someone across a table and just connect, when I need a friend. Even if I don't know if we will always be friends, even if I can't predict the future. All I have is today. And I will live. And I will love. And I will be okay.

I will walk across the earth for the women who have done the same for me—however momentary, however brief the way we saw each other may have been. I am just lucky to have been in your presence. I hope you feel the same about mine.

Does Anyone Else Feel Like They're in a Funk?

Are you there God? It's me—Eli.

Well, I don't know if you're there because I don't know if you're real. I want you to be real. Because these days I need something to believe in. I don't know if I'm real. I look in the mirror, and I can't tell what I look like anymore. My features are far from a nose and a pair of eyes; they are an endless to-do list of how to be better-looking. This is the youngest I'll ever be. Why can't I appreciate that? Why can't I just live? Everyone is having the best time ever on Instagram, and I am having the worst time ever at the OB-GYN. I am scared. I am failing at being twenty-five. I hear things get better at thirty. I don't know if I want to press fast-forward or rewind.

I want to pause. I need to pause. I can't pause. There's more to do. There's always more to do. It is my mom's birthday. I have to take care of that because I have to take care of her. I take care of everything. I take things apart and fix what's inside and put them back together. I anticipate their needs. And it is about time for my mental breakdown. I called the paramedics on myself last night because I was having a panic attack. But I was sure I was dying. I was sure I was dying. I feel like a fool now. In the shower, I think about their faces and their features, things I will one day forget. Better sooner than later. My mind is occupied with something else already. Something about tomorrow. I feel like a freak.

Every day is sardonic. Every night is peace and then hell. Next week I will wear a dress I actually like and will feel like a queen for three hours. But that will go away because it always does. And then I will get home from the function, and my ears will ring from the music, and I'll wonder what the point is. When I'll settle down. When I'll stop feeling like I'm in fight-or-flight all the time. There are bricks sitting on my chest. There is an elephant in every room I'm in, and that elephant is me. Except I am not large and all-consuming. I am nothing. I am the wallpaper and the walls. I am the smoke fading into the mirrors. I just want to be a girl who likes herself and knows what's going on. I am stuck.

I am weird. Misshapen. The internet tells me to change everything about my face. I change some things about my face, and then I feel awful for doing it, but also hungry to do it again and again and again. The world tells little girls they are ugly from the time they are old enough to understand what the word means. I spent all day doomscrolling and spent all night regretting it. I am in a funk, and I am stuck to the floor. My limbs are heavy, and they won't move. I just want to wake up. I just want to claw my way out.

•

I'm in a funk. I miss myself. I miss my sparkle. I'm stuck in my routine. How do I break free?

I am in my midtwenties, so all of my friends and I are in a funk. We ebb in and out of funks and in and out of shitty routines and in and out of fight-or-flight. We never relax. It feels like we can't. The excitement of college and adolescence faded quickly into rigid days that begin at nine a.m. and then begin again at five p.m. We sit around a table at six p.m. for dinner on a Wednesday. It is 2021, and we've rushed from our office buildings and meetings and other obligations to be around one table for once, a moment of exhale. To forget about everything we don't want to do that we have to do. To share a bottle of wine. To take turns talking about our bosses (whom we hate) and our jobs (which we put up with) and our dating lives (which are messy) and how much we love one another (all we have). One of us has sworn off dating. Another just met some guy in a wine bar I've never been to and probably will never go to because there are too many wine bars and not enough weekend nights.

"I'm not depressed, I just hate my life," one of them says. And we laugh because it is funny. Because it is relatable. And we tip our glasses of wine back into our pink mouths and we keep laughing and we order more wine. Because what is there to do anymore but laugh about how lost at sea we all feel? And then one of my friends starts crying because she feels stuck. And we all comfort her with our little words and things we have to look forward to and love and love and love, but we all feel this underlying pool of dread because we all know that feeling stuck is an inevitability in this chapter. *Isn't it?* We don't really know what we know and what we don't. We just know we feel stuck, that the days are fading one into the next, into the next, and everything feels the same.

I go home after our dinner and lay out my ugly outfit for the next day at work. I pack my gym bag, and I brush my teeth, and tears prick at my eyes as I do. I am not miserable. I like my life enough. It just feels like Groundhog Day each morning, and I wonder if that dust will ever settle but I see no way out. *Is this what it is?* I thought, while I wait for a text back from my very new boyfriend and wonder if he thinks I'm boring. I try to recover before bed by telling myself it could be far worse than it is. But tomorrow I will do the same thing I did the day before. And I stare up at the ceiling and I wonder if I am wasting my one and only chance at living on this job I hate and this routine that feels like a chore.

I can't sleep. I listen to my neighbors fight next door because we share a wall. It is comforting to know all of us are just doing our best. Just feeling what there is to feel. Cycling into and out of regret and remorse and celebration and then back to the drawing board. Their voices are so recognizable to me, and so is their pain. They know nothing about me. I try not to grab for my phone in the middle of the night when I'm unable to sleep because doesn't everyone always say that's what you're supposed to do? Stay off your phone? I think I read that on the internet. How fitting.

It gets to be too late. Even my neighbors surrender their argument to exhaustion. I have earned my phone, so I grab for it and open up the notes app to a fresh page. It is 4:01 a.m., May 27, 2021. I save all the notes in my iPhone notes app. I can never get rid of my fleeting thoughts. Can never break up with my foregone feelings. They're all a part of me.

> I don't want to live a boring life. It sounds so dumb but I need to live a life like the ones I read about and have read about. I think I just have to move abroad when I'm 24 or 25 so I need to start saving money for that now and once I get where I want to be I'll get a job but I need to have experiences that I can write about. I'm just so sad today.

That's what I wrote. And then I put my phone at my bedside and finally went to sleep.

After floating through the following days—morning workouts fading into conference rooms in beige office buildings with the air-conditioning far too high, collapsing into subway rides home, making the same dinners, texting the same people—something woke me up. A girl whom I was mutual with on TikTok had been diagnosed with cancer. She passed away. This had happened a few months prior, and her friends and family were sharing content she had archived over the months since her diagnosis that she wanted shared after she was gone. And the video on my For You page that afternoon was just her in the car with the world's brightest smile and sparkly eyes, belting Taylor Swift's "All Too Well (10 Minute Version) (Taylor's Version) (From The Vault)" at the top of her lungs. This was a person who knew she only had a few months left. This was a person who hadn't given up even when the doctors around her told her to. This was a person who, despite her incredibly heavy, incredibly monumental set of circumstances, and her incredibly shitty hand of cards, was smiling. Was laughing. Was gripping onto her joy as tightly as she could and holding it close to her heart. Sure, I don't know what her life and mental health looked like then, outside of sixty-second clips on TikTok. But I do know that despite all the hardship she was faced with, she chose to present joy and giddiness to the world. Meanwhile, with my health intact and my opportunities stretched out before me, all I could find the energy to do was mope and complain. To be stuck in a sticky funk.

Of course we can have bad moments. Of course we can fall into funks. Of course we can find ourselves thrust into moments of melancholy—even when our circumstances are good. Even when life is going well. I am not suggesting that you cannot be sad. Cannot feel depressed. Cannot feel stuck. I am not suggesting that you need a life-altering diagnosis or a terrible set of circumstances to feel pain. You can feel pain on a random Tuesday for no reason at all. You can feel pain even when the sky is cloudless and you are surrounded by all of your favorite people. Comparing two struggles is pointless and energy draining, and doesn't make either suck less, even if one happens to suck more. You'd never tell someone with a broken arm not to go to the hospital because they don't have a life-threatening illness. We shouldn't do this for our mental battles and emotional struggles either. But that doesn't mean we cannot understand that broken arms can suck and can hurt. But they can also heal. You can heal.

In my routine that I had chosen (despite the fact that it was the only job that offered me a position, I'd still chosen it, to apply, to accept), in my day-to-day that I crafted for myself, in MY own routine, I was miserable. I was not depressed—I was just lost—but I was choosing, daily, to continue down this rabbit hole of misery. This was a life that I created for myself. Therefore, in many ways, I had created this funk for myself. And I want to make it known that I am speaking to a simple funk, or a period of unhappiness—not medical issues such as clinical depression or other mental health disorders, which do require treatment by a mental health professional. I had gotten myself into a funk. And I had accepted it as my reality and decided to drown myself in this sardonic, shitty pool of hopelessness. Meanwhile, a beautiful girl with such tragic news resting on her shoulders about her own fate could find a small pocket of joy.

She reminded me that I could too.

•

I understand that for some, a simple TikTok video is not enough of a spark to get your engine reinvigorated, but I always try to look for signs everywhere—even in my doomscrolls. Ways I can learn, ways I can feel inspired, new ideas, and now I was determined to build a life for myself that I liked. A life for myself that sparked joy. A life for myself in which I was not doing anything (other than what was necessary) that I didn't want to do. Outside of a funk or a boring, monotonous routine, there was a chance for me to actually enjoy my days. And it was really only up to me to make sure it could happen. Outside of a portion of my day, writing about insurance news, staring at the clock (or occasionally my boss's feet, as he insisted on wearing flip-flops to the office . . . every day), I had the chance to live. I had been waiting to live at that point. Waiting until I could move on to a different job, waiting to find more time for myself, waiting to find more time for joy. Waiting. I was waiting for life to happen to me. And sometimes life does happen to you, but other times you need to get up and go to the gas station and fill up your tank. This girl on TikTok, whose life was so tragically taken from her, didn't have the time to wait around. She just had to live. You cannot waste your own life waiting for it to begin. Waiting for it to be joyful. Waiting for it to be exciting. Sometimes it is up to you to make it all of those things.

The first thing I needed was a game plan. Because at that point I had been floating through my days like a ghost just visiting a girl. I had forgotten that I had agency—one of the things that makes adult life palatable at all—to do (almost) anything I wanted to. Why was I wearing ugly, boring outfits to work instead of expressing myself in a way that would make me feel good? Why was I eating the same thing for lunch and dinner day in and day out, when I could be exploring new recipes? Why was I moving my body in the same banal way, listening to the same playlists, rewatching the same things, neglecting my books? It was almost like once I had accepted misery as my standard, once

I had lost my spark, I decided I'd never find it. This was my new baseline. This was my new normal. Because losing your spark and getting into the funk is easy. It happens without you even realizing. It is this invisible gas in the air that you inhale until you are under its spell. But getting out of a funk and finding your spark again takes work. It takes time and energy and effort. And we can be honest: it's bullshit that losing our way comes so easy to us, and finding it requires time and dedication—but that doesn't mean that said time and dedication is not worth it.

My very first act of business was making a list of everything I had never done or tried before. Why? Because I was bored. Because I was doing the same things over and over and over again, failing to realize there were infinite foods and activities I'd never tried, places I'd never gone, things I'd simply never done. I called this my never-have-I-ever list. And these things do not need to be extravagant, like traveling to Bali or skydiving (but they can be). I had never tried a lychee martini or had omakase sushi. I had never gone on a run over the Brooklyn Bridge. I'd never tried pole dancing, volunteered at an animal shelter, gone to drag bingo. I had never learned to knit or crochet. I had never baked a cake from scratch. I had never tried pottery or watercolor painting or taken a cooking class. There was an infinite number of things I'd never tried—some of them free. An infinite number of places I'd never visited—some of them in my own city. I listed out one hundred things and decided over the next year I would simply try to do one thing each week that I'd never done before. I'd document the process. I'd keep close tabs on how I felt when I was there. I didn't have to be good at the activities I tried or the new creative avenues I ventured down. I didn't need to even like everything. I just had to try new things. To prove to myself that there was newness everywhere, that there was variety everywhere. That there would always, for the rest of the life I am so lucky to lead, be something to try that I had never tried before in my life.

I can recall the restaurant where I first tried a lychee martini. And I cannot recall the hundreds of times I have ordered and enjoyed one since. I can recall the studio where I took my first pole dancing class. I can recall the girl I shared the pole with (two people per pole). I can recall how challenging it was, and simultaneously how much easier it was than I ever expected it to be. I can recall how sore my arms were the next day. How welcomed I felt in a space I'd never ventured into before. How free it all felt. I can recall the jog I went on over the Brooklyn Bridge. Running past New Yorkers on their commute and tourists taking photos of the view from the other side. A couple taking engagement photos. Another walking hand in hand. Experiencing all these tiny moments. Tiny moments they may never forget either. For as long as they are lucky to live, they are lucky to remember what the Manhattan skyline looks like from the Brooklyn side on a perfect fall day. I can recall the staircase in Midtown up to the studio where I took my first improv class. I can recall the way my inner child was ignited by the acting games we played that mirrored those of my childhood. I can recall how Wednesday evenings became something I looked forward to, because I knew I was going back up that staircase and back to the improv class, where we would just play.

And quickly it was no longer just about trying something new every week. It started to become a ritual, a practice, a religion—of looking out into the world for newness. For something to try. I was no longer afraid to fail because I learned failure wasn't even really an option anymore—I'd either try something new and adopt it into my life, or try something new and decide it wasn't for me, but learn something along the way. I began to crave moments of trial and error. Moments when I could do something without arranging or planning for it first. Moments of happenstance and spontaneity.

I wrote out all one hundred things I wanted to try and taped them to the wall next to my bed. I found such great joy and such great relief in crossing each item off. It felt like peeling back layers of myself, discovering the way I could move through the world with joy licking at my heels. Each scratch of my pen felt like a slow becoming, like I was discovering the meaning behind the mundane.

•

The funk I found myself in during the spring of 2021 is a universal one—the postgrad funk. A period of time where the ways we formerly defined success and failure fade, and we're met with entirely new circumstances, routines, and lifestyles. In college and even high school, we derived purpose from our extracurricular activities, social lives, and studies. In our postgrad haze, our purpose is no longer clear or even cut out for us—purpose is something we must seek ourselves, and oftentimes it isn't in the most obvious of places. For me personally, I was desperately seeking my purpose in my work—but my first job postgrad, working at a British insurance company writing articles about the insurance industry, wasn't fulfilling whatsoever. And when I couldn't find my purpose in my work, which was so often how I'd found my purpose in the twenty-one years that came before—I just surrendered to having none at all. I surrendered to the idea that postgrad was supposed to be awful and miserable and anxiety inducing and purposeless. I wish someone had told me that there were plenty of other places to discover my purpose, to rediscover my spark, that had very little to do with work at all. I wish someone had told me work could be a way I paid the bills, a way I kept myself fed—and that my life could exist so brilliantly and vibrantly outside of that. I wish someone had told me that this period of misery, where I felt so far from myself, and so detached from myself, wasn't written in permanent ink, but rather, was a signal. Whenever I find myself feeling off, or detached from myself, or far from home—I no longer see this as a life sentence, but rather, a signal. An alarm bell going off inside of me, telling me that something needs to change. Something needs to be altered. Something doesn't feel right. And I have all the tools within me to tend to those little leaks or maintenance requests. I now look at moments when I feel myself slipping into a funk or losing sight of my spark as an opportunity to find new ways to excite myself, an opportunity to learn something new about myself, an opportunity to live.

•

I spent six months working an insurance journalism job in a too-cold beige office building where I was pretty unneeded. I could usually complete all the tasks they gave me by two or three p.m., and then would be sent to the conference room to work on whatever busy work they could throw my way. It was in this conference room that I decided to start writing a newsletter. I had seen author after author launch and maintain newsletters, mainly on Substack—but I always felt like I wasn't "there" yet or wasn't well-known or established enough to start a newsletter of my own. I had around 300,000 followers on TikTok, but I hadn't monetized this following yet, and didn't know if I'd even have any readers. I was so bored and so uninspired, though, that I decided that if even just ten people were to subscribe, it would be enough for me. Nobody is ever truly ready for anything. You cannot wait to share your art until you have some arbitrary audience. You cannot wait to take the risk. You do not know how much time you'll truly have to wait. There is no waiting. Just living.

So, I published the blog and started to write. Because the truth is there is no right time to start something. There is no rule book. You must simply begin, and then you figure it out as you go. Just as every famous author and athlete and business owner and actor and mentor of yours did before people knew their name. They simply got started. And they got to work. And they fucked up, and they learned from it, and they backtracked, and they made more mistakes, and finally, eventually, they found their groove. But even when they found it, they still couldn't tell you what the hell they were doing. I garnered a few hundred readers, and eventually a few thousand. It was nowhere near the audience of some of the authors I looked up to or even other people I knew in real life. But it was something to do. It was an outlet. It was a productive way to spend the time in the conference room when I had nothing better to do.

And in some ways, it slowly became a purpose. A purpose does not need to be something you excel in. It doesn't need to be a first-place medal, or something tangible, or something you do for acclaim or money. A purpose can be the community you build, the chosen family you love, the way they love you in return. A purpose can be a pet. It can be a hobby you do that you aren't even very good at it. It can be the art you make that nobody sees. The way you stay busy. The way you move your body. The passion you've had for something since you were a child. It does not need to be a promotion at work or having crazy passion for what you do to make a living.

A purpose is just a tiny thread pulling you up out of bed in the morning and into this world we call our own. Nobody gets to decide what yours is but you.

Eventually, this very hobby, which I was so apprehensive to start, changed my life. This newsletter that I thought I wasn't established enough to launch, that I thought I wasn't good enough to publish, was the very reason literary agents reached out to me via email just six months after I launched it, and asked if I was ready to start working on my first book. If I hadn't begun, if I hadn't flung myself at the wind and committed myself to trying, if I hadn't dared to let other people watch me try—with every potential to fail laid out before me—I never would've heard from my now agents. And you would never be reading this book.

When I saw my funk as an opportunity to reclaim my life, to reconsider what mattered to me, to rediscover my purpose—an opportunity, open ended, to simply find my own will again—I unintentionally walked into a dimly lit room where all my dreams would come true.

Certainly, you can allege without my TikTok following, my literary agents would never have found my Substack blog. And you're certainly right; they wouldn't have. But you cannot deny this: If I'd feared failure more than I feared complacency, there would have been no TikTok following. There would have been no Substack blog. There maybe wouldn't have even been a cold and beige office building to be incredibly bored in. There is no such thing as failure when you view each opportunity as a chance to get what you wanted when you began, or to learn something about yourself or the world.

•

My postgrad funk was truthfully about trying to reconcile the lessons of my childhood with the reality of adulthood—of trying to learn about how to be a functional and, moreover, a happy and motivated adult, in a world that did not prepare me for the cold, murky waters that awaited me after graduation. A society that told me over and over and over again that college would be the best four years of my life (a myth I've rejected since the first time I heard it), then upheld their promise when I graduated and felt like I was on the receiving end of the worst joke in the world. And as I trudged along in those early days after graduating, I felt pretty hopeless. My worth was tied to my work, and my work was the most banal, uninspiring thing I'd ever done. My friends were all miserable and lost, and we couldn't rely on one another for answers. The guy I was dating would tell me I didn't have to wear so much makeup when we hung out. But he didn't know I felt like I had to. I hated being alone just as much as I hated going to parties and having to make small talk. I felt like a tourist in my own life. Visiting sometimes, just on occasion, with the proper documents and a camera to take pictures of all the good things I saw. I felt like I had lost myself. The sweet girl in the University of Michigan sweatshirt, so excited to arrive at college and begin her life. The heartbroken girl in the sweater, ending a relationship she had clung to for dear life for months. The passionate girl in the theater building, racing to rehearsal after class, scribbling down a poem in the margins of a script. But in those tearful moments, on those dark, sleepless nights, I hung on to the fact that you can't really lose yourself, because you are all that you have. All that you will ever truly, permanently have. You can feel lost. And that is a valid, truthful, and dark feeling. But you cannot lose yourself.

You are all you have. It is all you can do to give yourself the life you deserve. A good life. One full of variety and things you've never tried before. One where you take a new route to work sometimes so you can see new trees and new street corners. One where you eliminate anything killing your energy to make room for something that will give you more. One where you sign up for a class at random because you've always wanted to try, and one where you know you're never too old to try something for the first time. One where you are curious—desperately curious—to learn about new things, to investigate your why, to get to the center of yourself and grow outward from there.

Let us be honest with ourselves, and gentle with ourselves—change is hard. Change is fundamentally uncomfortable, and there aren't many people in the world who are overjoyed by change, excited to experience it, or actively welcoming it into their lives. The change we all experience after our days of education fade and we are faced with the real world are inevitably difficult. But without change, there is no growth, there is no variety, there is no exciting news. Nobody shares the pains of change behind the scenes; they only share the sparkly moments—which makes us feel like aliens, or out of our own bodies when we struggle to process transformations, even when they coincide with good things in our lives. We only see the promotions and the engagements and the marathon finish lines. But to get there, there was pain and work and bad nights that amount to this goodness. Because change is hard for all of us. The difference is what we decide to do when faced with it.

You can stay on the bench if you want. There is nobody stopping you from staying where you are. But you cannot hit a home run from the bench. To get off the bench is to risk striking out. To strike out is to learn something about yourself and the world that you didn't know before.

•

There is such a pressure, in today's world, to know what you want. To know what you want to do with your life; to know what you want to be when you grow up. There is such an unspoken pressure for us all to know our purpose and commit to it the second we walk into the real world and unpack our things at our cubicles, or in our first apartment all alone, or back at our childhood home. My grandmother Gail (my dad's mother) lost her life when she was in her early forties. She was an Aquarius (which is information you don't need to know, but for some reason it helps me to picture her better, considering we never got the chance to meet). I can't remember a time when I wasn't compared to my grandmother. Maybe it's the namesake: Eli *Gail*. Maybe it is just our ancestry, passed from one woman to the next, something I hold in my hands and try to make sense of. When I was growing up, my father never spoke of Gail. I was raised with the knowledge that my grandmother was an extraordinary, stubborn, spitfire of a woman who left the world too young. All other stories and memories were padlocked behind the doors my father and uncle kept shut at all times. I didn't even know where the doors were, let alone how to force them open. In my twenty-six years, I've collected facts about her and held them close: she was a Jewish woman who died of breast cancer; she left behind a collection of gold coins of various sizes that hang in my mother's closet and around my neck; she was vivacious and beloved by everyone, fiercely. I've never known where the rest of her things are. A few years ago, my grandmother's cousin, who was raised like a sister to her, gave me a few of her things that she was saving for me. A sweater she knit, for one, and her old high school yearbook, from the year she graduated. Each memento of her is something I cherish deeply. The yearbook took me a while to go through—I was almost too afraid to peek into the intimacies of my grandmother's high school days when I hardly knew anything about her days after that. But eventually, one night, freshly twenty-three years old, overcome with loneliness and unsure where else to turn, I decided to sift through the pages for a sign from her. Something that could tether me to her further. All the girls on the senior portrait page in the yearbook are looking over their shoulders submissively, but Gail is staring right at the camera. Next to each senior portrait is a list of each student's high school activities. Gail is hailed as Clifford J. Scott High School's fashion plate. The yearbook claims she "divides her talents between the designing board and the captain of the cheerleading squad." Beside each senior portrait is the word *Ambition* with a colon next to it. All the students included their post–high school ambitions, and upon searching through the yearbook, I found the vast majority had put college, higher education, or for many of the girls, considering this is the 1950s, secretary.

Gail, though, is different. Printed next to her *Ambition:* is the word *undecided*. I wonder about it for a second. Undecided. While every other kid in the yearbook felt so pressured to amount to greatness, or reach for insane heights, or brag about a seemingly perfect future life plan, Gail was apparently all right with not knowing. Perhaps I've read too far into it. But something about the *undecided* strikes me somewhere in my chest and tugs hard. That undecided went to the Fashion Institute of Technology for two years to pursue her dreams, but they didn't quite fit, so she dropped out because she got bored when she stayed in one place for too long. That undecided married my grandfather, and they opened the restaurants that I'd have memories of from the day I was born. That undecided gave my father and my uncle their lives. That undecided danced on bars and ran her cigarettes under the faucet to try to quit. That undecided gave me my eyes and the gold coin around my neck. That undecided wore mink coats through chemotherapy, had a cool and calm presence like the ocean's waves, and then left the largest, most gaping bright hole in this world. That undecided was the greatest person my father ever knew and was the greatest loss of his life. This woman was brave enough and bold enough to encompass the *taboo* unknown and still find her way. Still leave such a mark that, when I ask about her, her cousin or anyone else who knew her loses their breath for a second, so astounded to have even known someone so special, to have even loved her. And in that moment, in my bedroom with no windows, using my phone's flashlight to see, I hope I can be brave enough too.

•

I wish my grandmother were here to write a book and tell you this, but I will pass along her message instead. Your ambition does not need to be decided to live a big, good life full of everything you deserve. You are not what you accomplish. You are not the school you graduated from, or the job you have, or the contests you have won. You are a series of love stories passed down from one pair of lovers to the next. You are heritage and tradition, brilliance and the way your nostrils flare out when you get sad or excited. You are the bars you've danced on. The lives you've touched. The love you've given and the love you've received in return. You are not a funk. You are not the moments you've felt stuck or lost. It is freeing and miserable to realize that we, as individuals, probably won't be remembered. I'm sure you don't know the first name of your great-great-great-great-grandparent. It doesn't really matter, then, what you accomplish at work. Or what you accomplish at all. It matters how it felt. How it felt when you found a person who you realized would really matter to you, even if not forever. It matters how you felt when you tried something new and realized that it would be in your life for a very long time. It matters how you felt when you watched the most beautiful sunset of your life, when you heard a song and knew it would forever be one of your favorites. It matters how you felt and how you feel, and how you will feel.

It is so insanely difficult to deprioritize what we are told should matter by society and reprioritize what really matters. But it is something we must do in order to free ourselves. Yes, you have to work. And if you are lucky you will spend your days working at a job you enjoy. But that is not everything; that is not who you are. Yes, you will have a routine, and places you must be, and adult responsibilities. But those do not have to be all you do in a day. The postgrad funk was one of the most isolating times of my life, and I know, because I am human and because life is not easy, that I will find myself missing my spark or feeling lost or stuck or in a funk in the future too. But this is simply a part of you, looking out for you. This is simply a signal, telling you that you deserve better for yourself. And making that better, creating that better, starts with us.

•

At twenty-six, I go out to dinner with my friends at seven p.m. on a Wednesday. We no longer hate our lives all of the time. We have a standing date: we go to the same place, with mirrors on the ceiling and really good fries. We plan a trip together in December because we have been saving our paychecks, and we are desperate to spend time together outside of the chaos and hustle of the city. We love one another so deeply because we have seen one another at our lowest, we have been there to pick one another up off the floor, to press the reset button, to answer the four-way

FaceTime call and just listen. We do not know where we're going next. We have abandoned our former five-year plans, and we are letting the days take us. But we are not just moving through them like ghosts or trespassers or the wind. We are living them. And we have worked for these lives we love so much, that we cherish so deeply. And we toast to that.

Does Anyone Else Feel Like It's Okay Not to Know Everything?

I am ten years old and in a production of the musical *Annie* in a church basement with a local children's community theater. We hardly have a budget or a set, and I am instructed to go outside in my parents' backyard to rub actual dirt on my costume (made by my mother) to make it appear dirty. I am playing Molly—my first-ever role where my character has a name, and lines to memorize, and certain lyrics to sing, just me. All alone. It is opening and also closing night, and I am standing in the hallway leading up to the stage—which feels as vast and legitimate as a Broadway house, not just the church basement entertainment space. It is funny how our minds do this, wrap their arms around the faintest of moments, etching them into the permanent ink of our histories. I am standing with my director, telling him I feel nervous. I am afraid to forget my lines, well aware I have one real chance to get up there and wow the audience. To get the applause. To do a good job. I just want to do a good job.

"Well, it's a good thing to be nervous," he says. And I am startled by it. Surely the great performers of our lifetimes are never nervous—surely anyone good enough to make it to Broadway is never nervous. Surely I am the one who doesn't have what it takes, a bundle of nerves backstage to simply perform in front of her parents and grandparents.

"Being nervous means that you care. Having those butterflies means you have something invested in this. If you weren't nervous, it would show me that maybe you didn't care about this as much as you should. So take all those nerves and turn them into energy. When have butterflies ever been a bad thing?"

I don't remember what I said, or even if I said anything at all.

When have butterflies ever been a bad thing? was what stuck with me. What has stuck with me ever since. Because he's right. To be nervous about a performance or a new job or a new relationship or a big event or day in your life is to have a real, tangible example of how much you care.

And what an epiphany it is to accept and honor your care. To understand and value your care. To water your care, to raise it like a child you love more than you love yourself. To realize that your care, and the way you care, is vast and wonderful and something to be celebrated and protected.

That church basement was the first time I can remember feeling nervous because of my care, because of what I had invested, because of my stakes. It certainly wasn't the last. It was the last time, though, that I mistook those types of butterflies—that bubbly nervous energy—for anything other than exactly what they were and are: a real example of how much I care. A real example of the strength it takes to put myself out there. Perhaps it was not weak to feel this way. Perhaps, it was brave.

•

Twenty-two through twenty-four were years I felt I was slipping through my own grip. Twenty-two and disoriented and adrift, trying desperately to act the perfect adult and failing miserably, loudly, and chaotically at doing so. Each birthday came around with a shimmer of hope that I could get my shit together before the next, that in the next 365 days I could transform gracefully into a girl who has it figured out, that I could spend the following fifty or more weeks pushing through the fog and into a bright, cool clearing. A clearing I'd never seen but pretended existed nonetheless. What is life without hope? The internet tells me to give myself grace, but what grace is there to give a girl who doesn't even know what she's doing? Who doesn't even know who she is? It wasn't always like this, before twenty-two. We knew ourselves for so long, didn't we? Was I just naive, or too idealistic, or too young? Was being happy always so hard?

At twenty and twenty-one, I was on fire. An accomplished social butterfly with a blunt brunette bob. I knew so many people's names on campus, walked into crowded bars with an attitude finely sharpened. Feeling wiser than I'd ever been, I assumed my maturing, growing, and becoming days were past me. I never even thought there was more to come, more to do. I was a bright, feisty girl who never got hungover. And so much was ahead—so many never-felt-before highs and startlingly new lows. I'd never really lost a friend I cared deeply for. I'd been dumped, I'd broken hearts, I'd nearly graduated from college, I'd managed to keep myself sane while also ruining my hair by flat ironing it every day. But I had no real idea what was waiting for me past the iron gates of my school days. I thought I understood words like *lonely* and *grief* and *misunderstood*, but I'd be living them out in just a few months, carefully unpacking them, carefully undressing them. Shoving them under my bed and trying so hard to just be put together while reality grated against my soul and wore me down. Craving a cohesion, an understanding, that the grown-ups around me all seemed to possess—no flaws, no imperfections, no real-world bullshit. I'd never felt so out of place, so awkward, so brutal as I did when I settled into twenty-two.

On the Upper West Side in my first postgrad apartment, I was a newborn baby. But this time, there was no excuse for my not knowing. No excuse for my stumbles. No hand-holding, guiding, or protecting. It was just me and my failure to ever dress correctly for the weather outside. It was just me and my stolen confidence and my borrowed personality. Just me and my constant fear that I'd never be adored, my loose grasp on a reality everyone else seemed to be living so effortlessly in. I moved through the world with a clunky awkwardness and would've sworn to you all eyes were on me, analyzing and judging, at all times.

At twenty and twenty-one, I didn't care what anyone else thought of me. I liked myself. My clothes. My friends. The way I did my makeup. The way I took swirly notes in my notebooks during class and read on the bench outside the classroom while I awaited the next one. I liked how I appeared in the eyes of girls I don't talk to anymore. Laughing with them. Telling them everything. Unafraid, in many ways, of what would happen if we all fell apart. I liked how I appeared in the gaze of the guy I went home from the bar with. I did not fear scaring him off. I did not fear his eventual distaste of me. I was not there for his affection, nor his desire. I was there because it was fun. Everything I did at twenty years old I did because it was fun. Strictly that. I went to concerts in Detroit with Sadie, and we danced and drank White Claws until we were dizzy in the back seat on the way home, never sick of each other. Never thinking more than just a few steps ahead, a distance we could see to. Our lives together were an overlook on a mountaintop, a startling view, a sparkling sky, a vastness—the kind of thing that takes your breath away. I went on long, meandering runs around my sweet college town, never savoring the rhythm of my sneakers on the familiar concrete, passing by buildings and hardly remembering to taste the moment, to soak it through my pores, to hold it with me closely.

I was twenty-two years old, and the vastness was gone. I wondered why I didn't spend all the time back then reminding myself to savor its sweet flavor. My bedroom had no windows, and my Sadie was in another city, in another bedroom. I was twenty-two years old, and it was a memory. I was surrounded by the remains of them. Scared to death they were all I had left of my bygone joy. Tiny shards of broken glass poking into my palms, covering my floors so I was trapped in my bedroom by their sharp sentimentality. Forced to think each of them through. Forced to regret the way I failed to hold each of them tightly, to loop my arms through them. Instead, they dropped, and I spent months surrounded by their pieces. My parents in the basement of the Pretzel Bell on game day, the disgusting couch in my senior year house that constantly served as a bed for a male friend of ours who never made it home, Daphne waking up in our guest bedroom over the pandemic every morning—weeks when I failed to consider her life would start again in London and she'd have to go home. And that home wasn't me—somehow, when that's all we'd ever been for each other.

Now I was a grad student in journalism, and why—after all—did I give up on myself to go be "serious," to go be "practical"? I had no real answer. The world had paused for months in 2020, and it seemed like the only option for an eldest daughter with a good head on her shoulders. Go do the practical thing. Don't be the daughter your parents have to worry about. Don't be the sister your brothers wonder about. You are an eldest daughter who was supposed to hold it together for herself so she could hold it together for everyone else. Go to grad school. Go be sensible. Set an example. Do it for everyone else. Not for you. Never for you. Nothing for you.

At twenty-two, with eroded confidence, I am running marathons after boys from yesterday, desperate for their affirmation, needing them to want me like they did at eighteen. Maybe, then, that will mean I haven't grown from that sweet girl to some unrecognizable beast. We get by. We learn. We finish up grad school because we are a good girl. A good girl. A tired, broken girl, but still a good one. And nobody will know we are broken or tired because we will paste wellness on ourselves like it is a full face of makeup. Nobody will know we are so self-conscious. So aware of our impending failure, the dread we wake up with, like a drum in the center of our chest. Twenty-two with a wrecked sense of self. An accident you can't look away from, smoke still billowing from its exploded engine. Things will get better. Things will get better. We can't see it yet. We meet some guy and now we are his diamond of the season. We take a job, and it is boring and horrible, but we think it is exactly what we are supposed to do. Not making anyone proud. Surely not making ourselves proud.

Twenty-three, gaining weight when you want to lose it. Caring so deeply, so embarrassingly, what everyone else thinks, because twenty-three feels like you are under a microscope. Twenty-three feels like you are patient zero. Twenty-three feels more like sixteen than it does like twenty-one. A deep sense that you are being watched. The feeling of being an experiment. And behind closed doors you can melt down; you write your darkest, most pained thoughts in your notes app, you drown in the middle of a drought, but you have no choice but to about-face and do the boring day again and again. At the Seventy-Second Street train station, barreling toward downtown, you are a perfect adult. You are aged, gently, by the fifteen-year-old girls hustling down Columbus Avenue, arm in arm. You want to stop them and hold them in time. You are looked down on by the women in their thirties, who are shiny and beautiful and know almost everything about themselves. You are so young to them. What am I meant to be at this time in my life?

I am twenty-three, and I am so afraid I will never know the answer.

I am twenty-four, and feeling like the ground beneath my feet is lava I can finally withstand. Still pretending to understand what I'm meant to be. The grace period of postgrad fades and the credits of that chapter roll. And now, surely, I am supposed to be a good adult, just like I have been a good daughter, a good sister, a good friend. But I am not. I am always afraid, always nervous, and I have forgotten that this means that I care. The foundation I constructed so religiously, with surgical precision, no longer feels like home. In fact, I can't even find my way back to my most cherished of memorized addresses. Don't even remember etching my scripture below myself like a chair I can rest on when it all gets too tough. Some days I feel like I am just a girl who wants everyone to like her. Some days I feel like I will never stop loathing how my body looks in that outfit. I continue to put myself in the path of things that make me feel like shit. I call my Uber and have no destination. Not everything is bad, but every day is confused, and I just want to be plugged back in. I want to feel like myself again.

I am twenty-five and realizing that perhaps there is no true way to know. Twenty-five and crying at the spin class when they play that one song that feels like a sign I needed. Twenty-five and fearing wasting a life so much I decide I have to just live. Twenty-five and leaning into the crazy with my full body weight. A weight I am comfortable in. A body I honor. Twenty-five and realizing feeling like myself is simply going back to the basics and beginning again. There is no true way to have everything, or even *anything* figured out. So you must just live. Twenty-five and realizing that there is no such thing as a perfect adult. Twenty-five and realizing having it all figured out would mean you have nothing else to learn. Nowhere else to grow from here. Twenty-five and a fourth of the way to one hundred. Twenty-five and still a little scared.

Twenty-six and realizing that not even the adults feel like adults. We are all the children we once were. We are all the teenagers we once were. We've simply grown into our features, unlocked new privileges. But we still need our mothers. We still need to call home every now and again. We still need protecting. Guidance. Wisdom. Even at twenty-six. Even at twenty-six, you will feel like the newborn baby you once were. You will feel like a wise old broad who has seen it all. You will feel like a small child who has seen nothing. You will be all of those things, because you are all of them. Twenty-six and realizing every year will bring the full range of human emotions—from exhaustion to excitement, confusion to clarity. I am alive to experience these things. I am here to endure. I am grateful for the chance to have so many questions, to want to do my best. Twenty-six and terrified. Twenty-six and thrilled. Twenty-six and here. Time has mended these cracks in the foundation. I can stand on my own feet.

•

In clandestine ways, we teach young people to place so much importance on how others view them and what others may subsequently think of them as a result of this perception. We program our young people, from a very young age, to derive validation and affirmation from the world around them. We go on to expect young people to behave, dress, socialize, and act in ways that make them most palatable and digestible to society to attain said validation. We structure our world in "norms," "traditions," and "standards" that we see as the baseline, deeming everything that doesn't fall into these strict guidelines as the other. So many of the lessons we're taught from an early age teach us to value the perception other people have of us over the perception we have of ourselves. We're never truly taught, in fact, to value the perception we have of ourselves much at all. We have to be normal. We have to be traditional. We have to follow these little invisible steps and be perfect. Be sensational. Be sparkling. Be flawless.

In my early twenties—flailing, crooked, trying my absolute best for adoration—I was just doing as I was taught. You are just doing as you've been taught. Trying my absolute best to be a perfect adult who gets all the affirmation and validation from the adults and the world around her is what I have been programmed to do. It is what I thought I was supposed to do. The only preparation I walked into my early twenties with was this unspoken idea that it was my job to be put together, to be mature, to be serious, and that if I did that, the world around me would bend in my favor, would melt in my hands. I would tame the world so well, it would be something I owned or kept as my own.

But that isn't how it works. You cannot tame storms or divert them from their paths. You cannot predict the unruly winds of change, or the sea—most of which we have yet to even explore. By simply trying to be palatable and digestible for society—so I fit in, so I felt put together, so I had my shit together, shrinking myself in a desperate attempt to be perfect, to have it figured out, to ward off this moment of uncertainty—I became unrecognizable to myself, and my world became unrecognizable in tandem.

There is no way—no matter who you are—to have your entire life "figured out." To feel constantly at ease, to feel constantly settled, to stay put and have your shit "together." There is no one grand feeling that accompanies adulthood. There is no way to be a perfect adult. There is no one way to be an adult.

To be an adult is to be a person over the age of eighteen. To be perfect is to live your life as loudly, brilliantly, and individually as you possibly can. Even if your bedroom floors are never visible. Even if you are depressed or anxious or lost. Even if you are unemployed or undecided. You are perfect when you commit to being yourself, wholly, sometimes chaotically, brutally. You are an adult when you turn eighteen and become one.

It is a waste of time to pretend yourself into oblivion. It is a waste of your life to wait for it to begin, to wait until you are small enough or accomplished enough or successful enough to begin living. It is a waste of time to hate yourself so deeply, in a way that ruins your chances at joy and beauty.

At twenty-six, I am looking forward to a life of not knowing everything but of being nosy enough that my curiosity leads me in the direction of newness. Of gaining confidence and, with each passing day, gaining the ability to care only what I think of myself. We must teach our young people to care about what the younger version of them would think of who they are today, not what their next-door neighbors, classmates, enemies, exes, or acquaintances think of them. We cannot control the opinions or potential perceptions others have of us. We can only control how we live. We must teach our young people to not invite opinions into their homes if they wouldn't invite the people with said opinions in too. We must teach young people to trust themselves—stupidly, wonderfully, deliriously. We must teach young people to not take criticism from those they wouldn't take advice from. We must teach young people—at moments of crisis, at moments of disillusionment—to think not *What did these somewhat irrelevant strangers think of me?* and instead, *What does the version of me, from ten years ago, think of me?*

You are exactly who you were ten years ago, only now you spend your weekend evenings at wine bars with your friends and you make a paycheck and do your own laundry. You are in touch with that version of you—with all the versions of you—in touch enough to wonder what younger you would think of you today. You, with your innate sense of personal style and perfume collection and knowledge about a random topic you could go on about for days. You, and your favorite movie and your favorite book and your refined palate for art or music or theater or whatever medium you love. You, with a heart full of love, a world of possibilities ahead, who has circumvented challenges beautifully, who has achieved things your younger self never would have imagined. You, who will never fit in a box, will never be just one thing. You, who are so much more than a title you wear at work, or a hobby you're good at, or a trait you've stitched on your sleeve. You cannot be reduced to just one thing. You are not a writer or a singer or a doctor or a lawyer or any number of niche aesthetics or vibes or "cores." You are not, and do not have to be, just one thing. You can and will be one million different things at once. I cannot wait for you to discover each fold of you, each trapdoor, each attic bedroom and small, tiny window to your soul.

Keep an account of your life. Even if you start today. By way of simply being alive, you are interesting enough to log what has happened to you. To take photos of things just to remember them later. I revisit my college journals when I need to tap into the mind of the girl I used to be. I scroll through her playlists, and I listen to them, and I realize she is not so far away. The fears I had about cycling into and out of personalities—about never being or feeling just right, about having a limited, dim sense of self—fade away when I find her again. Sickeningly nostalgic, too sentimental, with all this love to give. I grew out the blunt brunette bob (for now), but I am the girl I have always been. We have grown into different pairs of pants, different bedrooms, different hands we hold. We have grown out of friendships and into other ones, carrying the same stuffed elephant from one year to the next that we've had since we were eighteen. We learn new recipes but never hesitate to reach for the old, learn new preferences but always prefer being too hot to too cold. You are not so far from yourself. You are the you that you always have been, with an opened mind, an expanded range of feeling, and an expanded vocabulary to describe these tugs of the heart. It gets more complicated, but it also gets better. And though it never gets easier, you do become better at handling it.

She would be proud of you. Thirteen-year-old you, having her first kiss under the tree at the park across the street from her elementary school. Fifteen-year-old you, winning a cross-country race. Sixteen-year-old you, losing her virginity on a couch in the basement. Ten-year-old you, learning for the first time that butterflies mean that you care.

•

This August I found myself in St. Louis, Missouri, at the historic Muny, a theater where I spent the summer of 2018, nearly six years prior. There are one thousand seats in the theater. They are green and plastic and have brought me to other ends of the universe, back in time and forward. That summer revealed so much to me, as summers often do. This hungry penchant, ever growing, eating away at me, to choose to create no matter the cost. This painful realization that many of the people who had been occupying my days no longer had a place where they once did. The startling realization that I was changing, shifting, and opening my eyes wider to the world around me. With the sun setting on the horizon, I felt myself growing up in the eye of this sticky Missouri summer heat. Watching the lead character in *Meet Me in St. Louis* sing "Have Yourself a Merry Little Christmas" to her younger sister to quell her fear about the future—one thousand people watching, all silent. Watching our Dorothy sing "Home" from *The Wiz* and thinking about home, how warm and foreign a word, how much its meaning changes as you grow. I turned twenty years old that summer. I acted like I knew everything, but deep down I was so scared of myself, so scared of my ambition and my passion, so scared of letting down this version of me, at twenty years old, with braids in her hair and a tendency to arrive far earlier and stay far later than she was supposed to.

This August, I returned for the first time to the green seats and the same sticky heat. They'd done renovations, put systems in place to help it run more smoothly, made changes to enhance without fundamentally erasing her history or her foundation. She was still everything I so fell in love with about her, six years earlier. And I was twenty years old again. When the orchestra began to play, a familiar swell of magic and wanting came over me like it always did back then—I am twenty years old, and I want to be a playwright and an author, and I spend my downtime at work writing stories and poems. I am twenty years old, ready to break up with my boyfriend, and I am in denial about it. I am twenty years old, a junior in college, and I am going to run a marathon and start dating the guy from drama class. I am twenty years old, and most of my friends are people I won't talk to at twenty-six. I am twenty years old, and Sadie and I are in the only fight we've ever been in. We made it out. I am twenty years old, and I am twenty-one years old. I am twenty-two and twenty-three, twenty-four and twenty-five. I am twenty-six, and I am holding all of us in my chest with the drum that still wakes me up in fear sometimes. I have so much of what I wished for at twenty years old when I sat in the same seat, experiencing the same love for art that I experience now, only it has been magnified as I have grown and discovered the vocabulary to describe how I feel about it. I am so proud of who I was at twenty years old, even when I royally fucked up. It is twenty-year-old Eli's fearlessness that I hold on to even now. Twenty was fearless. Twenty-one, spontaneous. Twenty-two, careful. Twenty-three, brave. Twenty-four, bright. Twenty-five, raw. Twenty-six is all of us at once. I have traveled back in time to the girl who I was, and I am the only audience member at the performance of my life I've been witnessing. The show has gone on, and it will continue to go on, and I will give myself a standing ovation even when I forget my lines. It is all I can do—live, liberate, and celebrate that life.

•

Now that I have stopped waiting for my life to begin, it has, in many ways, simply begun. I have this habit of putting myself in waiting rooms I have no business being in—locking the door and not allowing myself to leave until I interrogate every awkward thing I said at the party, every moment when I went somewhere and just felt like I didn't belong. In these waiting rooms, I'd remind myself that once I do X, I'll start to truly live. Once I get the promotion at my job, or find a new job and leave, I will be successful, I will be an adult worth showing her face in the world, I will be the version of me society will accept. Once

I get a boyfriend, I will be worthy of love, I will go out and enjoy it, and I will truly like myself. Once I lose ten pounds, clear up my skin, fix my hair, find my personal style, I will be stylish enough, pretty enough to get out of this room. To stop the waiting and begin the living.

But the goalposts are always moving when every day is judgment day and the judge is you. You will spend three months in that waiting room saying, *Tomorrow is the day I'll leave here*, and before you know it you've found yet another excuse, yet another reason you shouldn't start your life just yet. You will stay there forever because while it is hell, it is a hell in one single room that you can manage and control. It is scary to open your front door to the world and walk outside and bare your naked soul and all of your mess and hope to the universe—but it is even scarier to spend your days between four walls where nobody can see the cracks in your spirit and hear the way your laugh sounds when you get excited. You cannot wait until life gets easy to start living. You cannot wait to start chasing your joy. You will waste your life in waiting rooms. It is your duty to carry your younger self from one opportunity to the next, from one first date to the next, from one concert or dimly lit theater or birthday party to the next. It is your duty to show your younger self the best sunsets you'll ever see, the best meals you'll ever share with the best people you'll ever meet. It is your duty to love the things they loved, that younger person kept deep inside of you, and to bring them out into the world, risking being seen, to enjoy the abundance of goodness that awaits you.

I am painfully aware, by virtue of the fact that I am the writer and you are the reader, that there is a dynamic at play, wherein potentially, you might think I have my shit together. You might think I've made it, or that I feel like I've cracked the code or that I don't lock myself in waiting rooms, keeping myself from living.

You might think I feel confident and assured, put together and understood. And maybe this would be a better book if I could tell you that all of that is true. Maybe this would be a better book if I told you it wasn't a daily choice and an active practice to live now instead of waiting for the perfect moment. Maybe this would be a better book if I could tell you I wake up every morning and it is easy, seamless, to put myself out there, to be seen trying, to be alive and in my twenties. But it is an active practice, being present, understanding that this is the only time I will live this exact moment on this exact day. Living when I am imperfect and working on myself through days when I have to remind myself that life isn't all about working on yourself, or being "the best version" of yourself, unless it is defined by your own stripped-down standards. It is an active practice, understanding this is the youngest I'll ever be and that both everything and also nothing matters. It is a complicated, messy, and incredibly simple practice to live. It is also easy to put your life on pause in your midtwenties, to decide that your life will begin when things don't feel so turbulent or disorderly or mystifying. It is the hard thing to walk slowly toward the edge of the cliff, and to fall toward your life right off the edge. To be yourself in the world will always be a challenge. What you are able to gain from doing so will make it worth every trial, tribulation, and moment of self-doubt.

Growing up is sentimental in a way, and sometimes it is a little sad. It is also beautiful when you realize that growing up is and always has been a chance to learn more about yourself, the world, and what you want to get out of it. I grieve versions of my life I will never live—dreams of years spent in Paris have been traded for ones played out in New York; musings about what-ifs will always buzz by me when I am in the thick of big life decisions or next steps. I choose to surrender to the idea, day in and day out, that I cannot make a wrong decision for my life and myself, because the universe is guiding me, both a few steps behind and a few miles ahead, ready to greet me wherever I wind up next. I wonder about where I'd have lived if I hadn't abandoned my big Broadway dreams after college and hadn't gone to grad school. I wonder about who I'd be if I was a working journalist at a big company. I wonder what would've happened if I never went to Michigan or never applied for the internships I held in college. It is normal to get on an emotional roller coaster at twenty-two and stay on it, riding the same waves of highs and lows a hundred times. Sometimes you get back on whenever you need a reminder of just how brilliant it is to feel, how good it is to know sadness only because you know happiness, to only know fear because you know comfort. Your siblings are going to grow up too. Your friends are going to move on. Around every bend there is an experience you've never had, which you will navigate for the first time, accompanied by emotions you will feel for the first time too. I used to fear growing older until I realized that at no point in one life do you ever stop encountering newness—new experiences and emotions. During the course of writing this book, I got engaged. Now I am watching my parents experience the newness of their first child getting engaged and married, while I experience the newness of being engaged to be married. A new chapter will begin when I approach the next career venture I hope to. When I meet the friend who will change my life. When I have a sneaky experience that alters everything. It will be a new chapter when I become a mother, and I will watch my mother in wonder as she navigates how new it feels to be a grandmother. There is so much coming for you; there is so much you can get in the way of too. So much you can do, so much you can achieve and attain. You will never, ever run out of places to see that you've never seen. Songs to listen to that you've never heard. Feelings to unpack and undress on your floor that you've never engaged with before. Experiences you've never had. It is too much to even make sense of. But when I grow so sad, so lonesome in the hot, bright light of being twenty-six—I think about how many feelings there are to feel that I haven't had my turn with yet. And I remember it is worth it after all. To keep going.

•

Does anyone else feel like it's okay not to know everything? I know you are scared because I am too. Sometimes simply feeling less alone is a good enough place to land. We are here together, blinking on a page, breathing softly in tandem. In the five stages of grief, acceptance is the last step. To accept that you will never truly know. To accept that for some questions, there just aren't answers. To accept that life is challenging, occasionally meaningless and blank, until you give it your own definition and significance. To accept that the feelings you're searching for don't actually exist. To accept that you will never overthink your way into making sense of all of us and everything. To accept that the only way to figure out what you're meant to do with your life, or who you're meant to be, or how you're meant to navigate these early adult days is to face them head-on.

Across the breakfast table from my mom, I wonder how she felt at twenty-six, holding me in her arms for the first time. I wonder if she ever felt like she couldn't do it. I wonder if she felt like she was always meant to be my mom or if she had to adjust to being somebody else's everything. We grew up together, in some ways. Because no matter how old your mom was when you were born—seventeen or twenty-five or thirty-five—she was still growing up too. She was feeling new feelings for the very first time as you took your first steps. She was navigating new waters when you were navigating ones that were familiar to her and novel to you. Even at fifty-two, my mom is growing up still. Even at fifty-two, she is the girl she was at fifteen. She is the girl she was at twenty-one. Her childhood passions are still the things that she loves the most. Her college best friend is on speed dial, and sometimes when they're together, they'll tell me stories that remind me of ones I have with Sadie.

What are you meant to be at this time in your life?

Nothing to everyone else and everything else to yourself. Be a disaster, be a nightmare, unravel and stitch yourself back together again. Go back to all the places you've called home—revisit them and love them and rest in their arms when you need a place to close your eyes for a few hours. Stop comparing yourself to people from your high school who are married with a kid, or who have randomly gotten famous, or who post everything they're doing to look cool on Instagram. Start comparing yourself to the hopes, dreams, and joy you have the capacity to discover for yourself, over and over and over again.

I am over halfway to fifty today, and my twenties have been miserable and mayhem and everything good I've ever wanted for myself, waiting for me when I get home at night. My twenties have been an investigation of who I've been and who I want to be. And a realization of who I already am, without addendums, and how it feels to be just that. Me. I don't want to just be remembered as simply everybody else's lighthouse. I never want to find myself in a fitting room at a Zara, planning to skip dinner again. I want to savor these New York City days with my friends, and I never want anything to make too much sense because there'd be nothing left to wonder about if it did. I want to be okay with the fact that I am not, and never will be, perfect.

Much of my life has been in the service of pleasing others. And in so many ways, unlearning that will take the next twenty-six years. But I am aware of it. Aware that even here, between these lines, I've tried so far to please you. Aware that I want to be in the business of pleasing myself first. So I don't hold back, and it makes some people hate me, but they never would've loved me anyway, so I stop trying to make them. Over the last few years, I have learned that love is not some big feeling, but exactly how it feels for something to make sense when everything else feels impossible. I have learned that it is okay to be selfish, that we are at the center of our own universe and we must act accordingly. I have learned that I want a big life. A loud life. More love. More bread for the table. Another round. One more hour together before we go home. One more person to write a birthday card for. One more kiss good night. Ten more pages before lights-out. And that it is okay to have wants. It is okay if those wants take up a lot of space. I can't even reach the top shelf in my kitchen without a step stool, but my soul is the tallest girl in the room, and she is well fed, and she is full. On so many days I still feel like one of my childhood stuffed animals in need of repair from my mother's sewing kit—in need of mending and fixing and stitching back up again so someone else can love me. But you can be both the tallest soul in the room and the stuffed animal in need of TLC. You can be the tallest soul, and the stuffed animal, and the intern in Missouri, and the ten-year-old in the church basement hallway, so nervous that she'll forget her lines.

You are here with me because you are afraid and because you care. You have butterflies because you cherish this life and you want to make sure you're doing it right. It is so cool to be nervous. It is so cool to care. It is silly of us to forget how rare it all is—the way we find each other and hang on for as long as it makes sense, the coincidences that really aren't, the fruit that ripens so sweetly in the summer, days with twenty-four hours that feel never-ending, the ocean, the moon, soft-serve ice cream, that you and I are here on the same earth at this exact moment in time. How cluttered it can feel—trying to find room for all of this feeling and life's abstract souvenirs in the form of moments we'll only live once. How claustrophobic it can be, the mental gymnastics of deciding how you'd like to exist. But you already know yourself. You have only ever been you, and your heart has an endless capacity to hold whatever it is you wish to make space for. The universe will be cruel, decades of time will feel confusing, and life is unfortunately not a right, nor something that will always be given. So you must use this body you've been allotted to make your time here feel good and significant for you in a way that only you can. You are here with your name and your eyes and your unique set of circumstances just this once. To make joy, to love deeply and with abandon, to frequent the same restaurants a million times, to fuck up, to be forgiven, to make bad, and eventually really good, art, to try. Nobody will remember most of us, and that's okay. The whole point is to love and be loved, to be your own and to give yourself to a world that will only ever know one of you. The time is now. Let's see what you can do with it.

Acknowledgments

What a gift to have so many thank-yous to hand out. I mean each, deeply. This book is a product of a lifetime lived with the help of other people and, mostly, other women.

Thank you to my team at HarperCollins, especially Jessica and Jacqueline, for bearing with me as we launched one set of stories and cultivated another. I appreciate your time, your patience, your attentiveness, and your listening ear. I feel safe with you. That is a gift.

Thank you to Mia Vitale and Sarah Passick, who have believed in me since I was twenty-two years old. Who have helped me grow. Who are honest, energized, and a home to go back to. You make women feel heard, strong, and alive. I am lucky to live in a lifetime in which I know, collaborate with, and love you both. I am most lucky to grow with you.

Thank you to Keith Bielory, Melissa DeMarco, John Shealy, and my Gersh team. You guys have never thought, and will never think, I am crazy, even when you should. I can't believe I am lucky enough to exist in a time where I have people as hardworking, dedicated, and motivating as you on my side. John, to a million more DCs.

Thank you to my assistant, Jonathan Huey, who came to me like a literal miracle. You are everything I could've ever dreamed of in a collaborator and more. I am so proud to create in this life beside you. You are a lightning rod of good ideas and perfect taste. To us.

Thank you to my best friend, Julia, who tells me the hard truths, reads over my shoulder as I write, and is a constant in an ever-changing blur of midtwenties chaos. You were the gift of twenty-two. I don't want to ever do life without you.

Thank you to Allie Westra, a soulmate in best friend form. You are a muse, a rock, the antidote to every hard day. Thank you for standing by me through every bad decision and making all the good ones with me.

Thank you to Veronica Risucci, for holding my hand across continents. I have so few words to describe a connection that runs so deep. You make me better. Zero zero zero.

To my mom, for all the truth, the fashion advice, the being there. For reading me all those books and singing me all those songs when I was two and three and four years old. Thank you for your commitment to whom you love, most of all. Lucky doesn't begin to cover it.

To my dad, for always believing I can do it before I ever believe I can. For the home-cooked meals too. Knowing I always have someone on my side, and that person being you, is something I will never take for granted.

To my brother Jake, for always being proud of me and always giving me someone to be proud of too. Thank you for being a friend that I will have for life.

To my brother Jack, for being the calm before every storm, the calm through every storm. I am still with you. And for that I am unbearably grateful.

To all four of my grandparents, for loving each other so that my parents could eventually love me.

To my unbelievable chosen family, my friends who cannot begin to understand how much I need them. It is over bottles of shared wine and bowls of pasta that I come back to earth and heal. Your laughs, birthday cards, care, text messages checking in. Your understanding. I love you forever.

Thank you to my readers, those of you who loved this book and lent it to a friend, those who checked it out of the library or bought it at your favorite indie bookstore—I am astounded that it is my job to give you the gift of my stories. Thank you thank you thank you. Forever.

And to my someday husband, who has rubbed my back and filled my water bottle, reminded me of my worth and given me the room to grow into the most authentic version of myself I've ever been, thank you. For all of the stress and chaos that transpired under our roof as I toiled with this project, I hope you'll forgive me. You overwhelm my wholeness; you are truly one of a kind, and I love to see me from your point of view.